PracticePla

Arthur E. Jongsma, Jr., Series Editor

Helping therapists
help their clients...

Practice*Planners*

Second Edition

THE COMPLETE ADULT
PSYCHOTHERAPY
Treatment Planner

A new, fully revised edition of the bestselling *The Complete
Psychotherapy Treatment Planner*, this invaluable resource features:

- Treatment plan components for 39
  behaviorally based problems—including five
  completely new problem sets
- A step-by-step guide to writing treatment plans
- Over 500 additional prewritten treatment goals,
  objectives, and interventions
- Handy workbook format with space to record
  your own treatment plan options
- Over 100,000 **Practice*Planners*** sold

Arthur E. Jongsma, Jr., and L. Mark Peterson

Practice*Planners*
Arthur E. Jongsma, Jr., Series Editor

Brief Therapy
HOMEWORK
PLANNER

- Contains 62 ready-to-copy homework assignments
  that can be used to facilitate brief individual therapy
- Homework assignments and exercises are keyed to
  over 30 behaviorally-based presenting problems from
  The Complete Psychotherapy Treatment Planner
- Assignments may be quickly customized using the
  enclosed disk
- Over 100,000 **Practice*Planners*** sold

Gary M. Schultheis

Practice*Planners*

The Clinical
DOCUMENTATION
SOURCEBOOK

Second Edition

A Comprehensive Collection of
Mental Health Practice
Forms, Handouts, and Records

FEATURES

- Contains ready-to-use forms for managing
  the mental health treatment process
- Covers every stage of the treatment process
- Includes customizable forms on disk
- Over 100,000 **Practice*Planners*** sold

Donald E. Wiger

Practice*Planners*
Arthur E. Jongsma, Jr., Series Editor

The Adult Psychotherapy
PROGRESS NOTES PLANNER

This time-saving resource:

- Contains Progress Notes statements for all
  behaviorally based problems
- Covers the gamut of Diagnostic Statistical Manual-based
  presenting problems approved in the latest ongoing changes of
  the *Psychotherapy Treatment Planner, Second Edition*
- Includes 1,000s of prewritten session- and therapy-
  related Progress Note descriptions
- Provides a handy workbook format with space to
  record your own progress note entries
- Over 250,000 **Practice*Planners*** sold

Arthur E. Jongsma, Jr.

WILEY

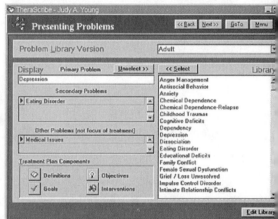

Practice*Planners*®   Order Form

Treatment Planners cover all the necessary elements for developing formal treatment plans, including detailed problem definitions, long-term goals, short-term objectives, therapeutic interventions, and DSM-IV diagnoses.

Documentation Sourcebooks provide a comprehensive collection of ready-to-use blank forms, handouts, and questionnaires to help you manage your client reports and streamline the record keeping and treatment process. Features clear, concise explanations of the purpose of each form—including when it should be used and at what point. Includes customizable forms on disk.

e Complete Adult Psychotherapy Treatment Planner, Second Edition
0-471-31924-4 / $44.95

e Child Psychotherapy Treatment Planner, Second Edition
0-471-34764-7 / $44.95

e Adolescent Psychotherapy Treatment Planner, Second Edition
0-471-34766-3 / $44.95

e Chemical Dependence Treatment Planner
0-471-23795-7 / $44.95

e Continuum of Care Treatment Planner
0-471-19568-5 / $44.95

e Couples Psychotherapy Treatment Planner
0-471-24711-1 / $44.95

e Employee Assistance (EAP) Treatment Planner
0-471-24709-X / $44.95

e Pastoral Counseling Treatment Planner
0-471-25416-9 / $44.95

e Older Adult Psychotherapy Treatment Planner
0-471-29574-4 / $44.95

e Behavioral Medicine Treatment Planner
0-471-31923-6 / $44.95

e Group Therapy Treatment Planner
0-471-37449-0 / $44.95

e Family Therapy Treatment Planner
0-471-34768-X / $44.95

e Severe and Persistent Mental Illness Treatment Planner
0-471-35945-9 / $44.95

e Gay and Lesbian Psychotherapy Treatment Planner
0-471-35080-X / $44.95

The Clinical Documentation Sourcebook, Second Edition
0-471-32692-5 / $49.95

The Psychotherapy Documentation Primer
0-471-28990-6 / $45.00

The Couple and Family Clinical Documentation Sourcebook
0-471-25234-4 / $49.95

The Clinical Child Documentation Sourcebook
0-471-29111-0 / $49.95

The Chemical Dependence Treatment Documentation Sourcebook
0-471-31285-1 / $49.95

The Forensic Documentation Sourcebook
0-471-25459-2 / $85.00

The Continuum of Care Clinical Documentation Sourcebook
0-471-34581-4 / $75.00

NEW AND FORTHCOMING

The Traumatic Events Treatment Planner
0-471-39587-0 / $44.95

The Special Education Treatment Planner
0-471-38873-4 / $44.95

The Mental Retardation and Developmental Disability Treatment Planner
0-471-38253-1 / $44.95

The Social Work and Human Services Treatment Planner
0-471-37741-4 / $44.95

The Rehabilitation Psychology Treatment Planner
0-471-35178-4 / $44.95

---

ame_____

ffiliation_____

ddress_____

ty/State/Zip_____

one/Fax_____

-mail_____

www.wiley.com/practiceplanners

To order, call 1-800-753-0655
(Please refer to promo #1-4019 when ordering.)
Or send this page with payment* to:
John Wiley & Sons, Inc., Attn: J. Knott
605 Third Avenue, New York, NY 10158-0012

❏ Check enclosed   ❏ Visa   ❏ MasterCard   ❏ American Express

Card #_____

Expiration Date_____

Signature_____
Please add your local sales tax to all orders.

The Rehabilitation Psychology
Treatment Planner

PRACTICE*PLANNERS*® SERIES

Treatment Planners

The Chemical Dependence Treatment Planner
The Continuum of Care Treatment Planner
The Couples Psychotherapy Treatment Planner
The Employee Assistance Treatment Planner
The Pastoral Counseling Treatment Planner
The Older Adult Psychotherapy Treatment Planner
The Complete Adult Psychotherapy Treatment Planner, 2e
The Behavioral Medicine Treatment Planner
The Group Therapy Treatment Planner
The Gay and Lesbian Psychotherapy Treatment Planner
The Child Psychotherapy Treatment Planner, 2e
The Adolescent Psychotherapy Treatment Planner, 2e
The Family Therapy Treatment Planner
The Severe and Persistent Mental Illness Treatment Planner
The Mental Retardation and Developmental Disability Treatment Planner
The Social Work and Human Services Treatment Planner
The Traumatic Events Treatment Planner
The Personality Disorders Treatment Planner
The Rehabilitation Psychology Treatment Planner
The Special Education Treatment Planner

Progress Notes Planners

The Child Psychotherapy Progress Notes Planner
The Adolescent Psychotherapy Progress Notes Planner
The Adult Psychotherapy Progress Notes Planner

Homework Planners

Brief Therapy Homework Planner
Brief Couples Therapy Homework Planner
Chemical Dependence Treatment Homework Planner
Brief Child Therapy Homework Planner
Brief Adolescent Therapy Homework Planner
Brief Employee Assistance Homework Planner
Brief Family Therapy Homework Planner

Documentation *Sourcebooks*

The Forensic Documentation Sourcebook
The Psychotherapy Documentation Primer
The Chemical Dependence Treatment Documentation Sourcebook
The Clinical Child Documentation Sourcebook
The Couple and Family Clinical Documentation Sourcebook
The Clinical Documentation Sourcebook, 2e
The Continuum of Care Clinical Documentation Sourcebook

Practice*Planners*®

Arthur E. Jongsma, Jr., Series Editor

The Rehabilitation Psychology Treatment Planner

Michele J. Rusin

Arthur E. Jongsma, Jr.

JOHN WILEY & SONS, INC.

New York • Chichester • Weinheim • Brisbane • Singapore • Toronto

Library of Congress Cataloging-in-Publication Data:

Rusin, Michele.
    The rehabilitation psychology treatment planner / Michele Rusin, Arthur E. Jongsma, Jr.
        p.   cm. — (Practice planners series)
    ISBN 0-471-35178-4 (pbk. : alk. paper) — ISBN 0-471-35179-2 (pbk. : disk : alk. paper)
        1. Clinical health psychology.   2. Medical rehabilitation—Psychological aspects.
    3. Mental illness—Treatment—Planning.   I. Jongsma, Arthur E., 1943–   II. Title.
    III. Practice planners.
    R726.7 .R865 2001
    616.89'1—dc21

                                                                                    00-066254

Printed in the United States of America.

10 9 8 7 6 5 4 3 2 1

To my husband, Michael Schmid.

In memory of my mother, Mary McDonnell Rusin, and to my father and step-mother, Michael and Dorothy Rusin.

To my friends and mentors Daniel Boroto, Brendan Muldoon, Billie Poon, Leonard Poon, Ilene Siegler, and the late Brian Gill.

You have all profoundly influenced my life. Thank you.

—Michele Rusin

To my brothers, Ed, Herm, and Ray. Thank you for your continuing interest and support.

—Arthur E. Jongsma, Jr.

CONTENTS

PRACTICE PLANNER SERIES PREFACE

The practice of psychotherapy has a dimension that did not exist 30, 20, or even 15 years ago—accountability. Treatment programs, public agencies, clinics, and even group and solo practitioners must now justify the treatment of patients to outside review entities that control the payment of fees. This development has resulted in an explosion of paperwork.

Clinicians must now document what has been done in treatment, what is planned for the future, and what the anticipated outcomes of the interventions are. The books and software in this Practice Planner series are designed to help practitioners fulfill these documentation requirements efficiently and professionally.

The Practice Planner series is growing rapidly. It now includes the second editions of the *Complete Adult Psychotherapy Treatment Planner,* the *Adolescent Psychotherapy Treatment Planner,* and the *Child Psychotherapy Treatment Planner*. Additional Treatment Planners are targeted to specialty areas of practice, including chemical dependency, the continuum of care, couples therapy, employee assistance, behavioral medicine, therapy with older adults, pastoral counseling, family therapy, group therapy, neuropsychology, therapy with gays and lesbians, and more.

In addition to the Treatment Planners, the series also includes *TheraScribe®*, the latest version of the popular treatment planning, patient record-keeping software, as well as adjunctive books, such as the *Brief, Chemical Dependence, Couple, Child,* and *Adolescent Therapy Homework Planners, The Psychotherapy Documentation Primer,* and the *Clinical, Forensic, Child, Couples and Family, Continuum of Care,* and *Chemical Dependence Documentation Sourcebooks*—containing forms and resources to aid in mental health practice management. The goal of the series is to provide practitioners with the resources they need in order to provide high-quality care in the era of accountability—or, to put it simply, we seek to help you spend more time with patients, and less on paperwork.

ARTHUR E. JONGSMA, JR.
GRAND RAPIDS, MICHIGAN

ACKNOWLEDGMENTS

I am grateful for the support that I have received in the process of compiling this book. I thank all the patients and families who have shared their lives with me through the years. It is their courage, their efforts to engage life despite substantial obstacles, that keep me engaged in this process of discovering the possibilities when a body and brain are changed. I am appreciative to Art Jongsma for the warm, respectful, and thoroughly enjoyable working relationship he created and maintained throughout the project, and to Judy Jongsma (always a pleasure to spend time with) who was inadvertently responsible for bringing Art and me together. Jennifer Byrne has been a faithful behind-the-scenes person, a friendly e-mail communicant, and a skillful manager of the manuscript. She has saved me more time and stress than I probably realize. I would also like to thank the staff of John Wiley & Sons, especially Kelly Franklin and Peggy Alexander, the editors of this work. I am also appreciative to my friends, colleagues, and family, whose encouragement and enthusiasm sustained my momentum.

—Michele Rusin

The Rehabilitation Psychology
Treatment Planner

INTRODUCTION

PLANNER FOCUS

The *Rehabilitation Psychology Treatment Planner* is designed for rehabilitation psychologists and neuropsychologists working with adult patients having cognitive disorders due to injuries or illnesses affecting the brain. It is targeted toward the types of problems that are customarily seen in acute and outpatient medical rehabilitation facilities. These include the affective, psychiatric, behavioral, and psychosocial issues most commonly encountered when working with neurobehaviorally-involved patients.

Interventions have been designed to cover the range of mild to severe impairments. Given that rehabilitation is characterized by a team approach, it is assumed that the psychologist is functioning not in isolation but is working in conjunction with a team of other rehabilitation professionals. Some interventions, indeed some entire chapters, focus on how the psychologist can support and contribute to the therapeutic outcome of another team member, such as a speech therapist or vocational rehabilitation counselor. While most interventions focus on patient needs, an underlying presumption is that the patient resides in a community, and the patient's functioning will be affected for better or worse by that community. Therefore, interventions are also included that account for family education needs and environmental modifications that would enhance functioning.

It is our hope that this book will serve as more than a shortcut to developing treatment plans. In each chapter, we have given careful consideration to diagnostic issues and available treatment options. We have put substantial effort into having the interventions flow logically. It is our hope that this volume may also serve as a resource during the clinical workday, as something of a roadmap to interns and fellows entering the perplexing and wonderful world of rehabilitation.

HISTORY AND BACKGROUND

Since the early 1960s, formalized treatment planning has gradually become a vital aspect of the entire health care delivery system, whether it is treatment related to physical health, mental health, child welfare, or substance abuse. What started in the medical sector in the 1960s spread into the mental health sector in the 1970s as clinics, psychiatric hospitals, agencies, and so on began to seek accreditation from bodies such as the Joint Commission on Accreditation of Healthcare Organizations (JCAHO) to qualify for third-party reimbursements. To achieve accreditation, most treatment providers had to begin developing and strengthening their documentation skills in the area of treatment planning. Previously, most mental health and substance abuse treatment providers had, at best, a "bare-bones" plan that looked similar for most of the individuals they treated. As a result, patients and third-party payers were uncertain about the direction of mental health treatment. Goals were vague, objectives were nonexistent, and interventions not specific to individual patients. Outcome data were not measurable, and neither the treatment provider nor the patient knew exactly when treatment was complete. The initial development of rudimentary treatment plans made inroads toward addressing some of these issues.

With the advent of managed care in the 1980s, treatment planning has taken on even more importance. Managed care systems *insist* that clinicians move rapidly from assessment of the problem to the formulation and implementation of the treatment plan. The goal of most managed care companies is to expedite the treatment process by prompting the patient and treatment provider to focus on identifying and changing behaviorally defined problems as quickly as possible. Treatment plans must be specific as to the problems and interventions, individualized to meet the patient's needs and goals, and measurable in terms of setting milestones that can be used to chart the patient's progress. Pressure from third-party payers, accrediting agencies, and other outside parties has therefore increased the need for clinicians to produce effective, high-quality treatment plans in a short time frame. However, many mental health providers have little experience in treatment plan development. Our purpose in writing this book is to clarify, simplify, and accelerate the treatment planning process.

TREATMENT PLAN UTILITY

Detailed written treatment plans can benefit not only the patient, therapist, treatment team, insurance community, and treatment agency, but also the overall psychotherapy profession. The patient is served by a written plan because it stipulates the issues that are the focus of the treatment process. It is very easy for both provider and patient to lose sight of what the issues were that brought the patient into therapy. The treatment plan is a guide that structures the focus of the therapeutic contract. Since issues can change as therapy progresses, the treatment plan must be viewed as a dynamic document that can and must be updated to reflect any major change of problem, definition, goal, objective, or intervention.

Patients and therapists benefit from the treatment plan, which forces both to think about therapy outcomes. Behaviorally stated, measurable objectives clearly focus the treatment endeavor. Patients no longer have to wonder what therapy is trying to accomplish. Clear objectives also allow the patient to channel effort into specific changes that will lead to the long-term goal of problem resolution. Therapy is no longer a vague contract to just talk honestly and openly about emotions and cognitions until the patient feels better. Both patient and therapist are concentrating on specifically stated objectives using specific interventions.

Providers are aided by treatment plans because they are forced to think analytically and critically about therapeutic interventions that are best suited for objective attainment for the patient. Therapists were traditionally trained to "follow the patient," but now a formalized plan is the guide to the treatment process. The therapist must give advance attention to the technique, approach, assignment, or cathartic target that will form the basis for interventions.

Clinicians benefit from clear documentation of treatment because it provides a measure of added protection from possible patient litigation. Malpractice suits are increasing in frequency and insurance premiums are soaring. The first line of defense against allegations is a complete clinical record detailing the treatment process. A written, individualized, formal treatment plan that is the guideline for the therapeutic process, that has been reviewed and signed by the patient, and that is coupled with problem-oriented progress notes is a powerful defense against exaggerated or false claims.

A well-crafted treatment plan that clearly stipulates presenting problems and intervention strategies facilitates the treatment process carried out by team members in inpatient, residential, or intensive outpatient settings. Good communication between team members about what approach is being implemented and who is responsible for which intervention is critical. Team meetings to discuss patient treatment used to be the only source of interaction between providers; often, therapeutic conclusions or assignments were not recorded. Now, a thorough treatment plan stipulates in writing the details of objectives and the varied interventions (pharmacological, milieu, group therapy, didactic, recreational, individual therapy, and so on) and who will implement them.

Every treatment agency or institution is constantly looking for ways to increase the quality and uniformity of the documentation in the clinical record. A standardized, written treatment plan with problem definitions, goals, objectives, and interventions in every patient's file enhances that uniformity of documentation. This uniformity eases the task of record reviewers inside and outside the agency. Outside reviewers, such as JCAHO, insist on documentation that clearly outlines assessment, treatment, progress, and discharge status.

The demand for accountability from third-party payers and health maintenance organizations (HMOs) is partially satisfied by a written treatment plan and complete progress notes. More and more managed care systems are demanding a structured therapeutic contract that has measurable objectives and explicit interventions. Clinicians cannot avoid this move toward being accountable to those outside the treatment process.

The psychotherapy profession stands to benefit from the use of more precise, measurable objectives to evaluate success in mental and behavioral health treatment. With the advent of detailed treatment plans, outcome data can be more easily collected for interventions that are effective in achieving specific goals.

HOW TO DEVELOP A TREATMENT PLAN

The process of developing a treatment plan involves a logical series of steps that build on each other much like constructing a house. The foundation of any effective treatment plan is the data gathered in a thorough biopsychosocial assessment. As the patient presents himself or herself for treatment, the clinician must sensitively listen to and understand what the patient struggles with in terms of family-of-origin issues, current stressors, emotional status, social network, physical health, coping skills, interpersonal conflicts, self-esteem, and so on. Assessment data may be gathered from a social history, physical exam, clinical interview, psychological testing, or contact with a patient's significant others. The integration of the data by the clinician or the multidisciplinary treatment team members is critical for understanding the patient, as is an awareness of the basis of the patient's struggle. We have identified six specific steps for developing an effective treatment plan based on the assessment data.

Step One: Problem Selection

Although the patient may discuss a variety of issues during the assessment, the clinician must ferret out the most significant problems on which to focus the treatment process. Usually a *primary* problem will surface, and *secondary* problems may also be evident. Some *other* problems may have to be set aside as not urgent enough to require treatment at this time. An effective treatment plan can only deal with a few selected problems or treatment will lose its direction. The *Rehabilitation Psychology Treatment Planner* offers 25 problems from which to select those that most accurately represent your patient's presenting issues.

As the problems to be selected become clear to the clinician or the treatment team, it is important to include opinions from the patient and often the patient's significant others as to his or her prioritization of issues for which help is being sought. A patient's motivation to participate in and cooperate with the treatment process depends, to some extent, on the degree to which treatment addresses his or her greatest needs.

Step Two: Problem Definition

Each individual patient presents with unique nuances as to how a problem behaviorally reveals itself in his or her life. Therefore, each problem that is selected for treatment focus requires a specific definition about how it is evidenced in the particular patient. The symptom pattern should be associated with diagnostic criteria and codes such as those found in the *Diagnostic and Statistical Manual of Mental Disorders, DSM-IV-TR (Text Revision)* or the *International Classification of Diseases*. The Planner, following the pattern established by DSM-IV, offers such behaviorally specific definition statements to choose from or to serve as a model for your own personally crafted statements. You will find several behavior symptoms or syndromes listed that may characterize one of the 25 presenting problems.

Step Three: Goal Development

The next step in treatment plan development is that of setting broad goals for the resolution of the target problem. These statements need not be crafted in measurable terms but can be global, long-term goals that indicate a desired positive outcome to the treatment procedures.

This Planner suggests several possible goal statements for each problem, but one statement is all that is required in a treatment plan.

Step Four: Objective Construction

In contrast to long-term goals, objectives must be stated in behaviorally measurable language. It must be clear when the patient has achieved the established objectives; therefore, vague, subjective objectives are not acceptable. Review agencies (e.g., JCAHO), HMOs, and managed care organizations insist that psychological treatment outcome be measurable. The objectives presented in this Planner are designed to meet this demand for accountability. Numerous alternatives are presented to allow construction of a variety of treatment plan possibilities for the same presenting problem. The clinician must exercise professional judgment as to which objectives are most appropriate for a given patient.

Each objective should be developed as a step toward attaining the broad treatment goal. In essence, objectives can be thought of as a series of steps that, when completed, will result in the achievement of the long-term goal. There should be at least two objectives for each problem, but the clinician may construct as many as are necessary for goal achievement. Target attainment dates should be listed for each objective. New objectives should be added to the plan as the individual's treatment progresses. When all the necessary objectives have been achieved, the patient should have resolved the target problem successfully.

Step Five: Intervention Creation

Interventions are the actions of the clinician designed to help the patient complete the objectives. There should be at least one intervention for every objective. If the patient does not accomplish the objective after the initial intervention, new interventions should be added to the plan.

Interventions should be selected on the basis of the patient's needs and the treatment provider's full therapeutic repertoire. The *Rehabilitation Psychology Treatment Planner* contains interventions from a broad range of therapeutic approaches, including cognitive, dynamic, behavioral, pharmacologic, family-oriented, and patient-centered therapy. Other interventions may be written by the provider to reflect his or her own training and experience. The addition of new problems, definitions, goals, objectives, and interventions to those found in the Planner is encouraged because doing so adds to the database for future reference and use.

Some suggested interventions listed in the Planner refer to specific books that can be assigned to the patient for adjunctive bibliotherapy. Appendix A contains a full bibliographic reference list of these materials. The books are arranged under each problem for which they are appropriate as assigned reading for patients. When a book is used as part of an intervention plan, it should be reviewed with the patient after it is read, enhancing the application of the content of the book to the specific patient's circumstances. For further information about self-help books, mental health professionals may wish to consult *The Authoritative Guide to Self-Help Books* (1994) by Santrock, Minnett, and Campbell (available from The Guilford Press, New York).

A list of reference resources is also provided for the professional provider in the Bibliography. These books are meant to elaborate on the methods suggested in some of the chapters. Some of this Planner's content leans heavily on the work of these listed authors, and recognition of this fact is found in the occasional footnotes located in the beginning of the particular chapters.

Assigning an intervention to a specific provider is most relevant if the patient is being treated by a team in an inpatient, residential, or intensive outpatient setting. Within these settings, personnel other than the primary clinician may be responsible for implementing a specific intervention. Review agencies require that the responsible provider's name be stipulated for every intervention.

Step Six: Diagnosis Determination

The determination of an appropriate diagnosis is based on an evaluation of the patient's complete clinical presentation. The clinician must compare the behavioral, cognitive, emotional, and interpersonal symptoms that the patient presents to the criteria for diagnosis of a mental disorder as described in *DSM-IV*. The issue of differential diagnosis is admittedly a difficult one that research has shown to have rather low interrater reliability. Psychologists have also been trained to think more in terms of maladaptive behavior than disease labels. In spite of these factors, diagnosis is a reality that exists in the world of mental and behavioral health care, and it is a necessity for third-party reimbursement. (However, recently, managed care agencies have become more interested in behavioral indices that are exhibited by the patient than the actual diagnosis.) It is the clinician's thorough knowledge of *DSM-IV* criteria and a complete understanding of the patient assessment data that contribute to the most reliable, valid diagnosis. An accurate assessment of behavioral indicators will also contribute to more effective treatment planning.

HOW TO USE THIS PLANNER

Our experience has taught us that learning the skills of effective treatment plan writing can be a tedious and difficult process for many clinicians. It is more stressful to try to develop this expertise when under the pressure of increased patient load and short time frames placed on clinicians today by managed care systems. The documentation demands can be overwhelming when we must move quickly from assessment to treatment plan to progress notes. In the process, we must be very specific about how and when objectives can be achieved, and how progress is exhibited in each patient. The *Rehabilitation Psychology Treatment Planner* was developed as a tool to aid clinicians in writing a treatment plan in a rapid manner that is clear, specific, and highly individualized according to the following progression:

1. Choose one presenting problem (Step One) that you have identified through your assessment process. Locate the corresponding page number for that problem in the Planner's table of contents.
2. Select two or three of the listed behavioral definitions (Step Two) and record them in the appropriate section on your treatment plan form. Feel free to add your own defining statement if you determine that your patient's behavioral manifestation of the identified problem is not listed. (Note that while our design for treatment planning is vertical, it will work equally well on plan forms formatted horizontally.)
3. Select a single long-term goal (Step Three) and again write the selection, exactly as it is written in the Planner or in some appropriately modified form, in the corresponding area of your own form.
4. Review the listed objectives for this problem and select the ones that you judge to be clinically indicated for your patient (Step Four). Remember, it is recommended that you select at least two objectives for each problem. Add a target date or the number of sessions allocated for the attainment of each objective.
5. Choose relevant interventions (Step Five). The Planner offers suggested interventions related to each objective in the parentheses following the objective statement. The entire list is eclectic and may offer options that are tailored to your theoretical approach or preferred way of working with patients. But do not limit yourself to those interventions. Just as with definitions, goals, and objectives, there is space allowed for you to enter your own interventions into the Planner. This allows you to refer to these entries when you create a plan around this problem in the

future. You will have to assign responsibility to a specific person for implementation of each intervention if the treatment is being carried out by a multidisciplinary team.

6. Several *DSM-IV* diagnoses are listed at the end of each chapter that are commonly associated with a patient who has this problem. These diagnoses are meant to be suggestions for clinical consideration. Select a diagnosis listed or assign a more appropriate choice from the *DSM-IV* (Step Six).

Note: To accommodate those practitioners who tend to plan treatment in terms of diagnostic labels rather than presenting problems, Appendix B lists all of the *DSM-IV* diagnoses that have been presented in the various presenting problem chapters as suggestions for consideration. Each diagnosis is followed by the presenting problem that has been associated with that diagnosis. The provider may look up the presenting problems for a selected diagnosis to review definitions, goals, objectives, and interventions that may be appropriate for their patients with that diagnosis.

Congratulations! You should now have a complete, individualized treatment plan that is ready for immediate implementation and presentation to the patient. It should resemble the format of the sample plan presented on the following pages.

A FINAL NOTE

One important aspect of effective treatment planning is that each plan should be tailored to the individual patient's problems and needs. Treatment plans should not be mass-produced, even if patients have similar problems. The individual's strengths and weaknesses, unique stressors, social network, family circumstances, and symptom patterns *must* be considered in developing a treatment strategy. Drawing upon our own years of clinical experience, we have put together a variety of treatment choices. These statements can be combined in thousands of permutations to develop detailed treatment plans. Relying on their own good judgment, clinicians can easily select the statements that are appropriate for the individuals they are treating. In addition, we encourage readers to add their own definitions, goals, objectives, and interventions to the existing samples. It is our hope that The *Rehabilitation Psychology Treatment Planner* will promote effective, creative treatment planning—a process that will ultimately benefit the patient, clinician, and rehabilitation community.

SAMPLE TREATMENT PLAN

Problem: MEMORY IMPAIRMENT

Definitions: Unable to recall information about personally experienced events at the level expected for someone of his/her age and education.

Unusually high rate of forgetting.

Difficulty recalling routes.

Fails to follow through on intentions to perform a planned activity, such as keeping an appointment, transferring laundry from the washer to the dryer, or taking medication.

Failure to meet time-related commitments such as paying bills, given history of good management of responsibilities.

Goal: Use external memory aids to track appointments and commitments.

Establish habits and routines to use procedural memory to one's advantage in completing recurring activities.

Short-Term Objectives	**Therapeutic Interventions**
1. Cooperate with an evaluation of acute and chronic factors influencing current memory performance. (3/1/01)	1. Review the patient's medical record to identify factors (e.g., developmental delay, central nervous system disorders, previous brain injuries, exposure to toxins, anoxic events) that might be influencing his/her current memory functioning.
	2. Obtain a history of the onset and course of the patient's memory disturbance, including all treatments and results.
2. Participate willingly in neuropsychological testing. (3/14/01)	1. Arrange for neuropsychological testing to identify the types and degree of patient's memory deficit, and to determine how other cognitive processes (e.g., attention, aphasia, visual-perceptual deficits) might be influencing the patient's ability to learn, recall, recognize, and utilize information.

(Continued)

3. Cooperate with assessment of "everyday" memory skills. (3/21/01)

    1. Refer for or administer tests of everyday or ecologic memory (e.g., Rivermead Behavioral Memory Test by Wilson, Cockburn, and Baddeley).

    2. Consult with the patient's rehabilitation therapists and family regarding his/her current memory functioning (e.g., remembering route to therapy area, learning exercise routines, reporting on recent events that are of personal interest).

    3. Give feedback to the patient (patient's family), physician, rehabilitation team, and other designated persons regarding assessment results and recommendations.

4. Describe changes in memory that seem to have occurred since the medical event. (3/21/01)

    1. Determine the degree to which the patient has insight into memory deficits by inquiring directly whether he/she has noticed any changes in memory, or by asking him/her to explain why he/she failed to succeed at a memory-related task.

5. Use a memory/organizer book to record important information and to keep up with appointments and other commitments. (3/28/01)

    1. Arrange for the patient to develop a memory/organizer book, creating sections in which he/she can file information that is most pertinent to his/her current needs (e.g., personal information, therapists' names, facts about injury/illness, monthly calendar, daily schedule, to-dos, etc.).

    2. Cue the patient to refer to the memory/organizer book to answer questions and to remind self of appointments and upcoming activities (e.g., when the patient asks, "When can I go home?," say "Let's look at the calendar in your book to find out," or when the patient asks,

(Continued)

"What happened to me?" say "Let's look in your book. Which section would have that information?").

6. Establish habits and routines to increase the percentage of time one accomplishes recurring activities with minimal or no cuing. (4/10/01)

1. Identify recurring activities that can be linked to established routines (e.g., scheduling morning dressing and grooming to immediately follow bathing; arranging to turn on the computer, access software, and work on task immediately following a morning television show; planning patient's review of memory book to immediately follow completion of a meal), thereby taking advantage of procedural memory and reducing the burden on prospective memory.

7. Cooperate with the use of prompts to establish habits, and put effort into relying on naturally occurring cue (e.g., internal or environmental stimulus) instead of an "artificial" alarm or cue. (4/30/01)

1. Use a verbal prompt, wristwatch alarm, alarm strip, or other cue to remind the patient to perform designated tasks at specified times.
2. Fade use of alarm or prompt, maintaining the patient's successful response rate at 80 percent or greater.

DIAGNOSIS

Axis I:	294.0	Amnestic Disorder Due to Cerebral Vascular Accident
Axis II:	V71.09	No Diagnosis or Condition

Note: The numbers in parentheses accompanying the short-term objectives in each chapter correspond to the list of suggested therapeutic interventions in that chapter. Each objective has specific interventions that have been designed to assist the patient in attaining that objective. Clinical judgment should determine the exact intervention to be used, including any outside of those suggested.

AGITATION, AGGRESSION, AND VIOLENCE

BEHAVIORAL DEFINITIONS

1. Frequent, unpredictable, or restless movements that are not goal-directed, accompanied by irritable mood state.
2. Thrashing or kicking movements.
3. Inability to maintain focus on activity, accompanied by "bursts" of movements or verbalizations with no clear goal.
4. Strikes out physically at staff, family, or others such that physical injury nearly occurs.
5. Strikes own body in ways that threaten or cause injury.
6. Hits, kicks, bites, or scratches rehabilitation professionals, family, friends, or other patients.
7. Verbally threatens physical injury.

__. _____

_____

__. _____

_____

_____

__. _____

_____

LONG-TERM GOALS

1. Coordinate actions in order to make them goal-oriented.
2. Protect integrity of own body, terminating all self-imposed injury.
3. Manage behavior so that others do not fear for safety.
4. Tolerate experience of frustration, anger, and upset while using socially acceptable methods to resolve difficulty.

5. Understand and accept restrictions or limitations imposed to protect safety.
6. Use words or problem-solving methods to resolve emotional distress.
7. Demonstrate ability to successfully participate in fundamental social interactions.

—. _____

_____

—. _____

_____

—. _____

_____

SHORT-TERM OBJECTIVES

THERAPEUTIC INTERVENTIONS

1. Cooperate with efforts to identify the circumstances surrounding episodes of agitated, aggressive, or violent behavior. (1, 2)

2. Allow staff to observe activities so that they might identify the factors associated with increased or decreased agitation or aggression. (3, 4)

3. Provide access to information concerning neurological, psychiatric, or other medical factors that might be influencing behavior. (5, 6)

4. Family and friends demonstrate understanding that current agitation represents a time-limited stage of brain-injury recovery. (7)

5. Family (legally designated decision maker) and reha-

1. Consult with the patient's rehabilitation team, physician, family, or other pertinent persons to identify specific agitated, violent, or aggressive behaviors that have occurred. Determine the circumstances surrounding the activity, the frequency of the activity, and the consequences.

2. Interview persons who know the patient well to determine whether significant episodes of violence or aggression had occurred prior to the neuropsychological impairment.

3. Observe the patient's social interaction during an activity that has been associated with agitation, aggression, or violence. Attend to triggers that precede the pa-

bilitation staff agree on a plan to assure safe management of agitated or aggressive behaviors. (8, 9)

6. Tolerate interventions that will allow safe freedom of movement and decrease need for physical restraints. (10, 11, 12)

7. Cooperate with actions designed to maintain an optimal level of environmental stimulation. (11, 12, 13)

8. Reduce agitation that is stimulated by environmental cues. (11, 12, 13, 14, 15)

9. Reduce agitation or aggression that has been maintained through environmental conditions and through reinforcing responses of others. (16, 17, 18, 19, 20)

10. Sign a contract describing the goals of rehabilitation and what is expected of all parties. (21)

11. Reduce the impact of fatigue on mood, agitated or aggressive behavior, and performance. (22, 23)

12. Acknowledge successful accomplishment of therapeutic activities and demonstrate willingness to work on increasingly more challenging rehabilitation tasks. (24, 25, 26)

13. Accept positive comments about successful task accomplishment and appropriate conduct. (25, 27)

tient's dyscontrol, the response of the person who is the target of the aggression, and the effect of the response on the patient's behavior.

4. Observe the patient interacting with a person who rarely or never experiences the patient as agitated, aggressive, or violent. Determine, if possible, what allows this person to maintain effective interaction with the patient.

5. Review medical records and consult with physician to determine how the patient's brain impairment, medications, medical factors, or psychiatric conditions may be contributing to the agitation, aggression, or violence.

6. Determine the patient's level of brain injury recovery using the Rancho Los Amigos Levels of Cognitive Functioning Scales (Hagan, Malkmus, and Durham).

7. If the patient is at the Rancho Level Four stage of recovery, educate the patient's family, friends, and other pertinent individuals about the agitation that occurs during this phase of recovery from severe brain injury. Inform them that this agitation typically passes with time.

8. Consult with the patient's rehabilitation team, physician, family, and other per-

14. Maintain rapport and working relationship with the rehabilitation therapist despite frustration with activities. (28)

15. Give best efforts to cognitive evaluations. (29)

16. Agree to evaluation for medications to improve cognition, mood, or behavior. (30, 31, 32)

17. Take medications regularly as prescribed and report effectiveness and side effects. (33, 34)

18. Cooperate with psychometric testing to determine how cognitive, affective, or other neuropsychiatric factors might be affecting ability to manage behavior. (35, 36, 37)

19. Family or legally designated decision maker, (the patient), and rehabilitation professionals agree on actions to reduce risk of injuries should the patient become violent. (38, 39)

20. Recognize authority of local police or safety officers and follow their directives to restore a safe environment. (40)

21. Family, friends, and staff position themselves in ways that reduce opportunities for the patient to inflict injuries. (41, 42)

22. Describe understanding of medical condition, changes in functioning, and purpose

tinent persons to specify how the patient's behavior will be managed safely in current environment.

9. Coordinate efforts to identify institution or other setting that can provide necessary level of security and assist with the patient's transfer to that facility.

10. Recommend that the patient have a trained attendant present constantly during those hours in which the patient's agitated or aggressive behavior poses a threat to the health or safety of himself/herself or others.

11. Recommend use of Vail bed, Craig bed, or other "bed" that will keep the patient safely confined during period of agitation, avoiding use of posey vest or other physical restraints, if possible.

12. Reduce the level of stimulation to which the patient is exposed (e.g., placing the patient in private room, lowering light level, keeping the television turned off, directing telephone calls to a location outside the patient's room).

13. Educate family and friends about ways to avoid overstimulating the patient (e.g., limiting visitors to no more than three persons at a time, assuring that only one person talks at a time,

of rehabilitation interventions. (43)

23. Verbalize an understanding of the debilitating medical event, imminent implications, and what is required for improvement. (44)

24. Family and others show skill in using redirection rather than logical argument at earliest sign of irritation. (45, 46)

25. Implement physical or cognitive relaxation strategies to reduce levels of arousal. (47, 48, 49)

26. Engage attention as much as possible in constructive conversations and activities in order to avoid ruminating about upsetting topics. (10, 50, 51, 52)

27. Honestly describe thoughts, intentions, and plans to cause injury or death to specific persons. (53)

28. Accept measures to prevent injuries/death and to protect welfare of self and others. (54, 55)

29. Obtain inpatient psychiatric or neurobehavioral care. (56, 57, 58)

30. Willingly listen to others' opinions about one's effectiveness in communicating and interacting. Verbalize an understanding of how they arrived at this point of view. (59)

31. Implement positive social and conflict resolution skills

speaking slowly, using short sentences, speaking in a calm tone).

14. Consult with rehabilitation team, (the patient), and the patient's family regarding visitation policies (e.g., how many visitors allowed at a time, specific persons who should be prohibited from visiting, etc.) and establish a mechanism to manage visitation (e.g., sign on the patient's door stating that all visitors must check in at nursing station).

15. Assess the environmental cues to which the patient is being exposed (e.g., television news coverage of a disturbing incident, mesh covering around bed that might make the patient feel like being in a jail cell); eliminate, if possible, what might be misinterpreted by the patient and/or contributing to agitation.

16. Add or emphasize environmental cues that will help the patient realize that he/she is in a medical care setting (e.g., a sign posted at the patient's eye level reading "X Hospital," a sign with a photo of a physician using a stethoscope, a photo showing a physical therapist helping someone walk with a walker).

17. Develop a behavioral plan describing how the environment is to be arranged, and

in interaction with staff and family. (60, 61, 62)

32. Accept referral for and begin psychotherapy focused on building self-esteem. (63)

33. Accept referral to social worker or case manager to identify resources required for ongoing therapy. (64)

34. The patient and/or legally designated decision maker agree to intensive therapy for patient to replace violent behaviors with those that are socially appropriate and also effective in meeting the patient's needs. (65)

35. Family report understanding of the reasons for the aggression, the plan for addressing this problem, and the likely prognosis. (7, 37, 66)

36. Family obtain support to help members maintain good family functioning while coping with the patient's aggression and/or violence. (67, 68)

__. _____
   _____

__. _____
   _____

__. _____
   _____

how others are to respond to specified agitated or aggressive behaviors of the patient (e.g., calmly orienting the patient by saying, "You are in a rehabilitation center where the staff will help you get well"; redirecting patient's attention to neutral stimulus by saying, "Let's look at this television program"; telling patient when stressful task will end, such as, "When you finish two more problems, we will stop and you can rest").

18. Develop a simple charting mechanism that will allow staff, family, and others to record occurrences of designated agitated or aggressive behaviors.

19. Communicate behavioral plan to the patient's rehabilitation team, (the patient), family, and others involved in the patient's recovery.

20. Educate family and friends about the importance of responding consistently to targeted behaviors.

21. Prepare a contract specifying the patient's rehabilitation goals, responsibilities of all parties (e.g., the patient, [family], physician, and rehabilitation therapists), and the consequences for not adhering to the points of the agreement. Have all involved sign the

contract. Post a copy in a noticeable place in the patient's room.

22. Schedule the most challenging activities into times when the patient is likely to be most rested.

23. Point out to the patient and family specific ways in which the patient acts, feels, and performs differently when rested versus when fatigued.

24. Recommend that rehabilitation therapists begin therapy session with an activity on which the patient is almost certain to succeed.

25. Point out the patient's success on activity.

26. Advise the patient that the difficulty level is about to increase and enlist his/her agreement by statements such as, "Are you ready to try something harder?" or "Now I'll give you something more difficult," or "You might find this hard, but would you be willing to try?"

27. Reinforce the patient's cooperation, participation, or other positive aspects of his/her behavior during recent activity.

28. If the patient becomes agitated and terminates an activity, instruct the rehabilitation therapist to make a short statement implying that the therapist remains

in charge of the treatment session and is labeling the previous participation as successful (e.g., "Let's stop now; you've done enough," or "That's enough for now; I can see you are getting tired").

29. Conduct or refer for periodic bedside or brief cognitive evaluations to monitor the patient's cognitive recovery by assessing orientation, insight, memory, and other pertinent cognitive functions.

30. Consult with the patient's physician regarding the use of medications to enhance the patient's level of alertness or ability to sustain attention.

31. Consult with the patient's physician regarding the use of medications to reduce the patient's irritability without impairing cognition or recovery.

32. Suggest or coordinate a referral to a physiatrist, psychiatrist, or neurologist with expertise in the treatment of brain injury, for medical management of behavioral problems.

33. Consult with the patient's physician regarding how medications will be prescribed, monitored, and managed.

34. Monitor the patient's use of prescribed medications and their effectiveness; address

issues affecting compliance and side effects.

35. Conduct or refer for neuropsychological testing to identify cognitive factors that may be contributing to the patient's difficulties with insight or self-control, and to determine what cognitive strengths might be used as resources in rebuilding acceptable social behaviors.

36. Conduct or refer for a psychological evaluation to identify psychiatric conditions underlying or contributing to the patient's aggressive or violent behavior.

37. Give feedback to the patient, (the patient's family), physician, rehabilitation team, and other designated persons regarding assessment results and recommendations.

38. Considering legal, ethical, and institutional policies, develop and communicate a plan for how the patient will be restrained if this is necessary to prevent danger to self or others.

39. Guided by institution's policies, develop a plan for use of a time-out room during violent episodes.

40. Alert the institution's security staff to the potential for violence and specifics concerning the patient's behavior so that they may be

prepared to assist quickly and appropriately in interrupting aggression.

41. Remind rehabilitation staff, family, and others to keep at a greater than arm's length distance from the patient, if possible.

42. Recommend that the rehabilitation staff, family, and others have a clear path of egress from the patient's room in the event of a violent episode.

43. Interview the patient to determine the degree to which he/she is aware of cognitive deficits or other functional changes associated with injury or medical illness.

44. Orient the patient frequently to medical condition (e.g., brain injury, aneurysm, stroke), immediate implications (e.g., hard to remember what's happened recently, doesn't pay attention to things on one's left, has hard time knowing how to put shirt on), and purpose of therapies (e.g., to help patient's memory to get stronger; to help patient pay attention to things on his/her left as well as on right; to help patient improve the way he/she works with shapes).

45. Teach family, caregivers, and rehabilitation therapists to avoid using arguing, joking, convincing,

confrontation, or any other "logical" efforts to change the patient's point of view.

46. Teach staff and family that at first signs of agitation, they should direct the patient's attention to a neutral topic using a calm yet firm voice.

47. Calmly and firmly tell the patient to "Take a deep breath. Hold it. Good. Relax." Repeat three or four times.

48. Engage the patient in a conversation about a neutral topic, or direct his/her attention to neutral activity (e.g., a nonviolent television program such as a baseball game).

49. With adequate supervision in place, take the patient for a walk or involve him/her in other physical activities that will help to decrease level of physical arousal.

50. Develop a 24-hour plan outlining the patient's activities at all times.

51. During waking hours, engage the patient's attention with specific topics as much as possible (i.e., avoid many periods in which the patient is left alone in room with nothing to do).

52. Arrange for designated family members and friends to spend time "in shifts" with the patient

in order to keep his/her attention occupied.

53. Evaluate the seriousness and consistency of the patient's threat against a specific individual(s).

54. Consult with other colleagues and legal counsel, if necessary, about seriousness of threat, the patient's ability to enact it, and need to warn intended victim(s). Document the major points of conversation, the impression, and the plan.

55. If the patient has the ability to carry out a serious threat against an individual's life, warn the potential victim, in accordance with state laws.

56. Talk with the patient about the importance of protecting own and other's welfare and urge him/her to sign self into a psychiatric hospital or other secure setting.

57. Coordinate plans to arrange involuntary psychiatric hospitalization for patient.

58. Identify and address the patient's (and family's) questions and concerns regarding inpatient psychiatric or neurobehavioral care.

59. Refer the patient to participate in group activities in which he/she will have an opportunity to get feedback about the social appropriateness of various behaviors.

60. In group or individual setting, teach the patient to rebuild positive social relationship skills (e.g., starting and maintaining a conversation, giving a compliment, asking someone for a date).

61. Teach the patient in group or individually to build or rebuild skills necessary to manage conflict or frustration (e.g., counting to 10 before reacting, assertiveness skills, "I" statements).

62. Use role-playing to model ways to handle disagreement, confrontation, or other difficult social interactions.

63. Conduct or refer the patient for psychotherapy to build self-esteem.

64. Coordinate the patient's referral to social services or case manager to identify resources for long-term therapeutic interventions (e.g., residential neurobehavioral rehabilitation, neurobehavioral day program, life-skills coaching services, intensive individual and/or family psychotherapy) for persistent aggression and violence.

65. Coordinate the patient's referral to long-term facility in which he/she can receive longer-term, intensive therapy targeted toward reducing aggressive or violent behavior and building prosocial behaviors.

66. Educate the patient's family about the neurological reasons behind chronic aggression, the plan for management, and the prognosis for resolving this problem.

67. Perform or refer the family for therapy to facilitate family's positive adaptation to the emotional and behavioral changes in their family member.

68. Refer the family to brain injury, stroke, or other support groups, respite care resources, or advocacy organizations.

__. _____
     _____

__. _____
     _____

__. _____
     _____

DIAGNOSTIC SUGGESTIONS

Axis I:	293.0	Delirium Due to (General Medical Condition)
	294.1	Dementia Due to (General Medical Condition)
	310.1	Personality Change Due to (General Medical Condition)
	293.9	Mental Disorder NOS Due to (General Medical Condition)
	309.3	Adjustment Disorder With Disturbance of Conduct
	309.4	Adjustment Disorder With Mixed Disturbance of Emotions and Conduct
	_____	_____
	_____	_____

Axis II: 301.0   Paranoid Personality Disorder
301.7   Antisocial Personality Disorder
301.83   Borderline Personality Disorder
799.9   Diagnosis Deferred
V71.09   No Diagnosis

_____   _____

_____   _____

ANXIETY/FEAR

BEHAVIORAL DEFINITIONS

1. Persistent worry or fear that exceeds the level typically seen for that situation.
2. Symptoms of motor tension such as restlessness, tiredness, shakiness, or muscle tension.
3. Symptoms of autonomic hyperactivity (such as rapid heartbeat, shortness of breath, sweating, dizziness, dry mouth, nausea, diarrhea) not explained by other medical condition or medication.
4. Hypervigilance such as feeling constantly on edge, concentration difficulties, trouble falling or staying asleep, and a general state of irritability.
5. A specific fear that significantly interferes with daily functioning.

__. _____
   _____
__. _____
   _____
__. _____
   _____

LONG-TERM GOALS

1. Reduce frequency and intensity of anxiety symptoms so that daily functioning is not impaired and acceptable comfort level is achieved.
2. Stabilize the anxiety level while increasing the ability to function on a daily basis.
3. Resolve underlying issues that may be creating or contributing to the anxiety.

4. Enhance ability to effectively handle the full variety of uncertain situations in life.

5. Patient and/or responsible party is able to identify signs of possible recurrence of anxiety, and is aware of behavioral, cognitive, and/or medical actions to take to reduce symptoms.

—. _____

_____

—. _____

_____

—. _____

_____

SHORT-TERM OBJECTIVES

1. Identify type, frequency, severity, and circumstances surrounding occurrence of anxiety symptoms. (1, 2, 3)

2. Cooperate with psychological testing to assess cause and severity of anxiety symptoms. (4, 6)

3. Cooperate with a neuropsychological assessment. (5, 6)

4. Tell the story of the anxiety, the attempts to resolve it, and the suggestions others have given regarding resolution. (7, 8)

5. Identify major life conflicts from the past and present that are associated with feelings of anxiety. (9, 10)

6. Complete anxiety exercises that identify cognitive distortions that generate anxious feelings. (11, 12, 13)

THERAPEUTIC INTERVENTIONS

1. Arrange for or conduct a psychodiagnostic evaluation to determine if an anxiety disorder is present, and to make treatment recommendations.

2. If the patient is a poor historian, obtain permission from patient or legally responsible party to interview person(s) familiar with his/her history.

3. Review medical records and/or consult with the patient's physician to identify medical conditions and medications that might be affecting his/her symptoms.

4. Arrange for or conduct psychological testing to identify severity of anxiety, and to rule out depression or other disorders as primary or coexisting conditions.

7. Report on the success of substituting positive, realistic thoughts for the distortions that precipitate and maintain anxiety. (14)

8. Implement thought-stopping techniques to interrupt anxiety-producing thoughts. (15)

9. List the advantages and disadvantages of the anxiety. (16)

10. Verbalize positive principles that reduce anxious thoughts. (17, 18)

11. Utilize paradoxical intervention to reduce anxiety response. (19, 20)

12. Identify problems that appear unmanageable and that threaten sense of survival or self-esteem. (21, 22)

13. Replace vague impressions about medical condition with accurate understanding of medical condition, treatment options, prognosis, and lifestyle implications. (23, 24, 25)

14. Complete physical evaluation for medications. (26, 27)

15. Take medications as prescribed and report on effectiveness and side effects to appropriate professionals. (27, 28)

16. Identify existing effective skills and preferences for relaxation. (29)

17. Apply physical relaxation techniques to lower physio-

5. Arrange for or conduct neuropsychological testing to identify cognitive problems affecting the patient's thought processes or behavior.

6. Give feedback to the patient (and family), treatment team, and other designated persons regarding assessment results and recommendations.

7. Actively build the level of trust with the patient in individual sessions through consistent eye contact, active listening, unconditional positive regard, and warm acceptance to help increase his/her ability to identify and express feelings.

8. Probe with questions (see *Anxiety Disorders and Phobias* by Beck, Emery, and Greenberg) that require the patient to produce evidence of the anxiety and logical reasons for it being present.

9. Ask the patient to develop and process a list of key past and present life conflicts that have created feelings of fear and anxiety.

10. Assist the patient in becoming aware of unresolved life conflicts related to anxiety feelings and in starting to work toward their resolution.

11. Providing assistance if necessary, have the patient complete the anxiety sec-

logic arousal levels.
(30, 31, 32, 33, 36)

18. Use imagery, memories, and/or music to lower physiologic arousal. (33, 34, 35, 36)

19. Trigger relaxation response with cue. (37, 38, 39)

20. Utilize "alternative medicine" interventions to produce and maintain sense of relaxation. (40)

21. Develop or use hobbies or other activities to decrease level of anxiety. (41, 42, 43, 44)

22. Increase the level of physical exercise sanctioned by medical personnel. (45, 46)

23. Identify a specific fear that interferes with daily functioning as well as the reinforcement contingencies that maintain the fear. (47)

24. Implement reinforcers that support improvement of functional skills. (48)

25. Clarify realistic and irrational components of this fear. (49)

26. Identify and attempt approximations to the feared activity, using relaxation techniques to keep arousal at moderate levels. (50, 51, 52)

27. Note success and congratulate self on progress in overcoming fear. (53, 54)

28. Verbalize insight into how past traumatic experiences

tion exercises in *Ten Days to Self-Esteem* (Burns).

12. Have the patient record in a journal thoughts associated with anxiety episodes.

13. Assist the patient in identifying catastrophizing, "what if" statements, fortune-telling, and other distorted thoughts that precipitate or maintain experience of anxiety.

14. Help the patient develop reality-based, positive cognitive messages that will increase self-confidence in coping with irrational fears.

15. Teach the patient to implement a thought-stopping technique (e.g., thinking of a stop sign and then a pleasant scene, or snapping a rubber band on the wrist) that cognitively interferes with distorted cognitive obsessions; monitor and encourage patient's use of technique in daily life between sessions.

16. Have the patient complete (or assist patient in completing) the "Cost-Benefit Analysis" exercise (see *Ten Days to Self-Esteem* by Burns) in which he/she lists the advantages and disadvantages of the negative thought, fear, or anxiety.

17. Read and process with the patient a fable from *Friedman's Fables* (Friedman) that pertains to anxiety.

are causing anxiety in present unrelated circumstances. (55)

29. Report tolerance for experiences that cannot be controlled. (56, 57)

30. Report increased confidence in ability to spontaneously handle situations effectively. (58, 59)

31. Verbalize an understanding of how the use of alcohol, marijuana, and other substances are ineffective as long-term solutions to anxiety and can interfere with effective problem solving. (60)

32. Accept referral for substance abuse treatment. (61)

33. Report understanding of own anxiety and ways to manage it using relaxation techniques, cognitive techniques, daily activities, and medications. (62)

—. _____
_____

—. _____
_____

—. _____
_____

18. Assist the patient in identifying philosophies that reduce anxieties (such as "The universe is a friendly place," and "Everything occurs as it should") and encourage him/her to think of these statements during times of anxiety.

19. Develop a paradoxical intervention (see *Ordeal Therapy* by Haley), in which the patient is encouraged to have the problem (e.g., anxiety) and then schedule that anxiety to occur at specific intervals each day in a specific way and for a defined length of time. Include in the schedule times of the day/night when the patient would clearly want to be doing something else.

20. Assign the patient to "worry on purpose" at specific times about specific topics that may or may not normally precipitate anxious thoughts.

21. Assist the patient in identifying problems that seem outside of his/her ability to solve or manage and then either develop a plan to enlist the help of others to solve the problem or turn it over to a higher power.

22. Identify need for resources and facilitate patient referral to appropriate professionals in the facility or community, such as social worker, social service agen-

cies, Social Security disability office, and so forth.

23. Assess the patient's need for education regarding medical condition, symptoms, and actions that patient can currently take to improve condition; coordinate with other treatment professionals in providing educational information.

24. Provide the patient and family with educational materials regarding medical condition and its treatment and/or refer to reliable Internet resources.

25. Inform the patient and family of support groups or advocacy organizations dealing with patient's particular medical condition.

26. Assess need for medications to reduce symptoms of anxiety and then refer to and consult with the patient's treating physician regarding how medication will be prescribed, monitored, and managed.

27. Address the patient's (and family's) concerns about medications and assist them in getting answers to questions about medication and side effects.

28. Monitor the patient's use of and results from prescribed medications; address issues affecting compliance and side effects, including habituation and dependence, if applicable.

29. Inquire into things that the patient has done in the past to relax that have been successful, and encourage their continued or renewed implementation.

30. Instruct the patient in deep breathing techniques.

31. Train the patient in progressive muscle relaxation techniques.

32. Perform or arrange for biofeedback to develop relaxation skills.

33. Select or allow the patient to select a chapter in *The Relaxation and Stress Reduction Workbook* (Davis, Eshelman, and McKay); then work with patient to implement the chosen technique.

34. Instruct the patient in guided imagery for anxiety relief.

35. Encourage the patient to identify and use music that promotes relaxation.

36. Facilitate the patient's obtaining audiotape of favorite relaxation technique(s).

37. Assign the patient to practice relaxation technique one to three times per day.

38. Have the patient select a verbal (e.g. "calm," "relax"), visual (e.g., beach scene), or other cue. Instruct patient to bring this specific cue to mind at the point of deepest relaxation.

39. Instruct the patient to bring the relaxation cue to mind during the session and have him/her notice how the cue is effective in facilitating a sense of relaxation.

40. Encourage the patient to explore potential benefits of yoga, massage, aromatherapy, tai chi, or meditation and support continued participation if effective for him/her.

41. Inquire into hobbies and other activities the patient has used in the past to create pleasure or enjoyment, and reinforce their continued or renewed implementation.

42. Encourage the patient to resume recreational activities that are within his/her medical or cognitive capabilities.

43. Facilitate referral to recreational therapist to assist the patient in resuming previous recreational activities, with adaptations, if necessary, or developing new activities suited to patient's current skills.

44. Assist the patient in working through loss or other emotions that interfere with him/her accepting adapted or new activities.

45. Identify exercises (e.g., water exercises, stationary bicycle, mall walking, armchair exercises) appropriate to patient's physical and

cognitive abilities, and support participation.

46. Assign the patient to read and implement programs from *Exercising Your Way to Better Mental Health* (Leith).

47. Assist the patient in specifying fear and contingencies surrounding occurrence of fear (e.g., antecedent and subsequent events, location, time, intensity, and duration).

48. Design reinforcements to support increases in functional activity and to minimize reinforcement of fear-related behavior.

49. Assist the patient in verbalizing both realistic risks and irrational concerns.

50. Use systematic desensitization methods to break the targeted activity into components that successively approximate the desired goal.

51. Enlist the patient's agreement to attempt the least risky components.

52. Direct the patient to use deep breathing or other rapid relaxation procedure before commencing activity.

53. Have the patient point out (or name for patient) the success in accomplishing component(s).

54. Direct the patient to acknowledge the courage demonstrated in working through fear.

55. Reinforce the patient's insights into past emotional issues and present anxiety.

56. Inquire into the patient's world view, life philosophy, or religious beliefs concerning what in life can and cannot be controlled.

57. Identify religious rituals and other practices from which the patient might draw strength, and support participation in them.

58. Utilize a brief solution-focused therapy approach in which the patient is probed to find a time or situation in his/her life when he/she successfully handled the specific anxiety or an anxiety in general. Clearly focus the approach he/she used and then encourage the patient to increase the use of this approach. Monitor and modify the solution as required.

59. Inquire into times in which the patient was impressed by his/her ability to handle unplanned for, difficult situations, and reinforce this resourcefulness.

60. Educate the patient (and family) about the impact of alcohol and other mood-altering substances on attempting to resolve anxiety disorders.

61. Assess the patient's substance abuse patterns and, if necessary, coordinate re-

ferral for therapy addressing substance abuse or dependence.

62. Refer the patient to written
information about anxiety
and its management, such
as *Thoughts and Feelings:
Taking Control of Your
Moods and Your Life,*
(McKay, Davis, and Fan-
ning), *The Anxiety and Phobia Workbook* (Bourne), *An
End to Panic* (Zuercher-
White), and *The Relaxation
and Stress Reduction Workbook* (Davis, Eshelman, and
McKay).

___. _____

_____

___. _____

_____

___. _____

_____

DIAGNOSTIC SUGGESTIONS

Axis I:

300.01	Panic Disorder Without Agoraphobia
300.21	Panic Disorder With Agoraphobia
300.29	Specific Phobia
300.23	Social Phobia
308.3	Acute Stress Disorder
300.02	Generalized Anxiety Disorder
293.84	Anxiety Disorder Due to (Axis III Condition)
291.89	Alcohol-Induced Anxiety Disorder
292.89	Substance-Induced Anxiety Disorder (Specify Substance)
300.00	Anxiety Disorder NOS
309.24	Adjustment Disorder With Anxiety
309.28	Adjustment Disorder With Mixed Anxiety and Depressed Mood

	309.4	Adjustment Disorder With Mixed Disturbance of Emotions and Conduct
	316	Psychological Factor (Specify) Affecting (General Medical Condition)
	_____	_____
	_____	_____
Axis II:	301.4	Obsessive-Compulsive Personality Disorder
	301.9	Personality Disorder NOS
	799.9	Diagnosis Deferred
	V71.09	No Diagnosis
	_____	_____
	_____	_____

ATTENTION AND CONCENTRATION IMPAIRMENT

BEHAVIORAL DEFINITIONS

1. Fails to notice significant stimuli in the environment.
2. Slow to detect and process pertinent information.
3. Unable to maintain focus on task until it is completed.
4. Unintentionally interrupts work on designated task when competing stimuli occur; distractible.
5. Requires unusual investment of energy and time in order to complete task.
6. Difficulty alternating between tasks.
7. Displays poor accuracy on primary task when working in a noisy or otherwise busy environment.
8. High error rate despite preserved skill (e.g., generates incorrect financial reports despite preserved mathematical skills; work is returned because it is incomplete).
9. Errors are inconsistent or explained by omission of details (e.g., gets multiplication problem wrong due to failure to place decimal point; misspells words at elementary school grade level while spelling several college-level words correctly).
10. Shifts topic of conversation abruptly.
11. Unable to follow two- or three-step commands.
12. Self-report of or described by others as having poor memory.

—. _____
   _____

—. _____
   _____

—. _____
   _____

LONG-TERM GOALS

1. Perceive and process essential information.
2. Persist in directing effort to specified task until it is complete.
3. Possess insight into residual attention and concentration problems.
4. Use compensatory strategies effectively to enhance performance.
5. Adjust environment to enhance performance.
6. Request necessary modifications in an assertive manner.
7. Refrain from activities that have potential to harm self or others because of changed attention or concentration skills.
8. Emotionally accept need to use strategies, adapt environment, and adjust goals.

___. _____
_____

___. _____
_____

___. _____
_____

SHORT-TERM OBJECTIVES

1. Cooperate with evaluation of attention and concentration abilities. (1, 2, 3, 7)
2. Participate willingly in neuropsychological testing. (4, 7)
3. Agree to assessment procedures to identify psychiatric conditions that might be affecting attention and concentration. (5, 6, 7)
4. Cooperate with efforts to use medications to optimize attention. (8)
5. Provide information about typical and recent sleep patterns and problems. (3, 9, 10)

THERAPEUTIC INTERVENTIONS

1. Review the patient's medical record to identify or rule out neurological conditions, learning disabilities, prior brain injuries, medications, substance-related disorders, psychiatric disorders, pain, or acute medical conditions (e.g., delirium) that might be affecting the patient's ability to focus attention and maintain concentration.
2. Interview the patient (patient's family) regarding the patient's ability to attend and concentrate prior to the most recent injury or medical event.

6. Implement changes designed to improve sleep quality. (11, 12)

7. Report on the impact of interventions on satisfaction with sleep and with daytime energy level. (13)

8. Agree to and participate in actions designed to address coexisting psychiatric disorders. (14)

9. Agree to temporarily eliminate sounds, sights, or other stimuli that might distract one from the main task. (15)

10. Family members consciously select sentence structure, speech rate, and intonation to help the patient concentrate. (16, 17, 18, 19, 20)

11. Verbalize accurate information about person, place, and time orientation. (21)

12. Provide information regarding positive and negative effects of visitors on mood and behavior and agree to arrange visitation to promote recovery. (22, 23)

13. Implement the visitation plan and provide information about the effectiveness of the plan. (24, 25)

14. Family members verbalize an understanding of a "catastrophic reaction" as a common response to overstimulation and demonstrate at least three actions they can take to help the

3. Consult with the patient (patient's family) and rehabilitation professionals regarding the adequacy of the patient's sleep.

4. Refer for or conduct a neuropsychological evaluation to identify the patient's ability to focus and maintain attention under various conditions, to identify other cognitive deficits affecting attentional skills, and to determine cognitive strengths that can be utilized in the rehabilitation process.

5. Refer for or conduct a psychodiagnostic evaluation to identify delirium, depression, bipolar disorder, anxiety, substance abuse, schizophrenia, or other disorders that might affect the patient's attention and concentration abilities.

6. Refer for or conduct psychological testing to assist in the diagnosis and clarification of psychiatric disorders that might impact the patient's attention and concentration abilities.

7. Give feedback to the patient (patient's family), physician, rehabilitation team, and other designated persons regarding assessment results and recommendations.

8. Consult with the patient's physician regarding adjustments in medications that might enhance his/her at-

patient regain a sense of control. (26, 27)

15. Accept the need for cognitive rehabilitation therapy and cooperate with the therapists in assessing and treating attention/concentration deficits. (28)

16. Acknowledge the potential of leisure activities to rebuild attention/concentration skills, and participate in recreational therapy. (29, 30)

17. Family members describe activities that they can do with the patient that will challenge him/her to pay attention without being overtaxing. (31, 32)

18. Challenge self to improve performance on computer and video games requiring attention to changing stimuli. (33)

19. Agree to have therapists, family members, and friends point out attentional lapses and to redirect to the topic of conversation. (34, 35)

20. Give best effort to understand and participate in structured therapy sessions in ways to accommodate limited concentration skills. (36, 37, 38)

21. Attempt to expand the length of time during which attention is focused. (39, 40, 41)

22. Describe ways in which participation in work, household responsibilities, and

tention (i.e., discontinuing medications that interfere with attention or adding medications to enhance the patient's ability to focus).

9. Inquire into the patient's typical, preinjury/preillness sleep patterns and routines, and identify any sleep abnormalities.

10. Consult with the patient (patient's family) and rehabilitation therapists to identify environmental factors (e.g., noise from the nurses' station, roommate who moans, patient too cold and unable to pull blankets up), medical factors (e.g., pain, unable to position self in preferred sleeping position due to hemiparesis, poor bladder control), or activity-related factors (e.g., misses evening bath, can't get back to sleep after being awakened for medication, naps during the day) that interfere with the patient's sleep.

11. Consult with the patient's physician about medical interventions to reduce hindrances and to improve the quality of the patient's sleep.

12. In consultation with the patient (patient's family) and rehabilitation team, develop and coordinate implementation of a plan to structure the patient's activities and environment in ways to be conducive to uninterrupted, restful sleep.

hobbies might be affected by attention deficits. (42)

23. Practice tasks that are designed to improve performance on relevant employment, household, and hobby skills. (43)

24. Tolerate background noise and other distractions while demonstrating concentration. (44)

25. Utilize external aids to remind self to accomplish important daily tasks. (45)

26. Implement and describe the benefits of rehearsal and repetition in maintaining concentration throughout a task. (46)

27. Implement a technique of reminding self prior to giving attention to the task of the consequences of successful/unsuccessful task completion. (47)

28. Schedule shopping, medical appointments, and other community activities to avoid crowded peak times or other situations that would be cognitively overtaxing. (48, 49)

29. Gradually attend community activities at busier (but not the busiest!) times in order to increase tolerance for stimulation. (50)

30. Incorporate behavioral strategies to reduce the chance of making errors. (51)

13. Monitor the implementation of actions to enhance the patient's sleep and assess the effectiveness of these interventions on both sleep quality and behavior during waking hours.

14. Initiate or arrange for treatment for depression, anxiety, substance abuse, or other psychiatric conditions that might be reducing the patient's ability to focus and maintain attention. (See Depression/Grief, Anxiety/Fear, Substance Abuse, and/or Posttraumatic Stress Disorder chapters in this Planner.)

15. Reduce or eliminate auditory stimuli (e.g., turn off radio, use private quiet room for therapies, allow only one conversation in the patient's room at a time) and/or visual stimuli (e.g., turn off television, close blinds to eliminate view of activities in courtyard) that interfere with the patient's ability to focus and maintain attention.

16. Teach the need for—and model for the family—speaking to the patient in short sentences having simple grammatical structure (i.e., subject, predicate, object).

17. Teach the need for—and model for the family—minimal use of sentences with negatives (e.g., instead of

31. Demonstrate an increased degree of productivity due to more focused concentration and less distraction. (52, 53)

32. Cooperate with a referral to evaluate the potential benefit of EEG biofeedback procedures on concentration ability. (54)

33. Cooperate with an evaluation to determine the need for supervision and/or accommodations to perform usual daily activities that may be dangerous or lead to self-defeating consequences. (55, 56)

34. Accept the recommendations of rehabilitation professionals regarding necessary modifications in daily activities to ensure personal safety and welfare. (57)

35. Work cooperatively with a vocational counselor to identify how to most successfully return to school or to work. (58)

36. Describe the accommodations that will likely be necessary in order to perform most successfully at school or at work. (59)

37. Verbalize knowledge of relevant laws regarding the right to accommodations and the procedures to follow to have them implemented. (60, 61)

38. Utilize legal counsel to pursue the right to accommodations. (62)

saying what is *not* going to happen, indicate what *will* be happening) in their communications with the patient.

18. Teach the need for—and model for the family and visitors—the use of a slowed, deliberate speech rate to give the patient sufficient time to process information.

19. Teach the need for—and model for the family—interaction with the patient that is calm, firm, and nonthreatening.

20. Instruct the family and visitors to allow only one conversation at a time when visiting with the patient.

21. Provide orientation information frequently and display it prominently in the patient's room.

22. Observe the patient's behavior with visitors and identify whether he/she has difficulty tolerating large numbers of visitors, specific visitor behaviors (e.g., children who are very active, friend who talks in a loud voice, brother who is hyper-talkative), or visitation at certain times of the day (e.g., in the morning before completing usual grooming activities, in the afternoon when scheduled to go to therapy, in the late evening when fatigued).

39. Engage in psychotherapy to deal with the emotional issues associated with changed abilities, changed lifestyle, and changed relationship roles. (63)

40. Family members report an awareness of the patient's residual attention/concentration deficits and their implications for the patient and all family members. (64)

41. Family members describe their emotional acceptance of the patient's cognitive changes and the ways in which their family life has been altered. (64, 65)

—. _____
   _____

—. _____
   _____

—. _____
   _____

23. Create guidelines for visitation that suit the patient's needs and are congruent with the institution's policies.

24. Inform the rehabilitation staff about visitation guidelines and determine how these will be implemented (e.g., placing sign on the patient's door, having family member call the patient's friends and ask them to visit in small groups, have family member request that friends indicate when they will visit to avoid having excessive numbers of visitors on any day).

25. Monitor the effect that the visitation plan has on the patient's mood and behavior and adjust visitation guidelines to suit his/her abilities and needs.

26. Discuss the signs of a "catastrophic reaction" (e.g., agitation, abrupt anger, sudden crying) with the patient and the patient's significant others and indicate that this is likely an indication that his/her ability to pay attention has been exceeded.

27. Identify specific steps that family members and significant others can take to restore the patient's sense of comfort in the event of a "catastrophic reaction" (e.g., stopping a conversation and calmly and firmly saying, "Take a deep breath; good;

that's enough [name of activity that had been ongoing] for now; let's take a break"; or taking the patient's hand or rubbing the patient's back in an effort to soothe him/her while arranging for the level of stimulation to be reduced).

28. Refer for and/or reinforce the patient's participation in cognitive rehabilitation therapy to increase his/her attention and concentration abilities.

29. Refer the patient to a recreational therapist for recommendations regarding leisure activities that can help build his/her attention and concentration abilities.

30. Teach the patient the value of recreational activities and address the possibility that he/she may believe that time spent on leisure activities might be better spent on "real" therapies.

31. When the patient is able to concentrate for at least five minutes, suggest activities that family or friends could do with him/her that would require focused attention without being too demanding (e.g., looking at photographs in an album or a magazine, reading headlines or brief news summaries, playing checkers).

32. When the patient is able to concentrate for 15 minutes or more, recommend addi-

tional activities that the family might enjoy with him/her (e.g., reading short human-interest stories, playing simple card games, planting and caring for potted plants).

33. Recommend that the patient play games on the computer that build attention span (e.g., video games requiring the patient to detect a target, solitaire, etc.).

34. Obtain the patient's permission for others to interrupt when he/she strays off topic to remind him/her of the topic of conversation.

35. Instruct the family to redirect the patient to the topic in a matter-of-fact, nonjudgmental way (e.g., "Let's go back to talking about the baseball game").

36. Schedule psychotherapy and other therapy sessions to be short (within the patient's concentration span) and perhaps more frequent.

37. Instruct the patient to take a brief rest break in the middle of a task when it is apparent that his/her attention is waning.

38. Plan the patient's therapy schedule so as to avoid putting cognitively demanding sessions back-to-back, without a rest break.

39. Using a stopwatch, time how long the patient is able to remain focused on a task.

Ask him/her to set a new goal, and challenge him/her to continue working until reaching or exceeding that goal.

40. Reinforce the patient's ability to stay on task for a specified period; gradually lengthen the amount of time that must go by before reinforcement is provided.

41. Graph or otherwise chart the length of time that the patient is able to concentrate on a task, and post this graph where he/she can refer to it frequently.

42. Assist the patient in identifying the negative impact that his/her attentional deficit has on his/her safety, accuracy, and productivity within the work or home setting or while pursuing a hobby; reinforce the patient's insight and encourage focused effort on overcoming this deficit.

43. Assign the patient therapy exercises and homework tasks requiring focused attention that are clearly relevant to his/her work or interests (e.g., make sure patient knows how a task will be personally beneficial; use cognitive exercises that relate to patient's profession, home responsibilities, or hobbies).

44. Build the patient's tolerance to distractions by gradually introducing com-

peting stimuli while he/she is working on a task (e.g., turn television on while patient is attempting to read a newspaper article; go grocery shopping when a moderate number of other people are also shopping; balance checkbook while listening to music).

45. Train the patient in the use of external aids (e.g., checklists, alarms, computerized reminder systems) to cue himself/herself as to what needs to be done and when to do it.

46. Recommend that the patient use verbal or visual rehearsal to maintain concentration (e.g., picturing a cheese sandwich and a glass of milk when writing "milk, bread, and cheese" on the list of groceries to be purchased; using a person's name several times in the conversation that follows the initial meeting; counting out loud when counting money).

47. Suggest that the patient cue himself/herself about the personal benefits of maintaining good attention just before beginning a task (e.g., considering how proud one's family will be if one can pay the bills accurately and on time; thinking about the inconvenience associated with failing to write expenditures in a checkbook ledger; imag-

ining how pleased the pa-
tient's spouse will be if the
patient is able to follow
his/her conversation) in
order to heighten the pa-
tient's arousal and interest
and therefore increase the
likelihood of performing the
task accurately.

48. Recommend that the patient schedule outings to
public areas (e.g., shopping,
attending church) during
those times that are typically least crowded.

49. Minimize the patient's exposure to situations where divided attention is required
for success (e.g., noisy party,
driving, social hour following church service).

50. When the patient is able to
tolerate public situations
under the quietest of conditions, obtain his/her agreement to go into the
community at times when
there will be an increased,
but still moderate, level of
activity.

51. Train the patient in the use
of behavioral strategies to
increase accuracy (e.g.,
using calculator; establishing habit of double- or
triple-checking work; setting a timer to remind self
to check on food that is
cooking).

52. Reward the patient for sustained concentration (e.g.,
pay per unit of accurate
work produced rather than

for the amount of time
spent at a job, provide reinforcement for completed accurate work, reinforce for
persisting on task).

53. Monitor the patient's level
of productivity and provide
feedback on a regular basis.

54. Coordinate a referral for
evaluation of the patient's
potential to benefit from
EEG neurofeedback to in-
crease his/her ability to concentrate.

55. Refer the patient for an occupational therapy evaluation to assess the impact of
his/her attentional deficits
on safety and accuracy in
performing everyday activities (e.g., cooking, paying
bills, using knives to cut
vegetables, etc.).

56. Refer the patient for a driving evaluation to assess
his/her ability to drive
safely under various traffic
conditions and to assess the
need for accommodations.

57. In consultation with the
treatment team, identify
those activities which the
patient (1) should not perform at all, due to safety
concerns, (2) should perform
with supervision, or (3) can
perform independently.

58. Refer the patient to a vocational counselor to identify
his/her potential to return
to the same or a different
job or academic program,

and to identify necessary accommodations.

59. Discuss accommodations that could be made at school or in the workplace to help the patient perform at his/her best (e.g., providing a quiet area in which to work, eliminating interruptions, allowing frequent rest breaks, simplifying tasks so that the patient attends to only one aspect of a task at a time).

60. Discuss with the patient the implications of the Americans With Disabilities Act (ADA), other legislation, or judicial rulings affecting his/her entitlement to accommodations at school, in the workplace, or in other areas.

61. Identify steps that the patient should take in order to request accommodations from a school, employer, or other entity, and determine that he/she has the knowledge and confidence to pursue obtaining necessary accommodations.

62. Discuss the possible utility of the patient obtaining legal counsel to compel school administrators, employers, or others to comply with legal guidelines regarding reasonable accommodations; make a referral to an attorney knowledgeable in this area of the law.

63. Refer for or conduct psychotherapy to support the patient in adjusting to changed abilities and the impact of these changes on self-image and on relationships.

64. Educate the family about the patient's residual deficits in attention/concentration, recommended activity changes, compensatory techniques, and accommodations, using examples that relate specifically to the patient's and family's life together.

65. Refer the family to resources (family therapy, support groups, reading materials, etc.) to assist them in coming to terms emotionally with the changes in their family life.

___. _____
     _____

___. _____
     _____

___. _____
     _____

DIAGNOSTIC SUGGESTIONS

Axis I: 294.9   Cognitive Disorder, NOS
             314.xx   Attention Deficit/Hyperactivity Disorder, (state type)
             314.9   Attention Deficit/Hyperactivity Disorder NOS
             _____   _____
             _____   _____

Axis II: V71.09   No Diagnosis or Condition

_____   _____

_____   _____

CHRONIC PAIN

BEHAVIORAL DEFINITIONS

1. Physical discomfort or distress of at least three months' duration.
2. Screaming, moaning, or phrases suggesting suffering (e.g., "Oh, oh, oh," "I have such a terrible headache today," "My back is killing me") apparently associated with physical sensation.
3. Grimacing or other facial expression suggesting physical discomfort and suffering.
4. Tensing or withdrawing body part in anticipation of or reaction to physical distress.
5. Refusal to engage in activity because "it hurts."
6. Decreased activity level attributed to physical discomfort, resulting in poor physical strength and endurance.
7. Reduction (or complete loss) in ability to engage in normal social, vocational, and recreational activities because of physical distress.
8. Relationships dominated or strongly influenced by pain.
9. Excessive use of over-the-counter analgesics.
10. Increased tolerance and perceived need for narcotic medication.
11. Use of street drugs or illegal substances with intent to decrease physical discomfort.
12. Troublesome cognitive and behavioral side effects from medication.
13. Excessive, nonproductive changing from one doctor to another in an effort to "cure" the pain.

__._____

_____

_____

Note: Some of the interventions in this chapter were based upon those in the "Chronic Pain" chapter in the *Behavioral Medicine Treatment Planner* (De-Good, Crawford, and Jongsma), with permission of the authors.

__. _____

    _____

    _____

__. _____

    _____

LONG-TERM GOALS

1. Reduce physical discomfort and emotional suffering to tolerable levels.
2. Refrain from frequent verbalizations or other communications about level of physical distress and suffering.
3. Participate in necessary and routine activities despite discomfort.
4. Maintain physical fitness through regular exercise suited to physical capabilities.
5. Manage activity level and energy expenditure to allow for participation in a variety of work, social, and recreational activities.
6. Reduce or terminate dependence on narcotic medications while utilizing medications that reduce pain according to physician's recommendations.
7. Identify and utilize benign interventions (e.g., heat, relaxation, transcutaneous neural stimulation) effectively to increase comfort level.
8. Become knowledgeable, active, and self-reliant in effectively managing pain.

__. _____

    _____

__. _____

    _____

__. _____

    _____

SHORT-TERM OBJECTIVES	THERAPEUTIC INTERVENTIONS
1. Describe the type and history of pain symptoms, efforts to manage pain, and	1. Conduct a behavioral analysis of the patient's pain by inquiring into the onset, location, duration, intensity,

others' reaction to the pain.
(1, 2, 3)

2. Discuss how the pain has affected one's life, including both negative and positive changes. (4, 5)

3. Provide accurate information about the amount, frequency, and history of the use of prescription and over-the-counter medications, herbs, and street drugs or illegal substances. (6, 7)

4. Identify how medical factors caused or contribute to physical distress. (7)

5. Report satisfaction that appropriate medical care has been obtained and that reasonable avenues to "cure" the pain have been considered. (8, 9, 10)

6. Agree to work with physician to gradually withdraw medications to which one has become addicted.
(11, 12)

7. Take medications to reduce pain levels as directed by physician and report as to effectiveness and side effects. (13, 14)

8. Cooperate with psychodiagnostic procedures to identify coexisting or contributing psychiatric conditions.
(15, 16, 18)

9. Accept a treatment plan for depression, anxiety, and/or substance abuse. (16)

10. Cooperate with neuropsychological testing. (17, 18)

and frequency of the pain. Ask about the outcome of treatments the patient has tried so far, factors that affect pain levels, and others' reactions to the pain.

2. Assess the intensity and/or other characteristics of the patient's pain using a numeric rating scale, visual analogue scale, McGill Pain Questionnaire (Melzack), or other instruments.

3. Observe the patient while interacting with therapists, family, and friends. Identify the ways (words, moans, grimaces, body posture) in which the patient communicates that he/she is experiencing pain. Notice what others do in response to the pain communication.

4. Inquire into ways in which the patient's activities and relationships have changed since the onset of the pain. Listen carefully for statements suggesting that the patient's stress level may have been reduced in reaction to the pain. Notice voice inflections or body language that may signal some pleasurable outcome related to pain-related life changes.

5. Administer questionnaires (e.g., Functional Assessment Screening Questionnaire [Millard], Sickness Impact Profile [Bergner, Bobbitt, Carter, and Gilson], Chronic

11. State realistic, achievable rehabilitation goals. (19, 20)

12. Verbalize a resolution of the anger, grief, and other emotions that are associated with the realization that physical discomfort and the reduction in abilities are likely to be long-standing. (21, 22)

13. Verbalize an understanding of key concepts regarding comprehensive management of chronic pain. (23, 24, 25, 26)

14. Identify factors that influence pain level. (1, 27, 28)

15. Participate in aggressive treatments to interrupt muscle spasms, reduce tone, or otherwise address treatable neuromuscular conditions exacerbating the level of pain. (29)

16. Implement relaxation techniques to reduce physiologic arousal levels and levels of muscle tension. (30, 31, 32, 37)

17. Utilize hypnosis to interrupt pain experience and increase comfort. (33, 34, 37)

18. Use imagery, memories, and/or music to lower levels of muscle tension and physiologic arousal. (32, 35, 36, 37)

19. Apply heat or cold to reduce pain level. (38)

20. Use nerve stimulation devices as directed to interrupt pain signal. (39)

Illness Problem Inventory [Kames, Naliboff, Heinrich, and Schag]) to assess the impact of the pain on the patient's daily activities and relationships.

6. Gather a complete history from the patient of medications or other chemicals used to manage the pain problem (e.g., prescription medications, over-the-counter medications, herbal remedies, and street drugs); ask patient to report on the effectiveness, habituation patterns, and side effects of each.

7. Review the patient's medical record and/or consult with his/her treating physician regarding medical factors causing or affecting the pain problem, and his/her use of medication to reduce pain. Consider whether the patient may be currently addicted to pain-reducing substances.

8. Ask the patient's opinion about the quality of his/her medical care and whether anything obvious has been overlooked. Challenge the patient to consider the risk of iatrogenic effects of tests, surgeries, or other procedures that he/she would like to try in order to "see if they might help."

9. If the patient's medical care for the acute condition and chronic pain appear to have

21. Agree to a trial of acupuncture for pain reduction. (40, 41)

22. Explore the potential benefits of chiropractic care, if approved by one's treating physician. (40, 42)

23. Utilize massage to reduce pain levels and to relax muscles. (40, 43)

24. Incorporate yoga practices into schedule to reduce stress and build awareness of mind-body relationships. (44)

25. Identify hopelessness, helplessness, and other distorted, negative cognitions that lead to and reinforce higher stress levels. (45, 46)

26. Report on the success of substituting positive, realistic thoughts for the distortions that precipitate and maintain stress. (47, 48)

27. Identify negative emotions and experiences that have been reawakened by or are affecting the way in which the current pain problem is managed or experienced. (49, 50)

28. Identify and demonstrate willingness to work through ways in which the pain may be inadvertently reinforced. (51, 52)

29. Verbalize adaptive spiritual and philosophic attitudes toward pain and limitations. (53, 54)

been haphazard, piecemeal, or otherwise insufficient, refer him/her to a reputable physiatrist or pain specialist to review the treatment to date and provide overall medical management.

10. Inquire into the patient's level of trust and confidence in the physician who is managing the pain problem and help the patient decide how to address those areas in which he/she has ongoing concerns.

11. Consult with the patient's treating physician to develop a plan to safely withdraw patient from addictive pain medications (e.g., consult a psychiatrist, refer to an inpatient pain program, refer for inpatient medical-psychiatric care).

12. Address the patient's (and family's) concerns about how pain medications will be withdrawn, and how the patient's symptoms will be managed during the weaning period and after the medications are withdrawn.

13. Consult with the patient's treating physician regarding the need for pharmacologic interventions to manage pain levels and clarify how medication will be obtained, monitored, and managed.

14. Monitor the patient's use of prescribed and over-the-counter medications, herbs,

30. Utilize energy conservation techniques and good body mechanics to minimize physical strain. (25, 55)

31. Participate in physical therapy, conditioning, and exercise programs as directed by physician and therapists to maintain fitness and endurance. (56, 57, 58)

32. Report on interests and activities that can and will be maintained despite the pain. (59, 60)

33. Decrease or eliminate communications about pain. (61, 62)

34. Describe the positive impact of focusing conversations on activities and accomplishments. (63)

35. Plan daily schedule to allow for proper pacing of activity level. (27, 28, 64, 65)

36. Utilize assertive communications to set limits, avoiding situations that could cause pain levels to rise. (66, 67)

37. Describe a plan for carrying out activities and meeting responsibilities that takes into account lifestyle adjustments necessary to manage pain. (65, 68)

38. Participate in vocational counseling sessions to identify job opportunities suited to medical, cognitive, and physical abilities. (69, 70)

alcohol, or illegal substances and their effects. Address issues regarding compliance with the medical program and side effects.

15. Conduct or refer for a psychodiagnostic interview and/or psychological testing to identify mood, anxiety, or personality disorders coexisting with or contributing to the pain problem.

16. Develop a plan to address the patient's depression, anxiety, and/or substance abuse. (See Depression/ Grief, Anxiety/Fear, and/or Substance Abuse chapters in this Planner.)

17. Arrange for or conduct neuropsychological testing of the patient to separate acute (e.g., effects of depression, pain, etc.) from longer-term (e.g., effects from brain injury or illness) cognitive deficits to assist in treatment planning.

18. Give feedback regarding the evaluation results and recommendations to patient, (patient's family), physician, rehabilitation team, and other designated persons.

19. Talk with the patient about specific results he/she hopes to achieve through therapy. Using input from the rehabilitation team, give the patient feedback about what likely can be achieved and

39. Attend and cooperate with all aspects of a work-hardening program. (71)

40. Complete applications for Social Security Disability Income (SSDI) or other sources of financial assistance if there will be a significant delay in returning to full-time work. (69, 72, 73)

41. Make appropriate use of marital/family counseling as needed. (74)

42. Participate in support groups with others who are living with chronic pain. (22, 75)

—. _____
   _____

—. _____
   _____

—. _____
   _____

what may be beyond the scope of current pain management technology.

20. Assist the patient in establishing interim goals that appear to be achievable given his/her overall condition.

21. Refer for or perform individual psychotherapy to assist the patient in identifying and working through emotions associated with recognizing the long-term nature of the pain condition and the need for significant lifestyle changes.

22. Refer the patient to psychotherapy group in which participants are dealing with significant loss and lifestyle change brought on by injuries or illnesses.

23. Discuss with the patient the "gate theory" of pain and the types of factors (e.g., stress, activity level, depression) that often affect pain.

24. Teach the patient key concepts in pain management: rehabilitation versus biologic healing process, conservative versus aggressive medical interventions, acute versus chronic pain, benign versus nonbenign pain, cure versus management, appropriate use of medications, role of exercise, and self-regulation techniques.

25. Assist the patient in obtaining information about causes and management of chronic pain. Recommend reading *Learning to Master Your Chronic Pain* (Jamison), *The Chronic Pain Control Workbook* (Catalano and Hardin), or *Managing Pain Before It Manages You* (Caudill).

26. Evaluate the patient's understanding of how current therapy activities will help him/her achieve stated goals. Encourage the patient to ask occupational, physical, or other therapists to explain the purpose of those activities that he/she may not understand.

27. Instruct the patient to keep a daily log of activities, pain level, and mood for a two- to four-week period. Recommend that he/she rate *current* pain, rate *current* mood, and list activities since the previous rating at several defined points during the day (e.g., first thing in the morning, noontime, dinnertime, and bedtime).

28. Review the activity/mood/pain log with the patient, looking for factors that are associated with higher and lower pain levels.

29. Consult with the patient's treating physician regarding whether the patient might benefit from nerve

blocks, injections, intrathecal medications, or other interventions to interrupt excessive muscle tightness or interrupt pain signal.

30. Teach the patient to relax muscles and reduce physiologic arousal using behavioral and cognitive-behavioral methods (e.g., deep breathing, progressive muscle relaxation, hand or foot warming, breath control).

31. Perform or arrange for biofeedback to enhance the patient's relaxation skills.

32. Select or allow the patient to choose a chapter in the *The Relaxation and Stress Reduction Workbook* (Davis, Eshelman, and McKay) or *Thoughts and Feelings: Taking Control of Your Moods and Your Life* (McKay, Davis, and Fanning); then work with the patient to implement the chosen technique.

33. Perform or refer the patient for hypnosis for pain reduction or relief.

34. Teach the patient or arrange for him/her to learn self-hypnosis skills and posthypnotic suggestions to achieve a greater sense of comfort.

35. Instruct the patient in pleasant guided imagery for relaxation.

36. Encourage the patient to identify and use music that promotes relaxation.

37. Facilitate the patient's obtaining audiotape(s) of favorite relaxation and/or hypnotic technique(s).

38. With the physician's approval, recommend that the patient use heat (e.g., heating pads, hot baths, topical ointment) or cold (e.g., ice packs) as preferred to reduce pain level.

39. Refer the patient for evaluation for transcutaneous neural stimulation (TNS) to determine whether it might be effective in reducing his/her level of pain.

40. Initiate discussion with the patient's treating physician about the potential benefits or contraindications of acupuncture, chiropractic care, or massage for the patient's pain condition.

41. Coordinate a referral of the patient for acupuncture trial.

42. Coordinate a referral of the patient for a chiropractic evaluation and treatment.

43. Refer the patient for a massage by a credentialed massage therapist.

44. Recommend that the patient join a yoga class or practice yoga techniques at home.

45. Assist the patient in identifying distorted, negative thoughts that precipitate

feelings of stress, tension, or depression.

46. Recommend that the patient record his/her thoughts and experiences in a journal.

47. Assist the patient in identifying a positive, realistic cognition that can be substituted for every identified negative thought associated with higher stress levels. Suggest that patient record these realistic thoughts next to the negative ones in his/her journal.

48. Monitor the patient's use of positive cognitions and reinforce successful replacement of distorted thoughts of catastrophizing, polarized thinking, fortune-telling, mind reading, helplessness, and so forth.

49. Explore emotional pain from the past that contributes to the patient's reaction to current situation.

50. Inquire into present aspects of the patient's life that contribute to the emotional distress.

51. Using great sensitivity toward maintaining the therapeutic relationship, explore the possibility that the patient may be benefitting in some ways (i.e., secondary gain) from the pain (e.g., avoiding having to return to a job with a critical boss; delaying dealing with

serious marital distress; feeling justified in receiving caring and attention from other people).

52. Identify ways in which the patient could solve life problems if the pain were not present (e.g., applying for a different job; seeking marriage counseling; tolerating the discomfort of others' caring while challenging the thought that "I don't deserve to be treated well").

53. Facilitate the patient's exploration of issues relating to justice, fairness, fate, or why this pain happened to him/her.

54. Encourage the patient to use spiritual resources consistent with his/her belief system to address existential issues raised by the prospect of living with pain.

55. Coordinate a referral of the patient to a physical and/or occupational therapist for education about the most efficient and comfortable ways for the patient to accomplish daily activities (e.g., cleaning house, bathing, washing dishes, doing laundry, sleeping, etc.).

56. Coordinate a referral of the patient to a physical therapist for evaluation, treatment, and design of a therapeutic exercise program, and show interest in the patient's efforts and results.

57. Encourage the patient to participate in an aquatic exercise program, if approved by his/her treating physician.

58. Monitor and reinforce the patient's ongoing implementation of a recommended home exercise program.

59. Challenge the patient to list those interests, activities, and role functions that can be maintained despite the pain.

60. Refer the patient to a recreational therapist to identify ways to adapt participation in leisure interests to suit physical needs.

61. Educate the patient, the patient's family, and the patient's therapists about the importance of not communicating routinely about pain because of the negative effect such communications have on social relationships and on the pain level itself.

62. Instruct the family and therapists to ignore casual, habitual pain communications and to continue with the ongoing activity. Inform the patient of this plan.

63. Ask the patient to notice and describe the positive aspects of conversations centered on non-pain-related topics.

64. Explain to the patient (and family) the importance of

pacing activities in order to manage pain levels.

65. Assign the patient to develop a weekly schedule that incorporates activities and rest in ways that will likely avoid excessively high pain levels or an activity/inactivity "roller coaster."

66. Ask the patient to identify situations in which he/she might feel pressured to act in ways that will increase pain levels.

67. Assist the patient in developing responses that will effectively define what he/she is or is not willing to do (e.g., asking for help in putting heavy groceries in the car; responding to challenges that he/she is using a handicapped parking space without cause). Role-play these situations and the patient's response in a psychotherapy session or contrived *in vivo* settings.

68. Assign the patient to develop a comprehensive pain management plan tailored to his/her particular pain response. Include work and household responsibilities, recreation, exercise, medications, stress management, and interventions to reduce pain levels.

69. Consult with the patient's treating physician and rehabilitation team about the patient's realistic potential

to return to paid employment, and the projected time line for doing so.

70. Refer the patient to a vocational counselor.

71. Recommend that the patient's treating physician refer the patient to a work-hardening program to develop the physical strength, endurance, and work habits necessary for successful job reentry.

72. Recommend that the patient (or family) initiate an application for Social Security Disability Income (SSDI) or other disability benefits if it appears that he/she will be unable to be employed for a significant time.

73. Refer the patient (family) to a social worker for information about eligibility for various financial resources.

74. Recommend that the patient participate in couple or family counseling to deal with the effects of the chronic pain on relationships, sexual functioning, and family lifestyle.

75. Refer the patient and family to support groups or advocacy organizations for persons living with chronic pain problems.

__. _____

_____

__. _____

_____

—. _____

_____

DIAGNOSTIC SUGGESTIONS

Axis I:

307.80	Pain Disorder Associated With Psychological Factors
307.89	Pain Disorder Associated With Both Psychological Factors and a General Medical Condition
300.7	Hypochondriasis
300.81	Somatization Disorder
300.82	Somatoform Disorder NOS
316	Psychological Factor (Specify) Affecting (General Medical Condition)
304.00	Opioid Dependence
305.50	Opioid Abuse
xxx.x	Pain Disorder Associated With a General Medical Condition
_____	_____
_____	_____

Axis II:

301.83	Borderline Personality Disorder
301.9	Personality Disorder NOS
799.9	Diagnosis Deferred
V71.09	No Diagnosis
_____	_____
_____	_____

CONFABULATION

BEHAVIORAL DEFINITIONS

1. "Makes up" information that has no particular relationship to historical events, and lacks insight into the fact that the information has been fabricated.
2. Creates information to fill in gaps in memory, and believes information to be true.
3. Reports events that occurred in one time and circumstance as having occurred in another, believing the new report to be accurate.

__. _____
   _____
   _____

__. _____
   _____
   _____

__. _____
   _____

LONG-TERM GOALS

1. Cooperate with family or other responsible persons to manage medical, personal, and financial affairs during period of profound memory impairment.
2. Tolerate redirection, restrictions, and supervision.
3. Report awareness of memory deficits.
4. Gain insight into the ability of the brain to create information to fill in gaps in memory.
5. Implement strategies to improve memory functioning.
6. Make lifestyle adjustments required to adapt to debilitated memory functioning.

—. _____
_____
—. _____
_____
—. _____
_____

SHORT-TERM OBJECTIVES

1. Family, friends, or medical personnel provide information about the fabricated information and what they understand to be historically true. (1, 2, 3, 4)

2. Family, friends, and/or medical personnel describe the onset of the patient's confabulation. (5)

3. Cooperate with evaluation of medical factors contributing to the impaired sense of personal history. (6, 7, 13)

4. Participate to the best of one's ability in an evaluation for delirium. (8, 13)

5. Cooperate with an evaluation of psychiatric problems that may be affecting ability to accurately report on one's personal history and present circumstances. (9, 10, 13)

6. Complete an evaluation of memory functioning. (11, 13)

7. Cooperate with psychological testing to help clarify the contribution of psychi-

THERAPEUTIC INTERVENTIONS

1. Identify the occurrence of the patient's confabulation by personal observation and by receiving reports from family, persons close to the patient, or rehabilitation therapists that the patient is making statements that are highly improbable.

2. Talk with the person(s) reporting the confabulation to identify, as much as possible, precisely what the patient said and in what context.

3. Talk with the patient's family or others who know him/her well to confirm that the information the patient is reporting is false, not historically true.

4. Talk with the informants and observe the patient to determine whether the confabulation is seemingly confined to one topic or occurs about many topics.

5. Interview the patient's family, others who know the patient well, and/or the

atric disorders to the ability to accurately describe one's history and circumstances. (12, 13)

8. Cooperate with efforts to treat delirium. (14)

9. Obtain treatment to address psychiatric disorders. (15, 16)

10. Verbalize insight into own confabulation and accept correction of mistaken beliefs. (17, 18, 19, 20)

11. Communicate the emotions raised by learning that others fail to see certain situations in the way that they seem to self. (21, 22)

12. Adjust conversation to neutral, present-focused topics. (23)

13. Cooperate with the therapist's effort to keep frustration levels within manageable limits. (24, 25, 26)

14. Demonstrate ability to control frustration due to others confronting confabulated beliefs. (27)

15. Improve orientation by cooperating with changes designed to minimize misleading environmental cues and emphasize those that provide accurate information regarding one's situation. (28, 29)

16. Put good effort into improving memory skills. (30)

17. Family describe an accurate understanding of confabula-

patient's rehabilitation therapists to determine when the fabrication of information began in relationship to the onset of the recent brain injury/illness.

6. Review the patient's medical record to identify factors (e.g., brain injury, central nervous system disorders, metabolic disorders, anoxic events, medications) that might explain the patient's confabulatory behavior and associated memory deficits.

7. Inquire into the patient's lifetime use of alcohol, street drugs, and other substances that could temporarily or permanently impair memory performance.

8. Refer for or perform an evaluation to rule out delirium as the cause for the concocted information.

9. Interview the patient (and family) to determine whether the patient has a history of serious psychiatric illness predating the medical condition.

10. Refer for or perform a psychodiagnostic interview to identify psychiatric conditions (e.g., malingering, dissociative disorder, somatization disorder, schizophrenia, paranoia) that might explain the patient's formulation of false information.

tion as a symptom that sometimes accompanies memory impairment. (31)

18. Family report responses (e.g., making fun of what the patient says, using logical arguments) that will likely irritate the patient while leaving the confabulatory material unchanged. (32)

19. Family identify the ability to redirect and reorient the patient when he/she begins to manufacture erroneous information. (33)

20. Family demonstrate empathy for the patient by speaking to the emotions that he/she is likely experiencing during the confabulation. (34)

21. A legally designated individual agrees to assume responsibility for making medical, personal, and/or financial decisions for the patient, if the patient is declared to be incompetent. (35, 36, 37)

22. Patient, family member, or legal representative complete applications for disability benefits or other sources of financial assistance if there will be a significant delay in returning to full-time work. (38)

23. Family members report an awareness of the patient's residual memory deficits and confabulation and their

11. Evaluate the patient's memory functioning. (See Memory Impairment chapter in this Planner.)

12. Refer for or perform psychological testing to clarify psychiatric conditions contributing to the patient's concoction of information.

13. Give feedback to the patient, patient's family, physician, rehabilitation team, and other designated persons regarding assessment results and recommendations.

14. Consult with the patient's treating physician about how the cause for the patient's delirium will be evaluated and treated.

15. Consult with the patient's physician, or coordinate a referral to a psychiatrist for treatment and management of schizophrenia, paranoia, or other psychiatric disorders.

16. Perform or refer for psychotherapy for treatment of psychiatric conditions that affect the patient's ability/willingness to provide accurate information.

17. Assess the patient's degree of insight into the confabulation by gently confronting him/her about the erroneous belief (e.g., "Actually, Mr. Smith, this is a hospital, not a prison," or "Mrs. Jones, I have carefully looked into

implications for the patient
and all family members.
(39)

24. Family members describe
    their emotional acceptance
    of the patient's cognitive
    changes and the ways in
    which their family life has
    been altered. (40)

—. _____
   _____

—. _____
   _____

—. _____
   _____

this, and it is true that this
is your daughter Marie"),
and notice the degree to
which the patient utilizes
this information to correct
his/her belief.

18. Ask the patient to consider
    whether there might be
    other explanations for what
    he/she is experiencing (e.g.,
    "Are there other places be-
    sides prisons in which they
    have locked doors?" or
    "Have you ever seen beds
    like these [with bars on the
    side] in hospitals, to keep
    people from falling out?" or
    "It must be hard to believe
    that Marie has gray hair
    and grown children").

19. Draw the patient's atten-
    tion to stimuli that could
    help orient him/her to the
    environment and circum-
    stances (e.g., other patients
    receiving therapy, doctors
    and nurses, calendars, the
    sound of his/her daughter's
    voice) and ask the patient
    about what he/she makes of
    this information.

20. Provide the patient with in-
    formation about his/her
    medical condition and mem-
    ory (e.g., "You had a brain
    injury that makes it very
    hard to remember things
    right now," and/or "Your
    brain is trying to fill in the
    gaps in your memory and
    sometimes makes up incor-
    rect information") consis-
    tent with the patient's level

of insight and tolerance for confrontation.

21. Notice the patient's emotional response to the confrontation (e.g., incredulous, irritable, distrustful, relief).

22. Give the patient feedback on observed emotions, and inquire into how well this reflects his/her internal experience.

23. Avoid reinforcing the patient's erroneous concept by avoiding prolonged discussions about the confabulated content and by changing the topic to a neutral, present-focused one (e.g., "Well, let's look at the menu and select what you would like for dinner tonight," or "Let's look in your memory book to see what you accomplished today," or "Would you like to watch the skating competition on TV?").

24. If the patient becomes irritable or upset, take measures to maintain rapport by acknowledging the patient's point of view as one of many possible viewpoints (e.g., saying "I can see how it might seem as if you are in a jail, because we are limiting you in what you can do right now," or "Tell me more about how it seems to you that you were taken hostage," or "Tell me what you remember about your daughter Marie").

25. Redirect the patient and reduce agitation by changing to a neutral topic of conversation.

26. Speaking firmly and calmly to the patient, indicate that you have taken the conversation as far as it can go for now and will continue at a later time. Then bring the session to a close.

27. Initiate actions to protect the patient and others if the patient becomes agitated or violent in reaction to others' failing to cooperate with his/her confabulated point of view (see Agitation, Aggression, and Violence chapter in this Planner).

28. Assess the environmental cues to which the patient is being exposed that might reinforce the theme of the confabulation (e.g., television news coverage about criminal trials, mesh covering around bed that might make the patient feel like he/she is in a jail cell, photos of daughter taken 15 years ago); if possible, eliminate those that might be misinterpreted by the patient.

29. Add or emphasize environmental cues that will help the patient orient to his/her present circumstances and will provide accurate information to replace the erroneous information (e.g., a memory book that the pa-

tient uses daily with the
name of the hospital
printed prominently on the
cover; therapists wearing
name badges that will be
easily seen by the patient;
captions on family photos
identifying who is in the
photo and when/where it
was taken).

30. Perform or refer for therapy
for memory impairment (see
the Memory Impairment
chapter in this Planner).

31. Educate the patient's family
(and others significant to
him/her) about the nature
of confabulation and its relationship to memory im-
pairment and brain disease/
injury.

32. Caution the family to avoid
reactions such as laughing
at the patient's confabu-
lated information, making
statements that the patient
could perceive as "making
fun of" him/her, or trying to
reason with the patient,
since these will likely irritate the patient and cause
him/her to feel misunder-
stood.

33. Model the use of redirection
and pointing out orienting
cues to respond to the confabulation.

34. Suggest that the patient's
family respond in an em-
pathic way to his/her
presumed emotional
experience (e.g., "I'll bet

you are very frightened right now," or "It must be hard for things to be so confusing").

35. Taking into account the provisions of state law, clarify whether the patient is competent to make imminent medical, personal, and financial decisions. Document this opinion in his/her medical record.

36. In accord with state laws and the policies of the institution, talk with the family (and/or partner) about the patient's presumed incompetence. Assist the patient's family and/or significant other in identifying who would be eligible and appropriate to assume decision making for the patient, and inform them about the steps necessary to obtain guardianship.

37. Following the provisions of state law and the policies of the institution, identify the person who is legally authorized to make specific decisions for the patient. Obtain legal counsel, if necessary. Document this information in the patient's medical record.

38. Refer the patient's family (or other responsible person) to a social worker, community social service agency, and/or the patient's personnel officer to apply

for sources of financial as-
sistance/disability for which
he/she may be eligible.

39. Educate the patient's family
about his/her memory
deficits, confabulation, recommended precautions,
activity modifications, compensatory techniques, and
accommodations, using ex-
amples that relate directly
to the patient's and family's
life.

40. Refer the patient's family to
resources (family therapy,
support groups, advocacy
groups, educational materials, etc.) to assist them in
understanding and coming
to terms with the changes
in their family life.

__. _____
   _____
__. _____
   _____
__. _____
   _____

DIAGNOSTIC SUGGESTIONS

Axis I: 293.0   Delirium Due to (General Medical Condition)
293.xx   Psychotic Disorder Due to (General Medical
         Condition)
294.0   Amnestic Disorder Due to (General Medical
         Condition)
290.xx   Dementia
294.1   Dementia Due to (Axis III Condition)
294.9   Cognitive Disorder NOS
300.xx   Factitious Disorder

	300.14	Dissociative Identity Disorder
	300.81	Somatization Disorder
	300.82	Somatoform Disorder NOS
	V65.2	Malingering
	_____	_____
	_____	_____
Axis II:	V71.09	No Diagnosis or Condition
	799.9	Diagnosis Deferred
	_____	_____
	_____	_____

DENIAL AND IMPAIRED AWARENESS

BEHAVIORAL DEFINITIONS

1. Refutes others' statements about having sustained a brain injury or other medical event affecting brain.
2. Refuses to acknowledge an obvious change in motor and/or cognitive abilities.
3. Explains functional problems as caused by some factor other than brain damage.
4. Acts surprised or quizzical when someone refers to his/her brain-related deficit.
5. Indifferent or unconcerned regarding deficits and their effect on life.
6. States "This can't be happening to me," "I feel like I will wake up from this dream any time now," or other statement suggesting awareness of condition mixed with difficulty in accepting it as having occurred to self.
7. Reports feeling numb and/or detached, or experiences a sense of unreality concerning occurrence of brain impairment.
8. Verbally acknowledges condition and/or deficit while maintaining exaggerated optimistic outlook regarding deficits and implications.
9. Cheerful or giddy demeanor when discussing medical condition and its effects.

Note: This chapter will discuss three types of denial: (1) the neurologically based inability to recognize deficits that accompanies damage to certain parts of the brain (anosognosia); (2) the defense mechanism of denial that occurs acutely as an early stage of coping with life- or ego-threatening situations; and (3) hysterical denial associated with a characterologic manner of dealing with stress. Refer to the chapter on Stimulus Neglect in this Planner for additional interventions that may be applicable to anosognosia, one manifestation of a neglect syndrome.

10. Markedly unrealistic point of view about the neurological condition, which minimizes the severity and duration of deficits.

__. _____

_____

__. _____

_____

__. _____

_____

LONG-TERM GOALS

1. Name functional results of the brain condition.
2. Emotionally accept lost abilities and changed lifestyle.
3. Respond realistically to the challenges of life following damage to the brain.
4. Make lifestyle changes necessary to compensate for deficits, and maintain safety and optimal level of independent functioning.
5. Find satisfaction in relationships and activities in spite of losses caused by neurological condition.

__. _____

_____

__. _____

_____

__. _____

_____

SHORT-TERM OBJECTIVES	THERAPEUTIC INTERVENTIONS
1. Family members and patient provide information about the patient's recent medical event, and describe his/her reactions to past stressful life events, significant losses, frustrations, or hurts. (1, 2, 3)	1. Review medical records and/or consult with the patient's physician to determine whether the patient has had damage in areas of the brain (frontal, parietal) most commonly associated with neurological denial.

2. Describe understanding of medical condition, its immediate effects, and its potential implications, to the best of one's abilities. (4, 5, 6)

3. Communicate the emotional reaction to the recent medical event and functional changes. (7, 8)

4. Cooperate with psychological testing. (9, 10, 11)

5. Perform ordinary activities that demonstrate the deficits resulting from the brain condition. (12, 13, 14)

6. Compare predicted versus actual performance to develop understanding of the deficits that have resulted from the brain condition. (15, 16, 17)

7. Examine videotapes, audiotapes, and/or other records of own performance and state a conclusion that the brain condition is causing difficulties. (15, 18, 19, 20)

8. Verbalize an understanding of the fact that the brain often tries to fool a person into thinking that nothing has changed after the brain has been injured. (21)

9. Family members report an understanding that brain damage can affect a person's awareness of the physical and cognitive changes that have resulted. (22)

10. Family members demonstrate the ability to respond to the patient's emotional

2. Talk with the patient (and the family) about past stressful situations. Inquire into how the patient coped with the stress, asking for specific examples. Listen for statements suggesting the predominant use of repression or hysterical-type defenses (e.g., "Oh, no matter what happens, he is always happy," or "I never allow myself to think negative thoughts," or "Things always turn out for the best").

3. Ask the patient (and/or others who are close to the patient) about past significant losses, or times that he/she has been sad, discouraged, or angry. Note whether the patient (or others) reports having experienced these "negative" emotions, or whether he/she seems "blocked" in his/her ability to experience them.

4. Talk with the patient about the reasons for receiving rehabilitation. Notice whether the patient is able to name (even generally) his/her medical condition and report physical and/or cognitive changes.

5. Gently confront the patient about problems that he/she may have omitted (e.g., "Your chart says that you had a stroke," or "I understand you are getting physical therapy to help you learn to walk," or "I see that

denial in a respectful way that helps him/her gain insight and promotes effective coping. (23, 24, 30)

11. Describe the significance of and feelings associated with acknowledging an injury or illness affecting the brain. (25, 26)

12. Verbalize acceptance of the immediate circumstances and report hope for the possibility of improvement. (27, 28, 29, 30)

13. Verbalize an understanding that reports of wholly positive affect in the face of significant loss or difficulty are frequently indicators of being severely stressed. (31, 32)

14. Identify life circumstances that taught the use of repression, denial, or other hysterical defenses as ways of managing emotional pain. (33)

15. Describe constructive actions that can be taken to manage or reduce emotional pain and that do not involve denial. (34, 35)

16. Agree to a treatment plan for grief, depression, or anxiety. (36)

17. Patient and family (and others significant to the patient) verbalize an understanding that the emergence of sadness, frustration, anxiety, or other painful emotion is evidence

you are using a memory book; tell me what problems you are having with your memory") and notice the patient's degree of awareness of the condition and emotional reaction.

6. While talking with the patient about his/her medical condition, notice whether the patient has poor insight into specific deficits, has general difficulty believing that such an event has happened to him/her, or acknowledges the event while severely minimizing the significance of it.

7. Notice the patient's affective response when discussing his/her medical condition. Note whether he/she appears quizzical, unconcerned, numb, sad, giddy, or happy.

8. Give the patient feedback on observed emotions, and inquire into how well they reflect his/her internal experience.

9. Conduct or refer the patient for a neuropsychological evaluation to clarify cognitive factors contributing to impaired insight and awareness, and to identify cognitive factors (e.g., memory) that will be important in planning for the patient's rehabilitation.

10. Conduct or refer the patient for psychological testing to

of the patient's progress in the cognitive and emotional recovery process. (37)

18. Participate in therapeutic activities designed to improve cognitive and physical skills. (38)

19. Report accurately and without denial on progress or problems in achieving therapy goals. (29, 39, 40)

20. Implement recommended lifestyle changes to reduce risk of additional injury or other damaging event. (41, 42)

21. Participate in psychotherapy focused on difficult emotions and circumstances that come about because of the need to adjust one's life to suit one's abilities. (43)

22. Obtain ancillary services or benefits from community that support the rehabilitation process. (44)

23. Family (or other responsible persons) list actions they will take to protect the patient's and others' welfare if the patient fails to modify activities to match his/her abilities. (45)

24. Family (or other responsible persons) report having the resolve necessary to enforce restrictions and lifestyle changes on the patient. (46, 47)

___. _____

_____

identify current affective reactions, coping styles, and personality factors affecting his/her response to the neurological trauma.

11. Give feedback to the patient (patient's family), referring physician, rehabilitation team, and other designated persons regarding the assessment results and recommendations.

12. Engage the patient in familiar activities by which he/she will experience and realize his/her abilities and limitations. Inquire into the specific difficulties, asking whether he/she has noticed them and what he/she understands to be the cause.

13. Gently confront the patient by mentioning that many people experience difficulties similar to those he/she is experiencing after a medical event affecting their brain, and inquire whether the patient has considered this as a possible cause of his/her difficulties.

14. Remind the patient that the rehabilitation therapists will show him/her how to deal with the difficulties in order for him/her to regain as much of his/her previous ability as possible.

15. Recommend that the therapists identify a function (e.g., walking, recent memory) in which the patient is

__. _____

      _____

__. _____

      _____

having problems but deny-ing them. In collaboration with the patient, therapists should select an activity that could demonstrate the patient's skill level in that area (e.g., walking across the room, remembering items on a shopping list).

16. Suggest that the therapists ask the patient to predict how well he/she will do on a specific activity, and write this down. Therapists should ask the patient to perform that activity, pro-tecting him/her from injury, if applicable.

17. Ask the patient to rate how well he/she completed the task. Have the patient com-pare the predicted and ac-tual performance levels, and encourage him/her to ex-plain the differences. If the patient fails to name his/her brain condition as a pos-sible cause, say "Perhaps your brain injury (stroke, aneurysm, etc.) is making it hard for you to walk (re-member, etc.) right now."

18. Recommend that therapists videotape or audiotape the patient performing an agreed-upon activity that will demonstrate the deficits that have resulted from the neurological condition.

19. Review the video or audio recording and ask the pa-tient to rate his/her perfor-

mance based on what was just reviewed.

20. Go over the results of neuropsychological or other cognitive tests with the patient and point out problems thought to be caused by the brain condition.

21. Sensitively confront the patient when he/she tries to excuse difficulties doing customary tasks (e.g., "I didn't sleep well last night so I guess I was too tired to walk," or "I couldn't remember any items on that shopping list because I think it is silly to memorize lists") by educating the patient that damage to the brain can impair one's insight into the effects of the damage.

22. Educate the family and others who are significant to the patient about the nature of certain insight deficits as a neurologic symptom of his/her brain condition.

23. Acknowledge to the family members the temptation to point to the absurdity of what the patient is saying, but advise them to avoid responses that would hurt the patient's feelings or make him/her feel alienated (e.g., avoid direct confrontation that could be construed as being demeaning, such as "Don't you know that you can't walk because you had

a stroke?"). Do not laugh at or joke about the patient's explanation of his/her impairment.

24. Demonstrate to the family how they might facilitate the development of the patient's insight (e.g., "Let's look at the booklet the therapists gave us about strokes and learn about what happened to you"; or when the patient tries to stand on his/her affected leg, say "Wait; let's get help; your brain injury made that leg too weak to stand on"; or when the patient accuses spouse of ignoring him/her by not visiting, say "The doctor said that your memory is still weak since your injury; let's look at your guest book and see what I wrote when I visited last night").

25. Talk with the patient about what it would mean if it were true that he/she had experienced an event affecting the brain.

26. Process the patient's emotional and/or defensive reaction concerning the issue of brain impairment.

27. Assess the patient's need for education regarding medical condition, symptoms, and actions that he/she can currently take to improve condition; coordinate with other treatment professionals in providing educational information.

28. Provide the patient and family with educational materials regarding his/her medical condition and its treatment.

29. Assist the patient in identifying immediate therapy goals and actions that he/she feels capable of taking to achieve them.

30. Educate the staff and family regarding the patient's current need for an overly optimistic view about long-term prognosis in order to maintain motivation and hope, and inform them of how they might respond in a neutral, yet supportive way, using statements such as "We'll do everything we can to help you recover as much as possible," or "It would be wonderful for you to do that well."

31. Point out instances in which the patient makes a cheerful or unfoundedly optimistic remark in direct response to discussion of problem areas; interpret this as a possible response to the stress of acknowledging the reality of the neurological impairment.

32. Ask the patient what he/she is experiencing at the moment he/she attempts to shift the mood from grief to cheer. If appropriate, reflect that many people would be experiencing anxiety, anger, or sadness at this point in

the conversation, and inquire whether the patient could understand this reaction.

33. Inquire into life experiences that may have affected the patient's freedom to communicate sadness, anger, or anxiety (e.g., patient's alcoholic parent became enraged whenever patient was unhappy; patient had a depressed mother, who became overwhelmed and nonfunctional upon hearing about sad event).

34. Inquire into the patient's experience in using activity to foster and maintain a positive mood state (e.g., exercise, achieving goals, cleaning the garage) and ask him/her to identify two activities that could be tried now to enhance mood.

35. Assist the patient in putting words to painful emotions and then inquire into what he/she experienced after verbalizing this emotion. Process and reinforce the emotional expression with the patient.

36. Develop a plan to address painful emotions that occur as the patient becomes aware of his/her condition and its implications. (See Depression/Grief or Anxiety/Fear chapters in this Planner.)

37. Talk with the patient (family and/or others who are

significant to the patient) about the fact that feeling emotional discomfort is a stage in recovery from denial and shows that the patient is progressing.

38. Coordinate referral for or encourage the patient's participation in specific therapies (e.g., physical, occupational, speech, recreational, cognitive) designed to increase the patient's safety and functional abilities.

39. Working collaboratively with the patient and therapists, design a system to monitor and record changes in key performance areas.

40. Review progress regularly with the patient and encourage the patient to discuss thoughts and feelings regarding current status and recent changes; reinforce the patient's accurate assessment of his/her abilities and point out any inconsistencies based in denial.

41. Facilitate communication among the patient, (patient's family), physician, and rehabilitation therapists regarding lifestyle changes (e.g., need for supervision, limitations on use of vehicle, delay in resumption of work) that are required because of the patient's changed ability level.

42. Identify key factors impacting the patient's ability to resume specific activities, and develop a system for these to be monitored regularly and for recommendations to be periodically updated.

43. Conduct or refer for psychotherapy to assist the patient in dealing with the emotional impact of implementing lifestyle changes to accommodate limitations.

44. Refer the patient to a social worker, case manager, or community agencies for assistance in accessing attendant care, disability benefits, or other resources needed for the patient's successful rehabilitation.

45. Talk with the patient's family (or other responsible individuals) about steps they would be willing and able to take (e.g., taking the battery out of the car, arranging for guardianship, calling the patient's employer and explaining his/her need to spend more time in recovery) to protect the patient from harming self or others because of poor insight. (See Rehabilitation Noncompliance chapter in this Planner.)

46. Work through the family's (or responsible individuals') emotional reactions to setting limits with the patient that are necessary due to

the patient's unrealistic assessment of his/her abilities.

47. Refer the family and/or responsible individuals to support groups or advocacy organizations where they can communicate with others who are dealing with similar issues.

___. _____
_____

___. _____
_____

___. _____
_____

DIAGNOSTIC SUGGESTIONS

Axis I: 294.9   Cognitive Disorder NOS
293.81   Psychotic Disorder Due to (General Medical Condition) With Delusions
309.9   Adjustment Disorder Unspecified
316   Psychological Factor (specify) Affecting (General Medical Condition)
V15.81   Noncompliance With Treatment

_____   _____

Axis II: 301.9   Personality Disorder NOS
799.9   Diagnosis Deferred
V71.09   No Diagnosis

_____   _____
_____   _____

DEPENDENCY/COUNTERDEPENDENCY

BEHAVIORAL DEFINITIONS

1. Persistent requests for more assistance with tasks than person seemingly requires.
2. Failure to perform necessary activity such that someone else will intervene to assure that task is accomplished.
3. Family members (caregivers) report that patient won't do tasks he/she is able to perform for self.
4. Refusal to accept assistance when it is obviously needed, exposing person to risk of physical injury, emotional stress, financial reversals, or other significant negative consequence.
5. Act in ways that professionals consider unsafe for current level of recovery.
6. History of injuries or damage incurred while attempting to carry out activities against medical advice.
7. Family members (caregivers) report that patient ignores recommended activity restrictions.

__. _____

_____

__. _____

_____

__. _____

_____

LONG-TERM GOALS

1. Voluntarily perform tasks within range of current assessed ability to meet basic needs and fulfill responsibilities.

2. Request and accept assistance for tasks that current limitations interfere with or which preclude safe, successful accomplishment.
3. Family and/or caregiver report feeling comfortable with the way in which patient requests and accepts assistance.
4. Terminate performing tasks that are unsafe for current level of recovery.

__. _____

_____

__. _____

_____

__. _____

_____

SHORT-TERM OBJECTIVES

1. Family and patient identify dependent or counterdependent behaviors that are discrepant from therapists' and/or family's expectations, and clarify the circumstances surrounding these behaviors. (1, 2, 3)

2. Cooperate with evaluation to determine whether requests for assistance are commensurate with actual abilities and skills. (4, 5, 6)

3. Verbalize understanding of physician's and therapists' opinions about current ability level. (7, 8, 9)

4. Discuss reasons for current decisions to seek (or not seek) assistance. (10, 11)

5. Verbalize concerns about potential negative consequences associated with

THERAPEUTIC INTERVENTIONS

1. Interview the patient's therapists, family, and/or caregivers to identify the types of situations in which the patient's requests for or refusals of assistance are significantly different from his/her presumed ability level.

2. Determine whether the family's (caregiver's) expectations are similar to those of the therapists, and resolve discrepancies.

3. Clarify the circumstances under which dependent or counterdependent behavior occurs (e.g., where, when, and how often); determine how others respond to the behavior; and identify the usual and potential consequences.

obvious functional improvement. (12, 13, 14)

6. Provide information about family relationships and how they might be influencing current response to disability. (14, 15, 16)

7. Family members provide honest feedback about the impact of the patient's behavior on their lives and emotions. (17, 18, 19)

8. Discuss preinjury/preillness style of help-seeking. (20, 21)

9. Clarify cultural, religious, or other beliefs that are negatively affecting current decisions to seek (or refrain from seeking) assistance. (22, 23)

10. Provide forthright responses to psychological evaluation questions. (24, 25, 27)

11. Give best effort to neuropsychological evaluation procedure. (26, 27)

12. Cooperate with treatment for depression or anxiety. (28)

13. Identify the negative consequences of excessive dependence or premature independence on the likely progress in rehabilitation. (29, 30)

14. Acknowledge emotional needs that underlie excessive dependence or independence. (31, 32)

15. Attempt alternate prosocial methods to meet emotional needs. (33, 34, 35)

4. Review the medical record and consult with the patient's rehabilitation team to determine his/her current abilities and needs for assistance.

5. Interview the family (caregiver) to learn whether there are circumstances affecting the patient's independence of which treatment team is unaware (e.g., the patient's mattress at home is unusually high off floor; the patient's "driving" is actually operating a golf cart in a restricted retirement community).

6. Arrange for *in vivo* assessment of the patient's capabilities (e.g., observe the patient cooking a simple meal, refer for a driving skills evaluation).

7. Inquire into the patient's understanding of physician's and therapists' opinions about current abilities and needs for assistance.

8. Explore the patient's insight into the factors underlying the professionals' opinions regarding skills and deficits.

9. Coordinate education of the patient concerning current abilities, deficits, recommended assistance, and anticipated duration of this status.

10. Encourage the patient to verbalize his/her point of view about abilities and de-

16. Identify distorted, negative self-talk that maintains dependent/counterdependent behavior. (36)

17. Identify and implement positive, realistic self-talk that fosters more adaptive behavior. (37)

18. Obtain information about others' experiences in coping with similar conditions. (38, 39, 40)

19. Agree upon short-term and long-term therapy goals, and on an immediate plan to achieve them. (41, 42, 43, 44)

20. Report positive, rewarding aspects of adjusting behavior to current ability. (45)

21. Utilize compensatory strategies to retain awareness of current skills, needs for assistance, and activity prescriptions and restrictions. (46, 47, 48)

22. Family members verbalize accurate awareness of patient's ability level, precautions, and recommendations for when they should (or should not) assist. (49)

23. Family demonstrates skills in using reinforcement principles to impact patient's dependent or counterdependent behavior. (16, 50, 51)

24. Family uses natural consequences and positive reinforcement to build and sustain appropriate activity level. (52, 53)

cisions to request (or forego) assistance.

11. Inquire into previous experiences that may be affecting the patient's current decision making (e.g., a relative who was turned down for Social Security disability benefits after pushing to do as much for self as possible, a friend who is still driving after experiencing a similar stroke).

12. If the patient is involved in litigation, inquire into whether his/her attorney has suggested that rehabilitation progress might interfere with successful litigation outcome; suggest the patient consider the favorable impact that good motivation for recovery might have on a jury's opinions.

13. Identify and discuss opinions the patient may hold about needing to show how seriously he/she has been affected.

14. Inquire about behavior of family members or others significant to the patient, paying close attention to statements suggesting that the patient perceives their love and attention to be associated with the patient's level of need.

15. Explore the history of family relations, being attentive to unresolved anger that might influence the patient to "act out" via excessive de-

25. Accept assistance designed to protect self from potential harm. (54, 55, 56)

26. Family describes plan for dealing with patient's needs that takes into account the emotional and physical needs of all family members. (57, 58, 59)

—. _____
_____

—. _____
_____

—. _____
_____

pendence or independence during this illness episode in order to "get back" at family.

16. Observe the patient and family together. Notice the family's response when the patient asks for excessive assistance or refuses needed assistance, being attentive to family behaviors that might positively reinforce his/her dependence or unrealistic independence.

17. Interview family members to inquire how their lives are being affected now by the patient's limitations, and how they expect their lives to be affected in the months ahead by his/her condition. Be attentive to signs of emotional reactions (e.g., becoming tearful, voice cracking, drawing a deep breath) or efforts to avoid an emotional reaction (changing the topic to something light, talking in abstract, overly intellectualized manner). At the time of the reaction, interrupt the family member to inquire into his/her current experience and the factors behind it.

18. Ask about family resources and plans to manage the additional stress and work necessitated by the patient's condition.

19. Explore the probable consequences of the patient's illness on all family members

(e.g., if the patient's daughter quits a job to care for the patient, how will that affect the daughter's career or financial solvency?).

20. Ask the patient and his/her family members about the responsibilities the patient was attending to prior to the recent illness/injury. Be attentive to statements suggesting a dependent or ruggedly independent style (e.g., "When my wife was sick I just let the laundry and housework pile up until she was able to do it again," or "People should do without if they can't do for themselves").

21. With the patient's permission, interview family or other interested parties about patient's preinjury/ preillness personality, paying close attention to how he/she acted during any previous episode(s) of illness.

22. Explore the patient's belief system about behavior during episodes of illness, family responsibilities to a sick member, beliefs about sickness, and what people need to do to get well.

23. Talk with patient's family about any customs or traditions that might be affecting his/her current behavior. Inquire into approaches (e.g., have the patient talk through concerns about rehabilitation recommenda-

tions with a trusted person from cultural/religious community; agree that the patient can have a family member dress him/her as soon as patient demonstrates ability to dress self safely and adequately; if the patient states that he/she never cooks, have the patient demonstrate ability to place order for takeout food, receive it at the door, and calculate change accurately) that would increase the patient's willingness to alter his/her behavior to achieve a better rehabilitation outcome. Facilitate those interventions that do not violate the patient's cultural, religious, or other beliefs.

24. Perform, or coordinate referral for, clinical diagnostic interview to identify depression, anxiety, personality disorders, or other psychiatric conditions that might be affecting patient's current behavior.

25. Administer or refer for psychological testing to clarify diagnostic issues.

26. Perform or coordinate referral for neuropsychological testing to identify problems with memory, reasoning, deficit awareness, or other cognitive problems that might be affecting the patient's judgment about current capabilities.

27. Give feedback to the patient (family), treatment team, and other designated persons regarding assessment results and recommendations.

28. Initiate or refer for treatment for depression and/or anxiety associated with patient's behavior. (See Depression/Grief and/or Anxiety/Fear chapter in this Planner.)

29. Ask the patient to name the potential consequences of being too inactive (e.g., muscles will weaken; others will treat the patient as a burden or as unimportant; fewer opportunities will exist to participate in activities outside the home) or of resuming activities before therapists recommend (e.g., possibility of new injury requiring additional months of medical care; automobile accident that might cause family to insist that patient give up driving).

30. Request the patient to state the probability that these negative events might actually occur to himself/herself. If the patient says the consequences would not occur, inquire why he/she sees self as different from others in similar circumstances.

31. Inquire into the emotional needs that are being met through the patient's behavior.

32. Point out consistent patterns of behavior that might have reinforcing emotional consequences for the patient (e.g., "Did you ever notice that when you lie in bed, not attempting to dress yourself, both of your daughters come and spend 30 minutes helping you dress?").

33. Explore a variety of more adaptive ways by which the patient might meet his/her emotional needs (e.g., invite family or friends to join self for lunch; establish a routine schedule of telephone contact with family members; ask caregiving staff to participate in a recreational activity) while addressing concerns and considerations that interfere with using these alternatives.

34. Enlist the patient's agreement to try a more adaptive alternative for meeting emotional needs, reinforcing him/her for taking on this risk.

35. Ask the patient to describe the positive and negative aspects of his/her experience with prosocial, adaptive methods of addressing his/her emotional needs.

36. Assist the patient in identifying dysfunctional self-talk (e.g., "I can't do anything for myself anymore"; "The only way to tell if people care about me is to get them to help me"; "I have to prove

I'm still worth something by doing everything I used to do"; etc.).

37. Assist the patient in identifying positive, realistic self-talk (e.g., "I am making gradual progress in doing more for myself"; "People have shown caring for me in many ways"; "My self-worth is not measured by what I do but who I am"). Monitor implementation of these thoughts.

38. Refer the patient to support or adjustment group where he/she can listen to how others are dealing with their limitations and recovery.

39. Arrange for referral of the patient to a peer counselor, if available.

40. Provide the patient with information about advocacy organizations dealing with his/her particular medical condition.

41. Engage the patient in conversation to identify long-term goals for rehabilitation, and to determine the degree to which he/she expects to achieve that outcome.

42. In consultation with the patient's rehabilitation therapists, identify interim goals and the recommended steps to achieve those goals.

43. Talk with the patient regarding therapists' recommendations for immediate steps that should be taken

to help achieve desired long-term goals. Identify any concerns and negotiate plan with the patient and therapists until workable plan is achieved.

44. Monitor the patient's participation in agreed-upon rehabilitation program. Acknowledge the effort being put into rehabilitation. Identify any new or residual concerns about the rehabilitation program and assist patient in addressing them.

45. Inquire about any positive effects of the patient adjusting behavior to current abilities (e.g., increased confidence, sense of accomplishment, fewer disagreements with therapists and family).

46. Institute a trial of short, written notes to remind the patient of current ability level (e.g., weekly status report listing common activities—transferring, walking, etc.—and stating how much assistance is currently needed; signs placed strategically in home: "Microwave–YES; Stovetop–NO").

47. Develop a contract between the patient and the treatment team outlining the responsibilities of each. Specify anticipated benefits if the contract is followed, and state most likely harmful effects if parties do not uphold their agreements. Have all parties sign this

contract to demonstrate that it is to be taken seriously.

48. Develop an easily-read bar graph that shows when the patient has achieved independence in various skills (e.g., putting shirt on, donning pants, brushing teeth, bathing) and refer to this graph when it is time for each task.

49. Assess the family's understanding of the patient's need for assistance. Arrange for additional education, as needed.

50. Educate the family about basic behavioral principles (e.g., positive and negative reinforcement, punishment, extinction, fixed and random reinforcement schedules) and point out how they apply to the patient's current situation.

51. Assist the family in identifying alternative ways of responding to the patient's inappropriate behaviors that would decrease the likelihood of their persistence.

52. Encourage the patient's family to make activities that he/she enjoys (e.g., mealtime, television programs, trip to beauty salon) contingent upon the patient completing dressing, grooming, and/or exercise program.

53. Model complimenting and encourage the family to

compliment the patient on success in following recommendations regarding activity level and need for assistance.

54. Within limits of law, recommend that the patient's physician notify state driver's license bureau that the patient is not a safe driver because of medical event.

55. Recommend that the family limit the patient's access to potentially dangerous situations (e.g., take battery out of car, lock door to basement workshop where patient has power tools).

56. Support the family in firmly insisting on the patient maintaining scheduled activities and exercise (e.g., "Skipping therapy this morning is not an option").

57. Meet with the family and inquire about how each person is being affected by the patient's needs. Support the family in taking the needs of each member seriously, rather than always prioritizing the needs of the patient.

58. Refer for or conduct family therapy to work through stress the family is encountering in dealing with the "sick" member's behavior.

59. Refer the family to support groups for families of the neurologically impaired.

__. _____

_____

—.   _____

     _____

—.   _____

     _____

DIAGNOSTIC SUGGESTIONS

Axis I: 309.3   Adjustment Disorder With Disturbance of
                      Conduct
              309.4   Adjustment Disorder With Mixed Disturbance
                      of Emotions and Conduct
              309.9   Adjustment Disorder, Unspecified
              316   Psychological Factor (Specify) Affecting
                      (General Medical Condition)
              V15.81 Noncompliance With Treatment
              V62.4   Acculturation Problem

              _____   _____

Axis II: 301.6   Dependent Personality Disorder
              301.9   Personality Disorder NOS
              799.9   Diagnosis Deferred
              V71.09 No Diagnosis

              _____   _____

              _____   _____

DEPRESSION/GRIEF

BEHAVIORAL DEFINITIONS

1. Sad or flat affect.
2. Preoccupation with the subject of death.
3. Suicidal thoughts or actions.
4. Current stated preference to have died at time of medical event or injury.
5. High frequency of irritable episodes and/or complaints.
6. Avoidance of family and/or friends.
7. Markedly decreased interest in relationships and activities.
8. Poor effort or cooperation with rehabilitation therapy program.
9. Repeated requests for assistance with tasks person is reasonably able to do for self.
10. Lack of energy.
11. Frequent thoughts or statements of worthlessness or guilt.
12. Frequent pessimistic thoughts or statements about the future.
13. Significantly decreased or increased appetite.
14. Significantly decreased or increased sleep.
15. Experience of not being rested despite apparently normal sleep.
16. Poor concentration and indecisiveness.
17. Unresolved grief issues.
18. Mood-related hallucinations or delusions.
19. A family and/or personal history of major depression, bipolar disorder, or dysthymia.

__. _____
    _____
    _____
__. _____
    _____
    _____
__. _____
    _____

LONG-TERM GOALS

1. Return to normal mood state with ability to experience a variety of emotions in response to life situations.
2. Reinvest energy in relationships, work, and activities at level commensurate with physical and cognitive abilities.
3. Carry out behaviors to maintain health and functioning.
4. Patient and/or responsible party is able to identify signs of possible recurrence of depression, and is aware of behavioral, cognitive, and/or medical actions to take to prevent or interrupt recurrence.

___. _____

_____

___. _____

_____

___. _____

_____

SHORT-TERM OBJECTIVES

1. Define severity, course, and precipitant(s) of depression. (1, 2, 3)
2. Cooperate with psychological testing to assess depth of depression. (4, 6)
3. Cooperate with a neuropsychological assessment. (5, 6)
4. Acknowledge any suicidal thoughts, impulses, or attempts. (7)
5. Participate in plan to assure survival and safety while at risk for suicide. (8, 9, 10)
6. Accept the need for inpatient psychiatric care. (10, 11)

THERAPEUTIC INTERVENTIONS

1. Arrange for or conduct a psychodiagnostic evaluation of the patient to determine if depression is present, and to make treatment recommendations.
2. If the patient is a poor historian, obtain permission from the patient or legally responsible party to interview person(s) familiar with his/her history.
3. Consult with the patient's physician regarding medical conditions or medications that might be affecting his/her mood or behavior.
4. Administer psychological test(s) to identify severity of depression.

7. Contract with therapist to engage in no self-harming behavior. (12)

8. Take antidepressant medications regularly as prescribed and report as to effectiveness and side effects. (13, 14)

9. Express sadness, loss, irritability, anger, and other feelings or physical sensations associated with depression. (15, 16, 25)

10. Expand support system by contacting personal spiritual leader, attending a support group, and/or meeting with peer counselors. (16, 17, 18, 19)

11. Identify hopelessness, helplessness, and other distorted, negative cognitions that lead to and reinforce depression. (20, 21, 22)

12. Report on the success of substituting positive, realistic thoughts for the distortions that precipitate depression. (22, 23, 24)

13. Acknowledge an understanding of the relationship between poor cooperation, somatic symptoms, withdrawal, and self-destructive behaviors and the struggle with depression. (21, 22, 25, 26)

14. Identify past or recent experiences contributing to current depression. (21, 27, 28)

15. Verbalize accurate understanding of own medical

5. Arrange for or conduct neuropsychological testing to identify cognitive problems affecting patient's behavior and coping capabilities.

6. Give feedback to the patient (patient's family), treatment team, and other designated persons regarding assessment results and recommendations.

7. Assess suicide risk, history of previous suicidal ideation and/or attempts, availability of methods, and ability to implement suicide plan.

8. Within limits of law, inform the patient's physician, rehabilitation team, and family about suicide risk and coordinate implementation of precautions.

9. Inform the patient's family, within limits of law, about risk for suicidal behavior and ways to obtain help in an emergency.

10. Arrange for or conduct an evaluation for inpatient psychiatric care of the patient, using involuntary admission if necessary.

11. Identify and address the patient's (and family's) questions and concerns about inpatient psychiatric care.

12. Contract with the patient to not harm self, asking him/her to sign a written contract if appropriate.

13. Assess need for pharmacologic intervention and con-

condition, treatment options, and prognosis. (29, 30)

16. State a belief in self as being able to handle immediate circumstances and verbalize hope in possibility of improvement. (29, 30, 31, 32)

17. State realistic goals for recovery from medical condition. (33, 34)

18. Attend and cooperate with all aspects of the rehabilitation treatment program. (35, 36, 37)

19. Chart attendance at and progress achieved within rehabilitation sessions. (38, 39)

20. Verbalize acceptance of physical and/or cognitive limitations. (40, 41)

21. Report on the implementation of assertiveness skills in daily life. (42, 43)

22. Verbalize how religious beliefs and rituals that have been meaningful in the past can be supportive now. (44)

23. Implement the use of bright-light therapy to relieve seasonal affective depressive disorder. (45)

24. Attend and participate in family therapy sessions to increase communication, mutual support, and problem-solving skills within the family. (46)

25. Increase the level of physical exercise sanctioned by medical personnel. (47)

sult with the patient's treating physician regarding how antidepressant medication will be prescribed, monitored, and managed.

14. Monitor the patient's use of prescribed medications and effect on depressive symptoms; address issues affecting compliance and side effects.

15. Assist the patient in verbalizing and experiencing feelings of loss, anger, and other emotions associated with depression.

16. Facilitate referral to and encourage participation in emotional support or adjustment group.

17. Recommend that the patient contact chaplain or person from own religious community for support and counseling.

18. Educate the patient and family regarding support groups or advocacy organizations dealing with his/her particular medical condition.

19. Encourage the patient to meet with peer counselors, and facilitate referral.

20. Assist the patient in identifying distorted, negative thoughts that precipitate feelings of depression.

21. Recommend that the patient record thoughts and experiences in a journal.

22. Recommend that the patient read about managing

26. Take pride in appearance as evidenced by improved grooming and neat, coordinated clothing. (48)

27. Maintain level of activity and own responsibilities up to maximum capability. (49, 50, 51, 52)

28. Participate in potentially pleasurable activities and see possibility of obtaining satisfaction despite physical or cognitive limitations. (49, 51, 53, 54, 55)

29. Verbalize a plan to prevent relapse of depression. (55, 56, 57)

30. Verbalize an understanding of the negative impact of substance abuse on depression. (58)

31. Accept referral for substance abuse treatment. (59)

__. _____
    _____

__. _____
    _____

__. _____
    _____

depression, in books such as *Thoughts and Feelings* (McKay, Davis, and Fanning), *Control Your Depression* (Lewinsohn, Muñoz, Youngren, and Zeiss), and *Feeling Good* (Burns).

23. Assist the patient in identifying a positive, realistic cognition that can be substituted for every identified negative thought associated with depressive feelings.

24. Monitor the patient's use of positive cognitions and reinforce successful replacement of distorted thoughts of catastrophizing, polarized thinking, fortune-telling, mind reading, helplessness, and so forth.

25. Assist the patient in identifying physical sensations and interpersonal conflicts that substitute for direct emotional experience.

26. Point out physical sensations that appear or increase when the patient is stressed.

27. Explore the emotional pain from the past that contributes to the patient's reaction to current situation.

28. Inquire into present aspects of the patient's life that contribute to the depression.

29. Assess the patient's need for education regarding medical condition, symptoms, and actions that he/she can currently take to improve condition; coordi-

nate with other treatment professionals in providing educational information.

30. Provide the patient and family with educational materials regarding his/her medical condition and its treatment.

31. Assist the patient in identifying immediate therapy goals and actions that he/she feels capable of taking to achieve them.

32. Educate staff and family regarding the patient's current need for overly optimistic view about long-term prognosis in order to maintain motivation and hope, and inform them of how they might respond in a neutral yet supportive way, using statements such as "It would be wonderful for you to do so well."

33. Encourage the patient to prepare for an outcome that might include less than complete recovery, and support him/her in maintaining hope of resuming a satisfying life.

34. Work with the patient to set realistic, achievable goals.

35. Advise other members of the treatment team (e.g., physical therapists, occupational therapists, etc.) to set measurable therapy goals that can be accomplished in two weeks or less, and have therapists point out progress to the patient.

36. Recommend that therapists on the treatment team identify for the patient how current activities (e.g., muscle strengthening) relate to his/her long-term therapy goals (e.g., walking).

37. Advise therapists on the treatment team to provide the patient with positive social reinforcement for effort, participation, and objective progress that approximates goal.

38. Develop a chart that the patient, staff, and family will use to note the patient's participation and progress toward therapy goals.

39. Provide the patient and family with written feedback every week about accomplishments of that week and goals for the next.

40. Work with the patient to come to an acceptance of cognitive and physical limitations.

41. Be attentive to positive meaning the patient may find in loss and point this out.

42. Using modeling, behavior rehearsal, and role-playing, teach the patient healthy assertive skills; then apply these skills to several current problem situations.

43. Monitor the patient's implementation of assertiveness in daily life, reinforcing successes and discussing ways to enhance effectiveness.

44. Identify religious rituals from which the patient might draw strength, and support participation in them.

45. Recommend the patient's use of bright-light therapy.

46. Arrange for or conduct family therapy to resolve problems that interfere with effective communication, problem solving, or support within the family.

47. Identify exercises (e.g., water exercises, riding stationary bicycle, mall walking, armchair exercises) appropriate to the patient's physical and cognitive abilities, and support participation.

48. Encourage the patient to put effort into grooming and appearance, reinforcing progress as observed.

49. Encourage the patient to participate in activities related to previous interests and adapted to current abilities (e.g., pet therapy, adapted gardening, adapted golf, water exercises, painting, music).

50. Support expectation that the patient will receive only necessary help from family, staff, and friends.

51. Refer the patient and family to information regarding accessibility issues.

52. Refer the patient to vocational rehabilitation resources.

53. Express interest in the patient's preinjury/preillness activities and accomplishments.

54. Coordinate the patient's referral to recreational therapist.

55. Encourage and reinforce the patient for resumed participation in friendships and social groups.

56. Educate the patient and family about symptoms of depression, and actions that can be taken to prevent relapse (e.g., taking medication regularly, monitoring for and terminating use of distorted thoughts, maintaining exercise and social contacts, etc.).

57. Recommend that the patient read about treatment and long-term management of depression in books such as *The Depression Workbook* (Copeland) and *Depression: How It Happens, How It's Healed* (Medina).

58. Educate the patient and family about added negative impact of alcohol and other mood-altering substances on people experiencing depression.

59. Coordinate the patient's referral for therapy addressing substance abuse or dependence.

__. _____

_____

—. _____
   _____
   _____
—. _____
   _____

DIAGNOSTIC SUGGESTIONS

Axis I:

296.2x	Major Depressive Disorder, Single Episode
296.3x	Major Depressive Disorder, Recurrent
300.4	Dysthymic Disorder
311	Depressive Disorder NOS
296.5x	Bipolar I Disorder, Most Recent Episode Depressed
296.89	Bipolar II Disorder
293.83	Mood Disorder Due to (General Medical Condition)
292.84	Substance-Induced Mood Disorder (Specify Substance)
291.89	Alcohol-Induced Mood Disorder
296.90	Mood Disorder NOS
309.0	Adjustment Disorder With Depressed Mood
309.28	Adjustment Disorder With Mixed Anxiety and Depressed Mood
309.3	Adjustment Disorder With Disturbance of Conduct
309.4	Adjustment Disorder With Mixed Disturbance of Emotions and Conduct
309.9	Adjustment Disorder, Unspecified
V15.81	Noncompliance With Treatment
V62.82	Bereavement
_____	_____
_____	_____

Axis II:

799.9	Diagnosis Deferred
V71.09	No Diagnosis
_____	_____
_____	_____

DRIVING DEFICIENCIES

BEHAVIORAL DEFINITIONS

1. Significant deficiency in the ability to safely drive a motor vehicle due to brain-related injury or illness symptoms.
2. Inability to operate motor vehicle controls in usual way because of changes in motor functioning.
3. Lack of capacity to see vehicles, pedestrians, or other obstacles well enough to avoid a collision.
4. Changed visual-perceptual abilities affecting ability to judge distance between own vehicle and other objects.
5. Unable to keep vehicle consistently in designated traffic lane.
6. Failure to attend to relevant aspects of environment consistently enough to identify and react to changing circumstances.
7. Poor ability to divide attention between road conditions and vehicular operations.
8. Unable to remember route and/or destination.
9. Poor impulse control that puts driver at risk for acting on emotions without regard to safety.
10. At significant risk for interruptions in consciousness because of medical condition.
11. History of recently and frequently driving under the influence of alcohol or other drugs.

__. _____

   _____

__. _____

   _____

__. _____

   _____

LONG-TERM GOALS

1. Operate motor vehicle safely, making necessary accommodations for cognitive, perceptual, or motor impairments.
2. Refrain from driving while medical, cognitive, or perceptual problems put self at risk for an accident.
3. Terminate substance abuse and avoid driving while under the influence of substances.
4. Emotionally accept the need to terminate driving, suspend driving, or to implement accommodations because of changed abilities.
5. Arrange for transportation needs to be met through the assistance of family or friends.
6. Use public transportation systems, taxis, and other transportation methods to access necessary services and to continue social life.
7. Utilize mail-order and home delivery services to minimize need for transportation to stores.

—. _____

_____

—. _____

_____

—. _____

_____

SHORT-TERM OBJECTIVES

1. Cooperate with an evaluation of medical and behavioral factors affecting driving capability. (1, 2, 3, 4, 10)

2. Participate willingly in neuropsychological testing. (5, 10)

3. Implement recommended steps to improve vision and hearing. (6)

4. Utilize adapted equipment to operate motor vehicle

THERAPEUTIC INTERVENTIONS

1. Review the patient's medical record to identify medical conditions, sensory deficits, problems in motor functioning, perceptual deficits, or cognitive problems that might affect his/her ability to safely operate a motor vehicle.

2. Consult with the patient's physician or review the patient's medications to determine if he/she is routinely taking any that are thought

controls and to assess traffic conditions with necessary speed and accuracy. (7)

5. Cooperate with evaluation of driving-related skills. (8, 9, 10)

6. Identify the ways in which one's driving skills have been affected by the brain-related medical event. (10, 11, 12, 15)

7. Verbalize the need for modifications in driving and describe those that will be implemented in order to protect own safety and that of others. (13, 14, 15)

8. Update driver's license by following the procedures outlined by the state for evaluation of driving capability following medical events. (16)

9. Describe the difficulties anticipated in implementing the rehabilitation team's driving recommendations. (17)

10. List the specific responsibilities that had been met through driving prior to the medical event. (18)

11. Name at least one other way (i.e., besides driving) in which transportation needs could be fulfilled. (19, 20)

12. Cooperate with therapies to improve perceptual and cognitive skills required for safe driving. (21)

13. Put effort into therapies designed to improve motor

to affect level of alertness, response time, or other factors affecting driving skills.

3. Inquire into the patient's use of alcohol, street drugs, or other substances that might affect reaction time, judgment, or other skills necessary for effective operation of a motor vehicle.

4. Interview the patient (and patient's family) to assess his/her driving skills and driving record prior to the brain-related medical event.

5. Refer for or perform neuropsychological testing of patient to evaluate attention, concentration, memory, sensory-perceptual functions, judgment, and other cognitive factors that might affect his/her driving ability.

6. Refer for an evaluation of the patient's vision and/or hearing, or consult with his/her physician about how these skills will be assessed; facilitate treatments necessary to improve these sensory abilities.

7. Coordinate a referral to an occupational therapist to evaluate the patient's need for and ability to benefit from adapted equipment (e.g., knob on steering wheel, convex mirror, hand controls) to allow more effective operation of motor vehicle. Encourage the pa-

strength and coordination that will enhance safe operation of a motor vehicle. (22)

14. Describe the amount, frequency, and history of substance abuse. (23, 24)

15. Decrease the level of denial around substance use as evidenced by fewer statements about minimizing amount of use and its negative impact on life. (25, 26)

16. Obtain treatment for substance abuse problems. (27, 28)

17. Participate in supervised driving training to regain driving skills. (29)

18. Develop confidence in driving skills by gradually attempting more complex and challenging situations, while being accompanied by someone who is judged to be a safe, competent driver. (30, 31)

19. Agree to refrain from driving while rehabilitation team judges that residual deficits or medical conditions jeopardize driving safety. (32)

20. Participate in psychotherapy to facilitate coming to terms emotionally with the restriction/loss of driving ability. (33)

21. Family members (or others close to the patient) list actions they will take to prevent the patient from driving, if he/she will not

tient to acquire and use this equipment.

8. Refer the patient for an evaluation of specific driving-related sensory, cognitive, perceptual, motor, and perceptual-motor skills.

9. Refer the patient for an on-the-road driving evaluation with a trained rehabilitation professional to evaluate his/her skills and judgment.

10. Give feedback to the patient, (patient's family), physician, rehabilitation team, and other designated persons regarding assessment results and recommendations.

11. Describe specific cognitive, perceptual, and motor changes that have occurred with the brain injury or illness and discuss how these may affect the patient's driving skills.

12. Work with the patient to increase his/her awareness of brain-injury/illness changes. (See Denial and Impaired Awareness chapter in this Planner.)

13. Coordinate a meeting of the rehabilitation team to make a decision regarding the patient's current driving skills, need for adapted equipment, need for sensory prostheses (e.g., glasses, hearing aids, mirrors), and recommended restrictions (e.g., daytime driving only, non-rush-hour driving, etc.).

agree to follow recommen-
dations. (34)

22. Cooperate with an evaluation of ability to use public
transportation, taxis, and
door-to-door handicapped
transportation services.
(35, 36)

23. Demonstrate ability to effectively use transportation
services. (37)

24. Complete (or family complete) an application for
handicapped transportation
services. (38)

25. The patient (and family
members) identify and ad-
dress reservations about
the patient's use of various
transportation alternatives.
(39)

26. Patient and family verbalize a realistic, satisfactory
plan to have the patient's
transportation needs and
responsibilities met. (40)

—. _____
   _____

—. _____
   _____

—. _____
   _____

14. Guided by state law, make
recommendations about the
patient's current ability to
drive.

15. Assess the patient's (patient's family's) insight into
the patient's driving deficiencies and willingness to
implement the rehabilita-
tion team's recommenda-
tions.

16. Refer the patient to the
state's drivers' examination
agency for a reevaluation of
driving skills and update of
driver's license.

17. Assist the patient in verbalizing painful emotions or
identifying barriers (e.g.,
expense, driving during
daylight only not practical
with preteen children at
home) toward implementing
these restricted driving recommendations.

18. Identify the patient's transportation needs (e.g., getting
child to school, going to
work, grocery shopping) that
were met by the patient
driving prior to the brain-
related injury or illness.

19. Discuss the transportation
alternatives available to patient to meet each need (e.g.,
arranging rides with family
and friends, use of public
transportation, use of taxi-
cabs) and describe the pros
and cons of each alternative.

20. Brainstorm about ways to
reduce the patient's need to

travel to have basic needs met (e.g., utilize delivery services for groceries, use catalogs to order clothing and gifts, buy large quantities of nonperishable items when grocery shopping).

21. Refer the patient for cognitive rehabilitation therapy to address perceptual deficits, stimulus neglect, impulse control, attention deficits, and/or memory deficits affecting driving skills. (See Stimulus Neglect, Impulsivity, Attention and Concentration Impairment, and Memory Impairment chapters in this Planner.)

22. Coordinate referral of the patient for physical and/or occupational therapy to improve motor strength and coordination.

23. Gather a complete drug/alcohol history of the patient, including amount and pattern of use, signs and symptoms of use, and negative life consequences (social, legal, familial, and vocational) resulting from his/her chemical dependence.

24. Administer the Addiction Severity Index (McLellan, Kushner, Metzger, Peters, Smith, Grissom, Pettinati, and Argeriou), Michigan Alcoholism Screening Test (Selzer), Substance Abuse Subtle Screening Inventory (Miller), or other instru-

ments, and process the results with the patient.

25. Assign the patient to ask
two or three people who are
close to him/her to write a
letter to the therapist in
which they identify how
they saw the patient's
chemical dependence nega-
tively impacting his/her life.

26. Model and reinforce the patient's statements that reflect awareness of the
destructive consequences of
chemical dependence on self
and others.

27. Refer the patient for therapy to address substance
abuse problems. (See Sub-
stance Abuse chapter in
this Planner.)

28. Recommend that the patient attend Alcoholics
Anonymous (AA) or Nar-
cotics Anonymous (NA)
meetings and report to the
therapist the impact of the
meetings.

29. Encourage the patient to
participate in supervised
driving training with a rehabilitation professional to
build safe driving habits
and implement recom-
mended accommodations.

30. Talk with the patient about
ways to regain confidence
behind the wheel by driving
in a quiet, safe area (e.g., an
empty parking lot, streets in
an industrial park on a Sunday morning) with a family

member or friend who can supervise and give feedback.

31. Direct the patient to attempt driving in progressively more challenging driving situations, using his/her confidence and the feedback of a trusted individual to determine when it is time to progress to more complex situations.

32. Taking into account state laws concerning duty to report medical conditions affecting driving as well as laws concerning confidentiality of psychological information, consult with rehabilitation team regarding how the recommendation to suspend the patient's driving privileges should be implemented (e.g., the patient voluntarily refrains from driving, family withholds keys to car, state drivers' licensing board is notified of medical restrictions).

33. Refer for or perform psychotherapy to assist the patient in verbalizing and working through feelings associated with restriction/ loss of driving privileges.

34. Talk with the patient's family about actions they are prepared and willing to take (e.g., taking car keys away from the patient and storing them in a secure location, mechanically disabling the car's engine, installing a

locking device on the steering wheel) to prevent the
patient from driving.

35. Review neuropsychological
test results and consult with
the patient's rehabilitation
team regarding his/her ability to effectively and safely
use public transportation,
taxis, door-to-door handicapped transportation
services, and other transportation options.

36. Refer for an *in vivo* evaluation with a rehabilitation
therapist to determine how
effectively the patient uses
various types of public
transportation.

37. Refer the patient for occupational or recreational therapy to develop his/her skills
in effectively using specific
transportation systems.

38. Educate the patient (patient's family) about the
process of applying for eligibility to use door-to-door
public transportation for
people with disabilities.

39. Explore and work through
the patient's (and family's)
concerns (e.g., burdening
others, safety, convenience,
expense) regarding the use
of transportation alternatives.

40. In a family session, develop
transportation plans that
are acceptable to all to address the patient's identified transportation needs.

___.   _____

          _____

___.   _____

          _____

___.   _____

          _____

DIAGNOSTIC SUGGESTIONS

Axis I: 290.xx   Dementia
               294.1   Dementia Due to (Axis III condition)
               294.8   Dementia NOS
               294.9   Cognitive Disorder NOS
               303.90   Alcohol Dependence
               304.80   Polysubstance Dependence
               305.00   Alcohol Abuse
               309.0   Adjustment Disorder With Depressed Mood
               309.3   Adjustment Disorder With Disturbance of
                         Conduct
               309.4   Adjustment Disorder With Mixed Disturbance
                         of Emotions and Conduct
               309.9   Adjustment Disorder, Unspecified

               _____   _____

               _____   _____

Axis II: V71.09   No Diagnosis or Condition
               799.9   Diagnosis Deferred

               _____   _____

               _____   _____

EMOTIONAL LABILITY

BEHAVIORAL DEFINITIONS

1. Sudden, uncontrollable, spasmodic crying or laughing.
2. Emotional expression incongruent with the patient's internal experience.
3. Exaggerated emotional reaction to the environmental stimulus.
4. Inability to explain why laughing or crying is initiated.
5. Displays significantly more emotionality than prior to neurological illness or injury.
6. Emotional reactions are embarrassing, uncomfortable, or interfere with communication efforts.
7. Family or treatment team concludes that the patient is depressed because he/she "cries all the time."
8. Family or treatment team expresses frustration with the patient because he/she laughs inappropriately.

___. _____
_____
___. _____
_____
___. _____
_____

LONG-TERM GOALS

1. Return to preinjury style of emotional responding.
2. Learn to control expression of emotions to be congruent with environmental stimulus.

3. Patient and family successfully manage residual symptoms and their impact on social relationships and communication.

—. _____
_____

—. _____
_____

—. _____
_____

SHORT-TERM OBJECTIVES

1. Identify history, precipitants, and internal mood state associated with sudden crying or laughing. (1, 2, 3, 5)

2. Cooperate with psychological testing to identify disorders that underlie or coexist with lability. (4, 5)

3. Cooperate with treatment of psychiatric disorders. (6, 7, 8)

4. Acknowledge an understanding of the emotional behavior as a symptom of a neurologic condition. (9, 10)

5. Identify lability as distinct from sadness, grief, loss, or joy. (11, 12)

6. Apply rapid relaxation techniques to lower physiologic arousal levels. (13, 14)

7. Use rapid relaxation technique to interrupt labile episode. (15, 16, 17)

THERAPEUTIC INTERVENTIONS

1. Arrange for or conduct a psychodiagnostic evaluation to determine whether emotional lability is present, to identify or rule out concurrent psychological disorders, and to make treatment recommendations.

2. If the patient is a poor historian, obtain permission from patient or legally responsible party to interview person(s) familiar with his/ her history.

3. Review medical chart and/ or consult with the patient's physician regarding medical conditions or medications that might be affecting patient's emotional expression.

4. Arrange for or conduct psychological testing of the patient to identify depression, psychosis, bipolar, or other psychological disorders.

8. Take medication as prescribed to reduce or eliminate lability. (18, 19, 20)

9. Family reports understanding that the emotional expression does not reflect the patient's internal mood state. (21, 22)

10. Family members identify steps they can take to shorten or interrupt the lability. (23, 24, 25)

11. Family demonstrates ability to maintain effective, satisfying communication. (26, 27)

__. _____
   _____

__. _____
   _____

__. _____
   _____

5. Give feedback to the patient (patient's family), treatment team, and other designated persons regarding assessment results and recommendations.

6. Address the patient's (and family's) concerns and questions regarding need for psychiatric evaluation.

7. Coordinate referral for psychiatric evaluation and management.

8. Perform or refer for psychotherapy to address emotional and behavioral issues coexisting with lability.

9. Inform the patient regarding lability as a neurological symptom representing a changed threshold for emotional responding that has no particular significance to the patient's internal emotional state (i.e., an emotional "sneeze").

10. Advise the patient about anticipated duration and prognosis for labile symptoms.

11. Inquire into the patient's experience of sadness and/or joy and point out how this differs from experience during labile episode.

12. Encourage the patient to ask self "Am I upset (happy)?" during or immediately following labile behavior.

13. Lead the patient through deep breathing exercise and point out how this promotes relaxation.

14. Assist the patient in identifying image or memory that promotes feeling of relaxation.

15. Trigger labile response during session and instruct the patient to take several slow, deep breaths.

16. Encourage the patient to think of targeted image or memory to continue the experience of relaxation.

17. Reinforce the patient's ability to shorten labile episode.

18. Assess need for medication to reduce lability, and consult with the patient's treating physician about how medication will be prescribed, monitored, and managed.

19. Address the patient's (patient's family's) concerns about medications and assist them in getting answers to questions about medications and side effects.

20. Monitor the patient's use of and results from prescribed medications; address issues regarding compliance and side effects.

21. Educate the patient's family about emotional lability and how it differs from a genuine emotional response.

22. Encourage the family to inquire about the patient's internal experience by asking, "Are you sad (happy)?" if they are unsure whether crying (laughing) represents a mood-congruent emotional reaction.

23. Instruct the family to cue patient to take several deep breaths at first sign of lability.

24. If the family and/or patient are troubled by the patient's emotionality, suggest that the family change the topic of conversation from an emotional topic to something neutral.

25. Caution family members to avoid empathic or sympathetic responses to the patient's lability. For example, they should not say "What's wrong?"; "It will be okay"; "It's really not that bad"; or pat patient on the shoulder in response to lability.

26. Once it has been established that the patient (though emotionally expressive) is not experiencing intense sadness/happiness, recommend that family members ignore the patient's emotional behavior and continue the conversation.

27. Address family members' emotional reactions to the patient's changed communication style, allowing them to express their frustration and feelings of embarrassment or awkwardness regarding the patient's lability.

__. _____

_____

___. _____

_____

___. _____

_____

DIAGNOSTIC SUGGESTIONS

Axis I: 310.1 Personality Change Due to (General Medical
                   Condition)
         293.9 Mental Disorder NOS Due to (General Medical
                   Condition)

_____ _____

_____ _____

FAMILY STRESS REACTIONS

BEHAVIORAL DEFINITIONS

1. Family members describe the patient's condition or prognosis in overly optimistic (unrealistic) terms (e.g., "No one told us that something happened to his brain"; "The doctor said he'd be in rehab for about six weeks, and then he would be fine"; "Others may have limitations, but she will recover as if nothing ever happened").
2. Family members are irritable, angry, and/or accusatory with rehabilitation staff and/or the patient.
3. Family members do not make themselves available to support the patient's recovery and rehabilitation (e.g., family never visits, fails to return therapists' phone calls, does not appear for scheduled family education).
4. Family members report anxiety, depression, a sense of being overwhelmed, or other painful emotions.
5. Verbal abuse occurs on a regular basis within the family.
6. Physical abuse occurs within the family.
7. Family members experience physical symptoms (e.g., insomnia, nightmares, gastrointestinal problems, blood pressure problems) following onset of the patient's condition.
8. Family members report problems at school or at work following onset of the patient's condition.

Many of the interventions described in this chapter were based on ideas presented in the book *Head Injury and the Family: A Life and Living Perspective* (Dell Orto and Power). Additional information about working with families to manage chronic behavioral and emotional problems can be found in *Behavioral Family Therapy for Psychiatric Disorders,* Second Edition (Mueser and Glynn).

9. Family members are unrealistic about the implications of the patient's brain injury or illness and the effort that will be required from them to support the patient's recovery (e.g., "We'll easily be able to manage what she needs"; "I am sure he won't get angry and combative once he goes home").

10. The basic emotional or financial needs of family members are not met because an excessive amount of family resources are being allocated to the patient.

__. _____

     _____

__. _____

     _____

__. _____

     _____

LONG-TERM GOALS

1. Family members acknowledge brain-related changes, describe a realistic plan, and report confidence in their ability to manage the effects of residual cognitive and personality changes.

2. Family members identify own emotional distress and utilize available resources effectively to reduce emotional pain.

3. Family members' behavior reflects an understanding that brain injury/illness is a family problem rather than one that the patient alone must manage.

4. Family retains its sense of purpose and identity while it adjusts its resources and structure to include the needs of the member with impaired brain functioning.

5. Individual family members take actions to enhance emotional and physical health.

6. Family members pursue individual life goals while contributing to the family's needs.

7. Family members find positive meaning in building life to include the new circumstances.

8. Family members focus on present and future goals and put energy into realizing them.

9. Family members participate in recreational activities and experience having fun together.

__. _____

     _____

___. _____

  _____

  _____

___. _____

  _____

SHORT-TERM OBJECTIVES

1. Family members describe what has happened to the patient, and how they think this condition will affect the patient, themselves, and their family life. (1, 2)

2. Family members report their emotional state (e.g., shock, disbelief, bewilderment) and describe intellectual awareness that some patients with similar conditions experience long-term changes in their lives. (3)

3. Family members verbalize knowledge about the patient's brain condition, the effects this condition is having on the patient's thinking, emotions, and behavior, and the long-term changes that the patient might experience. (4, 5, 6, 7)

4. Family members acknowledge the need for (and accept support in working through) emotions associated with the family's losses. (8)

5. Parent(s) list ways they can communicate with their child(ren) about the patient's situation; how this will affect the family; and

THERAPEUTIC INTERVENTIONS

1. Establish rapport with all members of the family by inquiring about their concerns, questions, and emotions, and listening empathically.

2. Determine the family's stage of emotional coping (shock, denial, gradual awareness, reorientation) by inquiring into issues such as what the family members understand to be true about the patient's injury/illness and what they expect the long-term outcome to be.

3. Assist the family with early stages of emotional coping (shock, denial) by active listening, sensitive challenging of denial with gentle presentation of facts, informing family that help is available in the event that the patient's recovery is slower or more complicated than the family now expects.

4. Assist the family as they gain awareness of the seriousness of the patient's condition, by answering

that they as a family will handle this change. (9, 10)

6. Parent(s) name ways in which child(ren)'s emotional distress may be communicated through physical symptoms or behavioral change. (11)

7. Parent(s) arrange for psychotherapy for their child(ren) if physical and behavioral problems are excessive or fail to resolve. (12)

8. Family members identify the beliefs that have been triggered by the patient's brain injury/illness and describe the impact that these beliefs have on their moods and coping. (13, 14)

9. Family members report on the success of substituting positive, realistic thoughts for the cognitive distortions that precipitate stressful mood states. (15)

10. Family members discuss instances in which rehabilitation practices and cultural values may be at odds, and work collaboratively with the rehabilitation team to plan for the patient's recovery in a way that accommodates his/her cultural beliefs. (16, 17)

11. Family members tell the story of the family up to the time of the patient's illness/injury, describing what the experience of being in their family was like and also

questions, providing information about the patient's injury/illness, and discussing the most common outcomes.

5. Help the family to frame the questions they have about the patient's medical condition and prognosis and identify the best ways to obtain this information (e.g., meeting with the physician when he/she does rounds, calling the physician's office and scheduling a meeting, arranging a conference with the rehabilitation team).

6. Refer the family to written information (e.g., books, pamphlets, Internet Web sites) that will help them understand the patient's condition and treatments.

7. Inform the family about opportunities to meet with other families who have experienced a similar situation (e.g., peer counselors, support groups, advocacy organizations), and facilitate the contact, if needed.

8. Assist the family in naming and working through their emotions (e.g., sadness, anger, anxiety) associated with the family losses brought about by the patient's brain injury/illness.

9. Talk with the parent(s) about how to communicate with their child(ren) about the patient's condition; what this means to each

outlining the family's hopes and goals for the future. (18, 19)

12. Family members describe valued aspects of their family life. (20)

13. Family members consider how the family has previously dealt with stress and difficult situations, and describe the techniques that were most effective. (21)

14. Family members cooperate with an assessment of family communication, problem solving, and emotional support processes. (22, 23, 24)

15. Family members describe the family responsibilities and functions that had been filled predominantly by the ill/injured patient. (25)

16. Family members each describe how they have been and expect to be impacted by the patient's illness/injury. (26)

17. Family members discuss how they expect the family as a whole to be affected by the patient's condition. (27, 28)

18. Family members acknowledge the reality of the brain injury/illness, the need to adjust family plans, and commit themselves to incorporating this event into their family life. (29)

19. Identify the priority needs of each family member. (30)

child; and what it means to the family.

10. Recommend children's books dealing with witnessing a traumatic event, or the disability or death of a loved one, such as *A Terrible Thing Happened* (Holmes), *Tibby Tried It* (Useman and Useman), *I Don't Have an Uncle Phil Anymore* (Pellegreno), and *Homemade Books to Help Kids Cope* (Ziegler), or refer the parent(s) to a librarian for age-appropriate literature concerning coping with family illness, injury, and loss.

11. Talk with the parent(s) about physical symptoms (e.g., difficulty sleeping, changes in eating habits, vague complaints about not feeling well) or behavioral signs (e.g., nightmares, academic work not up to usual standard, withdrawal, change in friendship network) that might signal that a child is experiencing excessive emotional distress in reaction to the patient's injury/illness and its consequences.

12. Perform or refer for psychotherapy with the child(ren) to help identify stress, normalize experience, address concerns, and develop confidence that he/she and the family will be able to manage this situation.

20. Family members state the resources that the family brings to the problem of adjusting to the changed circumstances brought on by the patient's brain injury/illness. (31, 32, 33)

21. Family members describe other events that have drawn on the family's resources recently, affecting what might now be available. (34)

22. Family initiates actions to identify and utilize available resources. (35, 36)

23. Family members talk about their reluctance to utilize support. (37)

24. Family members verbalize that the wise and respectful use of available resources is an indication of family strength. (38)

25. Family members forthrightly acknowledge previous incidents that are making it more difficult for the family to come to grips emotionally with the current illness/injury. (39)

26. Family members take actions to enhance their ability to cope with the recent family stress. (40, 41)

27. Family members describe a plan to deal with the essential and priority needs of the patient and each family member. (42, 43, 44)

28. Family members report two or three indicators that the

13. Engage the family in conversation about what this injury/illness event means to their family life and listen carefully for beliefs (e.g., patient's condition is a punishment for not living right; patient's injury provides an opportunity to demonstrate family loyalty) that may hinder or assist the family in long-term coping.

14. Ask the family members to identify how their beliefs about the meaning of the brain-related event affect the family's mood.

15. Assist the family members in identifying a positive, realistic cognition that can be substituted for every identified distorted, negative thought associated with increased emotional distress.

16. Talk with the patient, family, and/or others who share the patient's culture to gain insight into how this illness/injury and the rehabilitation process might be viewed in his/her culture.

17. Coordinate a meeting with the family, (patient), (others who have knowledge of the patient's culture), and rehabilitation team to develop a rehabilitation plan that is medically sound and takes the patient's cultural practices into account.

18. Ask the family to talk about what their family life was

plan needs updating, and state their preferred method(s) to negotiate a new plan. (45)

29. Family members describe both the changes and continuity they are experiencing as they adjust to the new family situation. (46, 47)

30. Family members verbalize insight that the patient's emotional recovery typically will occur at a different pace than the family's emotional recovery, and describe ways to recognize the patient's progress in coping with his/her changed functioning. (48)

31. Family members describe the patient's expected residual cognitive and personality changes, and name several practical ways that they would be able to manage these changes. (49, 50)

32. Family members describe how their own behavior can affect the likelihood of the patient behaving in a certain way. (51)

33. Family selects one or two priority problems. For each problem, family members make observations about circumstances that affect the onset, frequency, and intensity of the problem, and describe how they react when the problem occurs. (52)

34. Family members implement changes in the environment

like prior to the patient's illness/injury.

19. Ask the family what events they were anticipating and/or planning for (e.g., patient was engaged to be married, couple were about to attempt conceiving a child, family was planning to use savings to finance early retirement) at the time of the patient's injury/ illness; facilitate expressions of grief or other emotions associated with this interruption in plans.

20. Assist the family members in describing what they value and like about the family (e.g., "Our family always pulls together when there is a problem"; "Our family makes a point to spend time together"; "Our family shows concern for other people"). Support and reinforce these strengths.

21. Inquire into the ways in which the family has dealt with crises in the past, identifying the degree to which various strategies were successful in reducing stress and resolving problems. Encourage renewed implementation of successful strategies.

22. Evaluate aspects of family functioning and adaptation by administering family functioning questionnaires such as the McMaster Family Assessment Device

or in own behavior and make notes about how these changes affect the occurrence of the target problem. (53, 54, 55, 56)

35. Family reports at least three actions that each member could take to protect the patient, himself/herself, and other family members from physical harm. (57)

36. Family discusses the implications of having the patient live in a residential or long-term care facility, and acknowledges the emotions that are elicited by these discussions. (58, 59)

37. Family members verbalize confidence in their ability to manage those problems that have arisen because of the patient's brain condition. (60, 61)

38. Family members describe actions they will take to reduce their own stress levels. (62, 63)

39. Report on the positive effect of family members' participation in recreational and social activities. (64, 65)

40. Family members describe the positive impact of keeping an activity that the family can look forward to on the family's calendar. (66)

41. Report on the effect of using humor to achieve perspective and to reduce family stress. (67)

(Epstein, Baldwin, and Bishop), the Family Environment Scale (Moos), and the Family Adaptability and Cohesion Evaluation Scale-III (Olson, Sprenkle, and Russell).

23. Assess the family's communication, problem solving, and support network using structured interview materials such as the Camberwell Family Interview (Brown and Rutter), the McMaster Structured Interview for Families (Bishop and Miller), and the Standardized Clinical Family Interview (Kinston and Loader).

24. Schedule a family meeting and ask the family to solve a hypothetical or real family "problem" (e.g., A couple has planned and paid for an out-of-town weekend to celebrate their thirtieth wedding anniversary. This weekend will occur one month after their son is scheduled to be discharged from acute rehabilitation. The patient's mother states she is nervous about leaving her son at this time.). Observe the family members while they solve this problem, noticing communication patterns, methods of establishing priorities, respect for input from various members, flexibility, willingness to compromise, and

42. Family members take periodic vacations from caregiving. (68)

43. On a daily basis, family members explicitly acknowledge the positive contributions and effects that other members have on them. (69)

44. Family members describe plans to continue participation with groups that are sources of pleasure, friendships, and support. (70)

45. Patient's partner describe ways to deal with changes in their sexual relationship since advent of the brain condition. (71)

46. Patient's partner acknowledge ways in which his/her life will be different because he/she must carry more of the responsibility that had formerly been shared with the patient, and share grief feelings associated with these changes. (72)

__. _____
   _____

__. _____
   _____

__. _____
   _____

other aspects of family problem solving.

25. Inquire into the patient's role in the family.

26. Ask how this injury/illness is affecting each family member by asking about their hopes, their responsibilities, their emotional ties to the patient, and the changes they have experienced since the patient's injury/illness.

27. Consider the effect that the stage of family life has on the impact that the brain injury will have on the family's ability to fulfill its goals and hopes.

28. Ask how the illness/injury might be affecting the family as a whole (e.g., need to move from family home to one that is accessible, postpone attempt to get pregnant, deplete family savings that would have paid for child's education); allow for expression of anger, disappointment, or other emotions.

29. Frankly discuss that the family will have to reexamine its mission, reallocate its resources, and form new relationships among its members.

30. Ask the family to name two or three priority needs for each member of the family, including the patient.

31. Identify emotional resources (e.g., satisfying employment, supportive extended family, coworkers, community resources, etc.) that the family has for dealing with the patient's illness/injury.

32. Identify the family's problem-solving strengths (e.g., creativity, "can-do" attitude, resourcefulness) that its members bring to the task of incorporating the effects of brain injury/illness into family life.

33. Identify the family's practical resources (disability insurance, savings, accessible home, car that patient can easily get into and out of) that will be helpful as they cope with the patient's new needs.

34. Explore other recent events that have drawn on family resources.

35. Assess the family's competence to access and utilize community resources effectively (e.g., Social Security Disability Income, handicapped transportation services, assistance offered by neighbors).

36. Refer the family to a social worker or provide its members with information about resources that will facilitate their meeting new family needs.

37. Identify factors contributing to the family's resistance to

using external resources; process these factors to resolution.

38. Assist the family in reframing the effective use of resources as a family asset rather than as a sign of a family weakness.

39. Identify unresolved family issues that have become more salient since the patient's injury/illness and refer for family, conjoint, and/or individual therapy as needed.

40. Refer for family psychotherapy or individual psychotherapy as needed to reduce levels of emotional distress that may be interfering with effective coping.

41. Inquire into family member's (members') desire to use medication to relieve symptoms of acute stress, and help them identify whom they would like to prescribe and monitor this medication.

42. Inquire into the family's initial plans for addressing the family's changed needs, exploring how they have come to this decision and to being attentive to the beliefs or values that are guiding their behavior. Draw the family's attention to major areas (e.g., finances, emotional support, supervision for patient) that have been overlooked, and ask them to

include these needs in their plan.

43. Explore how the plan for addressing the family needs will impact each family member, and determine whether the plan requires any member to sacrifice a need considered to be vital.

44. Adjust the plan for addressing the family needs so that essential needs of each family member are addressed.

45. Ask the family to describe how they will know that the plan requires updating (e.g., family members experience higher levels of distress, patient's need for assistance decreases, household composition changes) and how they will revise the plan (e.g., schedule appointment with therapist, hold family meeting, negotiate changes among themselves).

46. Openly discuss role changes and the reactions of family members to this new family structure.

47. Engage the family members in a conversation about ways in which they can continue to realize their sense of purpose and family identity, given the new circumstances that the brain injury/illness has introduced.

48. Discuss the typical emotional phases (e.g., denial, anger, depression) the patient will go through as

she/he attempts to cope and come to an acceptance of what has happened, and what these phases may appear like to the family.

49. Describe the residual cognitive, behavioral, and personality changes that the patient will likely experience, and ask the family to describe the challenges that these may present to them.

50. Brainstorm about ways to manage cognitive and personality changes in different family and social situations; reinforce those responses that will be most effective.

51. Educate the family regarding basic behavioral principles (antecedent events, reinforcement, etc.) and how these apply to their interaction with the patient.

52. Identify the one or two most problematic behaviors facing the family, and by prompting the family to provide specific information, conduct a functional analysis to identify antecedents and consequences of the target behavior(s).

53. Brainstorm with the family about how they might arrange the environment or their interactions to alter the likelihood of a target behavior occurring.

54. Develop a plan to change the frequency and/or the intensity of the target behavior.

55. Build the family's skill and confidence in responding to the patient's problematic situation by modeling, role-playing, and corrective feedback.

56. Talk with the family about ways they will monitor and document the effect of this plan on the identified behaviors.

57. Talk with the family about ways they can manage situations in which the patient or other family members are at risk for physical injury (e.g., calling 911, moving away from the patient so that he/she could no longer strike you, leaving the patient's presence and telling the patient to let you know when she/he has calmed down). (See also the Agitation, Aggression, and Violence chapter in this Planner.)

58. Talk with the family (and patient) about the positive and negative aspects of having him/her live in an assisted living environment, nursing home, or other residential facility separate from the family.

59. Facilitate the family's processing of emotions (e.g., guilt, loss, anger) associated with the decision making about placing the patient in a residential care facility.

60. Help family develop a sense of mastery (e.g., "We can

manage the problems associated with the brain injury if we take responsibility for doing so").

61. Assist the family in developing a well-rounded view of the patient/family situation (e.g., they are a family with goals, an identity, and assets who are now dealing with certain brain-injury/illness related problems; many aspects of family life remain intact).

62. Talk with the family about the variety of relaxation skills (e.g., deep breathing, guided imagery, progressive relaxation, hypnosis, yoga) and encourage members to develop both rapid and more sustained relaxation skills.

63. Encourage family members to engage in regular physical exercise to reduce stress levels.

64. Refer to a recreational therapist for assistance in identifying how the family's recreational activities can be modified to suit the patient's abilities, or to identify new recreational activities that are well-suited to the patient; monitor and reinforce activity implementation.

65. Encourage family members to pursue recreational and social activities individually and as a family. (See also Recreational and Social Life

Problems chapter in this Planner.)

66. Suggest that the family make specific plans for enjoyable family activities (e.g., vacation, outing, pizza and a movie at home); recommend that they keep something to look forward to on the calendar.

67. Encourage the family to find and share the irony and humor in even difficult life situations; solicit examples from family members.

68. Talk with the family about the importance of taking a vacation from caregiving responsibilities and of building in respite breaks; recommend use of respite care facilities or identify relatives and friends who might take over caregiving for limited periods.

69. Remind family members to reinforce and emotionally nurture each other (including the patient!).

70. Encourage the family members to continue involvement with friends, community groups, spiritual community, and support groups; monitor and reinforce their follow-through.

71. Talk with the patient's partner about changes in their sexual life since the injury/illness and discuss ways to obtain sexual relationship

satisfaction given the new circumstances. (See also Sexual Dysfunction chapter in this Planner.)

72. Talk with the patient's partner and help him/her address feelings of grief that are related to loss of the ways in which the patient had previously acted as a partner/spouse (and as a parent).

__. _____

_____

__. _____

_____

__. _____

_____

DIAGNOSTIC SUGGESTIONS

Axis I:
309.0   Adjustment Disorder With Depressed Mood
309.24   Adjustment Disorder With Anxiety
309.28   Adjustment Disorder With Mixed Anxiety and Depressed Mood
309.3   Adjustment Disorder With Disturbance of Conduct
309.4   Adjustment Disorder With Mixed Disturbance of Emotions and Conduct
309.9   Adjustment Disorder, Unspecified
316   Psychological Factor (Specify) Affecting (General Medical Condition)
V61.9   Relational Problem Related to a Mental Disorder or General Medical Condition

_____   _____

_____   _____

IMPULSIVITY

BEHAVIORAL DEFINITIONS

1. Behavior is initiated prematurely, seemingly out of volitional control, resulting in numerous negative consequences.
2. Unplanned or poorly coordinated activity, creating safety risk for individual.
3. Random activity not resulting in attainment of the desired goal.
4. Loss of control over aggressive impulses, resulting in assault, self-destructive behavior, and/or damage to property.
5. Overreactivity to mildly aversive or pleasure-oriented stimulation.
6. Seems to want everything immediately/decreased ability to delay pleasure or gratification.

___. _____
   _____
___. _____
   _____
___. _____
   _____

LONG-TERM GOALS

1. Reduce the frequency of impulsive behaviors.
2. Perform only activities that do not jeopardize safety.
3. Carry out a series of planned actions yielding the desired result.
4. Discover the probable etiology of impulsivity.
5. Develop an increased awareness of impulsive behaviors and their implications.
6. Achieve conscious control over behaviors.

—. _____

—. _____

—. _____

SHORT-TERM OBJECTIVES

1. Verbalize instances of impulsive behavior. (1)
2. Identify any known cause for a pattern of impulsive behavior. (2)
3. Describe use of alcohol or illicit drugs. (3, 4)
4. List all medications used or recently discontinued. (2, 5)
5. Verbalize feelings of depression or anxiety that could relate to impulsivity. (6)
6. Cooperate with treatment for depression and/or anxiety. (7)
7. Give good effort during neuropsychological assessment. (8)
8. Ask significant others and/or treatment team members to point out instances in which impulsivity has interfered with the logical flow or completeness of a project. (9, 10)
9. Agree to cooperate with a plan of receiving reaction from treatment team, family, and significant others to

THERAPEUTIC INTERVENTIONS

1. Ask the patient to give examples of impulsivity, noting precipitating environmental condition and resulting consequences.
2. Review medical, neuropsychological, and psychological information to identify medical, cognitive, emotional, and personality factor(s) reasonably explaining current impulsivity.
3. Assess the patient for chemical dependence or withdrawal problems (see Substance Abuse chapter in this Planner).
4. Refer for or develop a plan for substance abuse treatment.
5. If acute medical events (e.g., medication side effects, medication withdrawal, delirium) are the most likely explanation for the impulsivity, alert the patient's physician so that medical issues can be addressed and resolved.

impulsive behaviors that have already occured. (11, 12)

10. List the negative consequences of impulsive behavior as far as they are known or understood. (13)

11. Cooperate with a physician evaluation to determine if psychopharmacological intervention is warranted; then take medications as directed. (14)

12. Report as to compliance, effectiveness, and side effects of medications ordered to assist in control of impulsivity. (15)

13. Verbalize an understanding of the negative impact impulsivity will have on rehabilitation outcome. (16, 17)

14. Record impulsive behaviors and their consequences on a tally sheet that is carried at all times. (18, 19)

15. Report a reduction in impulsive behaviors and the positive consequences of such improved control. (20)

16. Practice and implement a mental rehearsal of Stop, Think, and Plan before enacting behavior. (21, 22)

17. Implement a technique of verbally describing actions before implementation as a means of reducing impulsivity. (23)

18. Utilize a daily planner to guide behavior rather than

6. Assess the patient for the presence of an affective, anxiety, and/or adjustment disorder.

7. Develop and implement a treatment plan for affective or anxiety disorders (see Depression/Grief or Anxiety/Fear chapters in this Planner).

8. Refer for or administer neuropsychological testing to assess cognitive factors contributing to the patient's impulsivity, and to identify cognitive strengths that can be utilized in addressing this problem.

9. Enlist the patient's agreement to seek others' feedback on planned behavior and to have others point out the impulsivity problem when it occurs.

10. Conduct a session with the patient and spouse, significant other, or family member to develop a contract for receiving feedback *prior to* impulsive acts.

11. Develop a plan of *reaction* to impulsive behavior (e.g., verbal confrontation, listing potential consequences, suggesting a stop and reconsidering recommended alternative behavior) from treatment team members, family members, and significant others.

12. Meet with treatment team, family members, and signif-

reacting impulsively to daily circumstances. (24)

19. Engage in vigorous physical exercise on a regular schedule. (25)

20. List the benefits or rewards of learning to control impulses. (26, 27)

21. Use "time-out" to remove self from situations and think about behavioral reaction alternatives and their consequences. (28)

22. Verbalize the steps of problem solving and apply them to specific conflicts in personal life. (29)

23. Implement relaxation procedures to reduce tension and physical restlessness. (30)

24. Cooperate with brainwave biofeedback to improve impulse control and reduce reactivity. (31, 32)

—. _____
   _____

—. _____
   _____

—. _____
   _____

icant others to solicit their consistent implementation of the plan of *reaction* to patient's impulsivity.

13. Assess and increase the patient's awareness of impulsivity by reviewing with the patient the consequences of his/her impulsive behavior.

14. Arrange for examination by a physician to determine if the patient might benefit from adding or discontinuing medications affecting his/her ability to maintain attention; encourage the patient to take medications as prescribed.

15. Monitor the patient's medication use as to compliance, effectiveness, and side effects.

16. Teach the patient the negative impact of impulsivity on rehabilitation program (e.g., causing frustration in relationships; canceling or forgetting appointments because of following an urge for a competing activity; placing self in danger due to poor judgment and overreacting, etc.).

17. Reinforce the patient for keeping rehabilitation appointment and following through with therapeutic homework and plan.

18. Assign the patient to keep a tally sheet of impulsive behaviors and their consequences.

19. Review the patient's record of impulsive behavior, rein-

forcing a reduction in frequency of impulsive acts and increased patient self-monitoring.

20. Reinforce the patient for improved behavioral control and relate this improvement to positive consequences (e.g., remaining unsupervised for longer periods of time, becoming a candidate for driving privileges, growing respect from self and others, etc.).

21. Use modeling, role-playing, and behavior rehearsal to teach the patient how to use Stop, Think, and Plan before action as applied to several different situations.

22. Reinforce the patient's use of Stop, Think, and Plan, underscoring its positive consequences.

23. Use modeling, role-playing, and behavior rehearsal to teach the patient how to verbalize behavior before enacting it impulsively.

24. Teach the patient to use a daily planner to guide behavior in a manner that is thoughtful, rather than simply reacting to a daily situation; encourage patient to delay responding until a planned reaction can be entered into daily planner.

25. Encourage the patient to regularly engage in physical exercise (if medically possible) to reduce energy that

goes into agitated impulsivity.

26. Assign the patient to list the benefits of learning to control behavior and to delay gratification of impulses (e.g., reduces risk of harm to self and of offending others, and allows for long-term planning, for weighing of consequences, and for choosing best alternative).

27. Review the patient's list of rewards for learning impulse control and assist in adding benefits to the list; assign patient to post list prominently in private living space.

28. Train the patient to use "time-out" intervention in which he/she regains self-control by withdrawing temporarily from the situation and calming down to think about behavioral alternatives and their consequences.

29. Teach the patient problem-solving skills (i.e., identify problem, brainstorm all possible options, evaluate each option, select best option, implement course of action, and evaluate results) and role-play their application to everyday life conflicts.

30. Instruct the patient in various relaxation techniques (e.g., deep breathing, meditation, guided imagery, etc.) and encourage him/her to use these techniques daily or when stress increases.

31. Refer for or administer brainwave biofeedback to improve impulse control and decrease reactivity.

32. Encourage the patient to transfer the biofeedback training skills of relaxation and cognitive focusing to everyday situations (e.g., home, work, social life).

__. _____
    _____
__. _____
    _____
__. _____
    _____

DIAGNOSTIC SUGGESTIONS

Axis I:	309.9	Adjustment Disorder, Unspecified
	300.02	Generalized Anxiety Disorder
	293.84	Anxiety Disorder Due to (General Medical Condition)
	291.89	Alcohol-Induced Anxiety Disorder
	292.89	Substance-Induced Anxiety Disorder (Specify Substance)
	293.83	Mood Disorder Due to (General Medical Condition)
	292.84	Substance-Induced Mood Disorder (Specify Substance)
	293.0	Delirium Due to (General Medical Condition)
	292.81	Substance Intoxication Delirium (Specify Substance)
	291.0	Alcohol Withdrawal Delirium
	290.xx	Dementia
	294.9	Cognitive Disorder NOS
	314.xx	Attention-Deficit/Hyperactivity Disorder
	_____	_____
	_____	_____

INITIATION DIFFICULTIES

BEHAVIORAL DEFINITIONS

1. Slowed or absent ability to begin a specific movement.
2. Difficulty in maintaining a motor sequence.
3. Requires external verbal, audio, tactile, or visual cue to begin a motor sequence that was formerly automatic.
4. Failure to spontaneously engage in typical or expected activities.
5. Does not follow therapists' or family members' action requests.

—. _____
_____
—. _____
_____
—. _____
_____

LONG-TERM GOALS

1. Demonstrate ability to volitionally begin and maintain desired movements.
2. Show typical motor behaviors for specific circumstances.
3. Patient and family state understanding of cause of residual psychomotor retardation and ways to compensate for motor impairment.

—. _____
_____

—. _____
    _____
    _____
—. _____
    _____

SHORT-TERM OBJECTIVES

1. Cooperate with evaluation to identify cause, course, and parameters of initiation difficulty. (1, 2, 3, 4, 6)

2. Participate in a neuropsychological evaluation. (5, 6)

3. Cooperate with a clinical interview and/or psychological testing to determine if psychiatric illnesses are affecting volitional movements. (7, 8, 9)

4. Provide information willingly about the impact of the initiation difficulty on everyday life and emotions. (10, 11)

5. Patient and family verbalize knowledge about the cause, prognosis, and planned treatment for the initiation problem. (12)

6. Accept referral for treatment of psychological or psychiatric conditions. (13, 14)

7. Complete evaluation for medications designed to facilitate motor functioning. (15, 16)

8. Take medications regularly as prescribed and report on

THERAPEUTIC INTERVENTIONS

1. Review medical records and/or consult with the patient's physician to identify the history and course of the initiation difficulty as well as neurological, psychiatric, or other medical conditions that might be affecting the patient's volitional movements.

2. Determine whether the patient has functional receptive language skills through a review of records, consultation with speech therapist, or by administering a language screening examination.

3. Consult with the patient's rehabilitation therapy team regarding the conditions under which the movement difficulty occurs.

4. Observe the patient during therapies and other activities to identify those motor functions that are affected and to identify those circumstances in which he/she appears better able to initiate activity.

5. Administer or refer for neuropsychological testing to

effectiveness and side effects. (17)

9. Participate in rehabilitation therapy sessions designed to improve initiation and maintenance of affected motor sequences. (18, 19, 20)

10. Demonstrate willingness to attempt first component of complex patterned movement. (21, 22, 23, 24)

11. Participate with therapists and family in using tactile cues to help initiate and maintain movement. (25, 26, 32)

12. Use auditory or verbal cues to help overcome initiation problem. (27, 28, 29, 32)

13. Use visual cues to help enhance movement. (30, 31, 32)

14. Demonstrate success in responding to specific movement request. (33)

15. Participate in activities using habitual, overlearned motor patterns to facilitate movement. (33, 34)

16. Report desire to continue working toward overcoming initiation difficulties. (35, 36, 37)

17. Spontaneously engage in variety of daily, self-initiated motor activities. (38)

18. Family and others who are significant in patient's life report satisfaction and comfort with patient's increased independence. (39, 40, 41, 42)

identify those cognitive processes underlying or contributing to the patient's initiation disorder.

6. Give feedback to the patient (patient's family), treatment team, and other designated persons regarding assessment results and recommendations.

7. Conduct a clinical interview to assess the patient for the presence of psychiatric disorders (e.g., schizophrenia, depression, or hysterical traits) that might be affecting initiation.

8. If the patient is a poor historian, obtain permission from patient or legally responsible party to interview person(s) familiar with his/her history.

9. Arrange for or administer psychological tests to clarify psychiatric diagnostic questions.

10. Explore and assess how the patient is affected psychologically by the initiation problem (e.g., suffering, secondary gain).

11. With the patient's or responsible party's permission, interview family members and other significant persons to learn more about motivational or reinforcement factors that might be causing or sustaining the symptoms.

—. _____
   _____
   _____
—. _____
   _____
—. _____
   _____

12. Educate the patient and family about the nature of the initiation problem and the planned course of treatment.

13. Refer for or initiate program to address psychiatric disorders causing, influencing, or coexisting with initiation difficulty.

14. Address the patient's (and family's) questions and concerns about diagnosis and planned treatment for psychiatric disorders.

15. Consult with the patient's treating physician about the possible benefits of medication to facilitate movement and decide how medication will be prescribed, monitored, and managed.

16. Assist the patient (and family) in getting answers to questions they might have about medications and their side effects.

17. Monitor the patient's use of prescribed medications and their effectiveness; address issues concerning compliance and side effects.

18. Facilitate referrals, if necessary, to specific therapies (e.g., speech therapy, physical therapy, occupational therapy, etc.) for treatment of apraxia, facial movement disorders, or ambulation difficulties.

19. Encourage the patient to participate in therapies that

will increase independence in grooming, hygiene, dressing, and other daily activities, and show interest in him/her by inquiring about progress and problems.

20. Reinforce the patient's participation in crafts, games, and recreational activities designed to encourage normal motor functioning as a byproduct.

21. Specify components of movement pattern, dividing complex movement into discrete steps.

22. Using verbal, tactile, or other cues, encourage patient to initiate and accomplish first discrete movement.

23. Provide additional cuing as needed to complete subsequent stages of complex movement.

24. Reinforce the patient on any success in initiating motor response.

25. Consult with therapists and/or observe the patient during activities to identify specific tactile cues that are effective in facilitating or maintaining movement.

26. Explore the effectiveness of having the patient tap rhythmically while speaking to help establish more normal speech fluency.

27. Observe the patient, confer with therapists, or initiate trial of auditory/verbal cues

(e.g., patient and therapist say "1, 2, 3, Go!" with patient and therapist beginning transfer on "Go!").

28. Suggest therapists attempt trial of clapping in a slow, steady rhythm (or of using a metronome) to cue the patient as he/she practices walking.

29. Inquire into the potential benefit of using rhythmic music to maintain the patient's motor sequences.

30. Assess benefit of visual cues to initiate and maintain movement. For example, place evenly spaced lines or dots on the floor, and then instruct the patient to move from line to line or from spot to spot (instead of saying "Take a step").

31. Evaluate whether the patient might benefit from visual feedback while carrying out designated movements (e.g., suggest that he/she look in a mirror while making an angry or happy facial expression, or observe self in mirror while brushing teeth or taking steps).

32. Identify to what degree the patient's family and friends know how to use sensory cuing to support his/her recovery. Facilitate communication between the family and the therapists if additional education is needed.

33. Use instructions that specify a familiar activity for the patient to undertake, rather than requesting a motion that would require patient to make a decision. For example, if the patient is tightly clutching a grab bar, interfering with egress from an elevator, the therapist (family member) might say "Put your hand in your lap" (specific), rather than "Take your hand off the grab bar" (patient must decide where to place hand).

34. Encourage the patient to undertake simple physical activities such as tossing and catching a beach ball, blowing bubbles with a bubble wand, and stirring a pitcher of juice.

35. Engage the patient in conversation about the particular ways in which improving initiation will be important over time.

36. Point out the ways in which the current activities may help the patient accomplish long-term goals.

37. Ask the patient to describe (assisting as needed) the progress that has occurred in the last week or two.

38. Reinforce motor initiation with pleasant natural consequences. For example, have the television tuned to a channel in which the patient has little interest.

Leave the remote control within his/her reach. If the patient reaches for and presses the control, he/she is rewarded with a preferred program.

39. Talk with the patient's family about their feelings and reactions as the patient becomes more independent.

40. Be attentive to signs of anxiety, sadness regarding loss, or strong needs to "help" that might cause the patient's family to inadvertently reinforce his/her dependence.

41. Help the patient's family examine their emotional response and identify ways in which these reactions might be unrealistic or might interfere with patient's progress.

42. Assist the family members in discovering ways they might show their caring and helpfulness to the patient without interfering with his/her initiative and moves toward independence.

___. _____

_____

___. _____

_____

___. _____

_____

DIAGNOSTIC SUGGESTIONS

Axis I:	290.xx	Dementia
	294.1	Dementia Due to (Axis III Condition)
	294.9	Cognitive Disorder NOS
	300.11	Conversion Disorder
	300.xx	Factitious Disorder
	309.3	Adjustment Disorder With Disturbance of Conduct
	309.4	Adjustment Disorder With Mixed Disturbance of Emotions and Conduct
	316	Psychological Factor (Specify) Affecting (General Medical Condition)
	V65.2	Malingering
	_____	_____
Axis II:	799.9	Diagnosis Deferred
	V71.09	No Diagnosis or Condition
	_____	_____
	_____	_____

MEMORY IMPAIRMENT

BEHAVIORAL DEFINITIONS

1. Unable to recall information about personally experienced events at the level expected for someone of his/her age and education.
2. Unusually high rate of forgetting.
3. Shows little or no benefit from recent learning experiences.
4. Difficulty or inability to recognize or report about events that have occurred since (and sometimes before) the illness or injury.
5. Not oriented to time, place, and/or purpose.
6. Difficulty recalling routes.
7. Poorer than expected ability to recognize faces.
8. Fails to follow through on intentions to perform a planned activity, such as keeping an appointment, transferring laundry from the washer to the dryer, or taking medication.
9. Failure to meet time-related commitments such as paying bills, given history of good management of responsibilities.
10. "Makes up" information, with no insight that the material has been fabricated and has no particular relationship to historical events; confabulates.

Note: Some of the interventions described in this chapter were drawn from procedures and concepts described in the following books; please see them for a detailed discussion of memory rehabilitation interventions: *A Therapy Technique for Improving Memory: Spaced Retrieval* (Brush and Camp), *Cognitive Rehabilitation of Memory: A Practical Guide* (Harrell, Parenté, Bellingrath, and Lisicia), and *Rehabilitation of Memory* (Wilson).

Note: The above behavioral descriptors presume that aphasia, visual-spatial disturbances, or other nonmemory cognitive or perceptual deficits have been ruled out as the primary cause of the patient's performance difficulty on "memory" tasks.

—. _____
   _____
   _____
—. _____
   _____
   _____
—. _____
   _____

LONG-TERM GOALS

1. Use external memory aids to track appointments and commitments.
2. Establish habits and routines to use procedural memory to one's advantage in completing recurring activities.
3. Attain insight into changes in memory functioning.
4. Use memory strategies to increase efficiency of learning and effectiveness of recall.
5. Emotionally accept changes in memory and consequences for lifestyle.
6. Adjust lifestyle to maximize performance in spite of memory deficits while maintaining manageable levels of stress.

—. _____
   _____
   _____
—. _____
   _____
   _____
—. _____
   _____

SHORT-TERM OBJECTIVES

1. Cooperate with an evaluation of acute and chronic factors influencing current memory performance. (1, 2, 3, 4, 18)

2. Provide information (and allow others to share infor-

THERAPEUTIC INTERVENTIONS

1. Review the patient's medical record to identify factors (e.g., developmental delay, central nervous system disorders, previous brain injuries, exposure to toxins, anoxic events) that might

mation) about own typical level of memory functioning. (5, 6)

3. Describe typical and recent sleep patterns and problems. (7, 8, 9)

4. Answer questions to the best of one's ability concerning emotional and psychiatric functioning, and allow family or others to give information as well. (10)

5. Participate in evaluation of basic sensory functions (e.g., vision, hearing) to determine if reception of environmental information is impaired. (11)

6. Participate willingly in neuropsychological testing. (12, 13, 18)

7. Cooperate with assessment of "everyday" memory skills. (13, 14, 18)

8. Cooperate with assessment procedures to identify psychiatric conditions that might be affecting memory. (15, 16, 17, 18)

9. Implement changes designed to improve sleep quality. (19, 20, 21)

10. Obtain treatment to address coexisting psychiatric disorders. (22)

11. Implement recommended steps to improve vision and hearing. (23)

12. Describe the ways in which learning occurs most/least easily, considering both the

be influencing his/her current memory functioning.

2. Obtain a history of the onset and course of the patient's memory disturbance, including all treatments and results.

3. Inquire into the patient's past and current use of alcohol, street drugs, and other substances that could temporarily or permanently impair memory performance.

4. Review the patient's recent and current medications to determine whether any could be affecting learning and memory.

5. Interview the patient (and the patient's family) to learn what his/her memory was like prior to the onset of the most recent brain injury/illness.

6. Obtain the patient's academic records, with his/her (or legally responsible person's) consent, to verify the description of his/her intellectual and academic performance.

7. Consult with the patient (patient's family) and rehabilitation professionals regarding the adequacy of his/her sleep.

8. Inquire into the patient's typical, preinjury/preillness sleep patterns and routines, and identify any sleep abnormalities.

nature of the information to be learned as well as the manner in which it is presented. (24)

13. Describe changes in memory that seem to have occurred since the medical event. (25)

14. Verbalize an awareness of memory deficit. (26)

15. Describe previously used methods that were helpful in learning and remembering information. (27)

16. Demonstrate improved cognitive skills that are important for accurate and detailed processing of information to be learned. (28, 29, 30)

17. Participate in cognitive rehabilitation therapies to improve memory functioning. (31)

18. Take or adjust medications as prescribed to optimize memory. (32)

19. Verbalize accurate information about person, place, time, and current personal circumstances. (33, 34, 35)

20. Use a memory/organizer book to record important information and to keep up with appointments and other commitments. (34, 35, 36)

21. Establish habits and routines to increase the percentage of time one accomplishes recurring ac-

9. Consult with the patient, his/her family, and rehabilitation therapists to identify environmental factors (e.g., noise from the nurses' station, roommate who moans, patient cold and unable to pull blankets up), medical factors (e.g., pain, unable to position self in preferred sleeping position due to hemiparesis, poor bladder control), or activity-related factors (e.g., misses evening bath, can't get back to sleep after being awakened for medication, naps during the day) that interfere with the patient's sleep.

10. Interview the patient (and family) to determine if pain or psychiatric conditions (e.g., depression, anxiety, posttraumatic stress disorder, malingering, dissociative identity disorder, psychogenic fugue state, or somatization disorder) might be interfering with his/her memory performance.

11. Consult with patient's physician and rehabilitation team to rule out problems in peripheral sensory registration (e.g., poor vision, poor hearing, impaired sense of touch) that might interfere with his/her ability to take in and learn new information.

12. Arrange for neuropsychological testing to identify the types and degree of patient's

tivities with minimal or no cuing. (37, 38, 39)

22. Cooperate with the use of prompts to establish habits, and put effort into relying on naturally occurring cue (e.g., internal or environmental stimulus) instead of an "artificial" alarm or cue. (38, 39)

23. Answer repetitive questions, spaced at increasingly greater intervals, in order to learn specific facts. (40)

24. Describe how the information one is trying to learn is important, and point out unusual details that will help in encoding information as distinctive. (41)

25. Utilize verbally mediated strategies to enhance learning and retention of information. (42)

26. Implement visually mediated strategies to facilitate learning and retention of information. (43)

27. Apply memory strategies to tasks of gradually increasing difficulty level. (44, 45)

28. Describe how a particular memory strategy might be useful for a variety of memory tasks in different settings. (46)

29. Implement a memory strategy in several settings, and make notes about how effective the strategy was for learning and retaining new information. (47)

memory deficit, and to determine how other cognitive processes (e.g., attention, aphasia, visual-perceptual deficits) might be influencing the patient's ability to learn, recall, recognize, and utilize information.

13. Refer for or administer tests of everyday or ecologic memory (e.g., Rivermead Behavioral Memory Test by Wilson, Cockburn, and Baddeley).

14. Consult with the patient's rehabilitation therapists and family regarding his/her current memory functioning (e.g., remembering route to therapy area, learning exercise routines, reporting on recent events that are of personal interest).

15. Arrange for a psychodiagnostic evaluation of the patient to identify depression, anxiety, posttraumatic stress disorder, dissociative disorders, somatoform disorders, malingering, or other psychiatric conditions that might impact his/her memory functioning.

16. With the patient's (or legally designated representative's) consent, obtain records of prior psychiatric/psychologic care or consult with those professionals who treated the patient.

17. Arrange for psychological testing to assist in diagnosing psychiatric disorders af-

30. Family verbalize an understanding of the types of information that the patient will likely acquire and recall more easily or have difficulty learning and recalling. (24, 48)

31. Family describe age-appropriate memory interventions to be implemented with the patient. (49)

32. Family describe five specific ways that the patient's memory functioning can be improved. (50, 51)

33. Family demonstrate appropriate interaction with the patient while he/she attempts to retrieve information: allowing the patient time to retrieve information, providing a cue, and then (if necessary) providing the correct response for the patient. (52)

34. Family members describe how they can foster the patient's independence for specific responsibilities by supporting the acquisition of habits and routines. (53)

35. Participate in leisure activities that are suited to current level of memory functioning. (54)

36. Cooperate with an evaluation to determine the need for supervision and/or accommodations to perform usual daily activities that may be dangerous or lead to self-defeating consequences. (55, 56)

fecting memory performance or reflecting the patient's difficulty in coping with memory and lifestyle changes.

18. Give feedback to the patient (patient's family), physician, rehabilitation team, and other designated persons regarding assessment results and recommendations.

19. Consult with the patient's physician about medical interventions to reduce hindrances to and improve the quality of the patient's sleep.

20. In consultation with the patient, family, and rehabilitation team, develop a plan to structure his/her activity and environment in ways to be conducive to uninterrupted, restful sleep and to coordinate its implementation.

21. Monitor the implementation of actions to enhance the patient's sleep and assess the effectiveness of these interventions on both sleep quality and behavior during waking hours.

22. Initiate or arrange for treatment for depression, anxiety, chronic pain, substance abuse, or other psychiatric conditions that might be interfering with the patient's ability to learn and recall information. (See Depression/Grief, Anxiety/Fear, Chronic Pain, Substance

37. Implement the recommendations of rehabilitation professionals regarding necessary modifications in daily activities to ensure personal safety and welfare. (57)

38. Work cooperatively with a vocational counselor to identify how to most successfully return to school or to work. (58)

39. Describe accommodations that are necessary in order to perform best at school or at work, and work toward implementing them. (59)

40. Verbalize knowledge of relevant laws regarding the right to accommodations and the procedures to follow to have them implemented. (60, 61)

41. Complete (or have family complete) applications for disability benefits or other financial assistance if there will be a significant delay in returning to full-time work. (62)

42. Responsible individual agrees to assist with decision making if patient is deemed incompetent to make medical, financial, and/or personal decisions. (63, 64)

43. Cooperate with assistance to terminate abusive treatment. (65)

44. Engage in psychotherapy to deal with the emotional is-

Abuse, Dependency/Counterdependency, Posttraumatic Stress Disorder, or other relevant chapters in this Planner.)

23. Consult with the patient's physician regarding how visual and auditory problems will be evaluated and corrected.

24. Review the neuropsychological test results as well as information gathered from the patient, and consult with the patient's rehabilitation team to determine the relative strengths and weaknesses of different memory types (e.g., declarative, semantic, episodic, prospective, procedural), and to identify how the mode of stimulus presentation (e.g., auditory, lexical, visual, motor) affects learning and recall, so that this information can be used in rehabilitation planning.

25. Determine the degree to which the patient has insight into memory deficits by inquiring directly whether he/she has noticed any changes in memory, or by asking him/her to explain why he/she failed to succeed at a memory-related task.

26. Institute actions to increase the patient's awareness of memory deficits. (See Denial and Impaired Awareness chapter in this Planner.)

sues associated with changed abilities, lifestyle, and relationship roles. (66, 67)

45. Family members describe their emotional acceptance of the patient's memory changes and the ways in which their family life has been altered. (68, 69)

__. _____
_____

__. _____
_____

__. _____
_____

27. Inquire about the patient's preinjury/preillness use of memory aids (e.g., organizer books, handheld computers, alarms) and strategies (e.g., clustering, coding, visual imagery), paying attention to why the patient liked/disliked each and how effective he/she perceived them to be. To the degree possible, plan new memory interventions to be consistent with the patient's preferences.

28. Refer the patient for speech therapy to address language-related deficits that may be interfering with his/her ability to comprehend and process verbal information.

29. Refer the patient for occupational therapy to address visual-perceptual deficits that may be affecting his/her ability to perceive and process visual-spatial material.

30. Arrange for treatment of patient for attention and concentration deficits that may be interfering with early registration and initial processing of information. (See Attention and Concentration Impairment chapter in this Planner.)

31. Arrange for cognitive rehabilitation therapy to address patient's memory deficits.

32. Consult with the patient's physician regarding adjust-

ments in medications to enhance his/her memory functioning (e.g., discontinuing
medications that might interfere with memory func-
tioning, adding medications
that may enhance learning
and recall).

33. Facilitate the patient's use
of an orientation board.

34. Arrange for the patient to
develop a memory/organizer
book, creating sections in
which he/she can file information that is most pertinent to his/her current
needs (e.g., personal information, therapists' names,
facts about injury/illness,
monthly calendar, daily
schedule, to-dos, etc.).

35. Cue the patient to refer to
the memory/organizer book
to answer questions and to
remind self of appointments
and upcoming activities
(e.g., when the patient asks,
"When can I go home?," say
"Let's look at the calendar
in your book to find out," or
when the patient asks,
"What happened to me?"
say "Let's look in your book.
Which section would have
that information?").

36. Reinforce the patient's use
of the memory/organizer
book to answer questions
(e.g., saying, "Great! You
were able to find the an-
swer to that question!").

37. Identify recurring activities
that can be linked to estab-

lished routines (e.g., scheduling morning dressing and grooming to immediately follow bathing; arranging to turn on the computer, access software, and work on task immediately following a morning television show; planning patient's review of memory book to immediately follow completion of a meal), thereby taking advantage of procedural memory and reducing the burden on prospective memory.

38. Use a verbal prompt, wristwatch alarm, alarm strip, or other cue to remind the patient to perform designated tasks at specified times.

39. Fade use of alarm or prompt, maintaining the patient's successful response rate at 80 percent or greater.

40. Utilize spaced retrieval techniques (Brush and Camp) to teach the patient personally relevant discrete facts (e.g., therapist's name, grandson's birthday, son's new teacher's name) by asking him/her to answer repetitive questions at increasing time intervals.

41. Teach strategies that will enhance the degree of meaning and attention to detail as the patient encodes new information (e.g., PQRST—Preview, Ques-

tion, Read, State, and Test [Robinson]; sketching image—such as a woman's face with bushy eyebrows "aiming" at her nose to remember the woman's name "Amy").

42. Teach the patient verbally-mediated strategies (e.g., chunking, categorization, clustering, acronyms, rhyming, associations, embedding information in a story) to enhance the learning and recall of information.

43. Teach the patient visually-mediated strategies (e.g., loci, peg words, drawing visual images, visualizing interacting images) to enhance memory performance.

44. Ask the patient to perform memory tasks on which he/she has a high likelihood of success.

45. Gradually increase the difficulty level of the memory tasks assigned to the patient, keeping his/her percentage of correct responses at a constant, high level.

46. Select a memory strategy, and challenge the patient to think of two situations or types of information for which this memory strategy might be useful, thereby encouraging generalization of strategy application.

47. Assign the patient to use a particular memory strategy to learn and recall informa-

tion in two new situations, and record the results so that he/she can discuss them in the next session.

48. Educate the patient's family about memory functioning, explaining that the patient will have difficulty learning new information but will typically remember things that happened long ago.

49. Explain to the patient's family why rote techniques and educational workbooks designed for children are usually not helpful in rebuilding memory after a brain injury and may in fact increase the patient's frustration.

50. Teach family members how to use strategies (e.g., chunking, peg words, visualization, etc.) and external orthotic memory aids (e.g., memory books, orientation boards, to-do lists, etc.) to assist the patient in learning and retrieving important information.

51. Refer the patient's family to written information that explains how memory strategies can be used to improve memory efficiency (e.g., *The Memory Book* by Lorayne and Lucas).

52. Model for the family how to assist the patient in retrieving information, by allowing two or three guesses, providing cues (e.g., "The person who visited last night was someone you work

with," or "The team that won the baseball game last night is from a city whose name starts with the letter "A") and then (if necessary) providing the correct answer. Explain to the family that repeated incorrect guessing is often counterproductive; the patient tends to "learn" the inaccurate information.

53. Teach the patient's family about procedural memory (i.e., tying one event consistently to the next event) and how it can be useful to build the patient's independence for accomplishing recurring activities; stress the importance of consistency in building and maintaining these habits.

54. Refer the patient to a recreational therapist to identify leisure and recreational activities that will provide enjoyment and reduce stress while challenging him/her to build memory skills.

55. Refer the patient for an occupational therapy evaluation to assess the impact of the patient's memory deficit on his/her ability to safely perform instrumental activities of daily living (e.g., cooking, taking medications, locking the house, paying bills, and caring for children).

56. Refer the patient for a driving evaluation to determine whether he/she can safely

drive given the current memory deficit, and to determine if he/she requires accommodations.

57. In consultation with the treatment team, identify those activities that the patient should not perform at all, due to safety concerns; should perform with supervision; or could perform independently.

58. Refer the patient for a vocational rehabilitation evaluation to determine how the memory deficit will affect his/her ability to return to school or to work, and to identify modifications necessary for successful reentry.

59. Assist the patient in identifying accommodations that could be made at school or in the workplace to help him/her perform at his/her best (e.g., taping lectures, reducing course-load, tests administered in multiple-choice format, checklists outlining procedures step-by-step) to compensate for residual memory deficits; facilitate implementation of such accommodations.

60. Teach the patient the general implications of the Americans with Disabilities Act (ADA) and subsequent related legislation and judicial rulings on his/her entitlement to accommodations. For specific questions or problems, refer the patient

to an attorney familiar with this area of the law.

61. Assist the patient in identifying steps that he/she should take in order to request accommodations from a school or employer; assess whether he/she has the knowledge and confidence to pursue the necessary accommodations.

62. Refer the patient (patient's family) to a social worker, community social service agency, or personnel office to determine what benefits he/she might be eligible for during the period when he/she is unable to resume work.

63. Taking into account the provisions of state law, clarify whether the patient is competent to make imminent medical, personal, or financial decisions.

64. Following the provisions of state law and the policies of the institution, identify the person who is legally authorized to make specific decisions for the patient. Obtain legal counsel, if necessary.

65. If there is evidence to suggest that the patient is being abused physically, financially, or in other ways, coordinate a referral to social services or to the state's adult protective services agency, following the institutional guidelines and the requirements of state law.

66. Perform or refer for psychotherapy to assist the patient in dealing with the emotions associated with the memory loss and resulting changes in self-image, relationships, and lifestyle.

67. Assist the patient in working through the emotions (e.g., embarrassment—"Everyone will know I have a memory problem"; frustration—"I hate having to carry this book everywhere and I don't have time to write down everything I want to remember"; ego-alienation—"I always just remembered things; this doesn't feel like me") associated with the need to use compensatory strategies and aids.

68. Educate the family about the patient's residual deficits in memory, recommended activity modifications, compensatory techniques, and accommodations, using examples that relate specifically to the patient's and family's life.

69. Refer the family members to resources (family therapy, support groups, advocacy groups, reading materials, etc.) to assist them in coming to terms emotionally with the changes in their family life.

—. _____
    _____
—. _____
    _____
—. _____
    _____

DIAGNOSTIC SUGGESTIONS

Axis I: 290.xx   Dementia
              294.0   Amnestic Disorder Due to (General Medical
                       Condition)
              294.8   Amnestic Disorder NOS
              294.1   Dementia Due to (Axis III condition)
              294.8   Dementia NOS
              294.9   Cognitive Disorder NOS

              _____   _____
              _____   _____

Axis II: V71.09   No Diagnosis or Condition

              _____   _____
              _____   _____

PERSEVERATION

BEHAVIORAL DEFINITIONS

1. Motor behavior sequences that repeat beyond the point of correct task completion and are apparently outside the patient's volitional control.
2. Inappropriate continuation of a category or type of activity.
3. Abnormal persistence or prolongation of an activity.
4. Repetition of a previous verbal response to a new question, topic, or stimulus.
5. Repetitive thought that dominates the patient's mind, interfering with the processing of new information.

__. _____
   _____
__. _____
   _____
__. _____
   _____

LONG-TERM GOALS

1. Behavioral sequence ends when task is accomplished.
2. Verbal responses are not repeated and are appropriate to current question or topic of conversation.
3. Behavior and words are responsive to current situation.
4. Track topic and shift mode of thinking to deal with changing situations.

—. _____
  _____
  _____
—. _____
  _____
  _____
—. _____
  _____
  _____

SHORT-TERM OBJECTIVES

1. Cooperate with assessment to identify cause of perseveration, stimulus events that trigger it, and how the perseveration presents. (1, 2, 3, 4, 6)

2. Participate in neuropsychological or psychological assessment. (5, 6)

3. Cooperate with referral for psychiatric evaluation. (7, 8)

4. Verbalize the degree of awareness of perseveration and its impact on the quality of performance. (9, 10)

5. Tolerate redirection by therapists and family that terminates ongoing behavioral, verbal, or cognitive perseveration. (11, 12, 13)

6. Verbalize an increased awareness of inappropriate repetitive or continuous response. (14, 15, 16, 17)

7. Demonstrate increased conscious monitoring, planning, and termination of perseverative responses. (18, 19, 20, 21)

THERAPEUTIC INTERVENTIONS

1. Review medical records and/or consult with the patient's physician to identify the history of the perseverative behavior, and to identify neurological and/or psychiatric conditions that might explain its occurrence or affect its presentation.

2. Consult with the patient's therapists to learn about when the perseverative behavior occurs, the degree to which the patient is aware that the perseveration is an incorrect response, and how therapists respond to the perseveration.

3. Interview the patient and engage him/her in tasks that will likely elicit the perseverative response.

4. If the patient is a poor historian, obtain permission of patient or legally responsible party to interview person(s) familiar with his/her history.

5. Administer or refer for psychological or neuropsycho-

8. Utilize audible self-cuing to assist in focusing and maintaining attention. (22)

9. Slow the pace of responding in order to inhibit verbal perseverative tendency. (23)

10. Agree to participate with therapist in using extinction and positive reinforcement techniques to shape goal-directed activity. (24, 25, 26)

11. Cooperate with assessment for medications to reduce perseveration. (27, 28, 29)

12. Take medications as prescribed and report any side effects. (29, 30)

13. Family verbalizes understanding of perseveration as an unintentional behavior not responsive to reason and demonstrates ability to respond in a therapeutic way. (31, 32)

14. Family identifies their own behavioral and emotional reactions as well as those of the patient in structuring social interaction and confrontation of patient's perseveration. (33, 34)

15. Family verbalizes patient's and own limits in dealing with perseveration. (35, 36, 37)

16. Terminate activities that have a risk of unintentional injury, financial loss, or other untoward effects caused by perseveration. (38, 39, 40, 41)

logical evaluation to clarify cognitive and/or psychiatric factors (e.g., impaired memory, decreased attention, decreased self-monitoring, or schizophrenia) causing perseveration and to guide the intervention plan.

6. Give feedback to the patient, (patient's family), physician, treatment team, and other designated individuals regarding the results of the assessment and the preliminary treatment plan.

7. Facilitate referral for psychiatric evaluation and care if patient's history or symptom presentation suggest that schizophrenia, bipolar disorder, or other psychiatric disorder may account for the patient's symptoms.

8. Address the patient's (and family's) concerns about the psychiatric referral and assist them in getting answers to their questions.

9. Assess the patient's awareness of perseveration by inquiring about behavior (e.g., "How many loops are in the model I asked you to copy and how many are in your drawing?" or "Did you notice that you have told me how to serve a tennis ball three times during this afternoon's conversation?").

10. Assess the patient's emotional reaction to therapists and to family when they

17. Family members attend support group or family therapy sessions to help manage emotional stresses associated with patient's symptoms of brain impairment. (42)

—. _____
_____

—. _____
_____

—. _____
_____

point out or interrupt a perseverative response.

11. With a calm yet firm tone, interrupt the patient's repetitive behavior, saying something like "Stop! We are going to do something different now," or "We are done copying designs," while removing pencil from patient's hand.

12. Interrupt a series of repetitive words or phrases and direct the patient's attention to an activity that will not require speech (e.g., "Let's look at the photos in this magazine," or "Let's watch this television program").

13. Interrupt cognitive sequence by directing patient's attention to physical sensations (e.g., "Take a deep breath and hold it; now breathe out and see how much you can relax your shoulders").

14. Explain to the patient that his/her medical condition has caused changes in the way the patient solves problems or communicates (e.g., gives identical verbal response to different questions, records same entry in checkbook multiple times, fails to follow conversation because of preoccupation with one idea) that may not be obvious to him/her.

15. Ask the patient's permission to interrupt in order to point out these problem-

solving or communication difficulties.

16. While maintaining rapport and observing the patient's frustration and cognitive energy levels, point out repetitive or continuous response.

17. With the patient's or other legally responsible person's permission, record the patient's perseverative activity on videotape or audiotape. Play it back to the patient, and assist him/her as needed in identifying repetitious behavior.

18. Using a warm, authoritative tone, interrupt a series of repetitious words or phrases by saying something like "Stop! Listen carefully to what I am asking you."

19. While maintaining empathy, inform the patient that the perseverative action or words are not correct (e.g., "You are saying 'Yes' to every question that I am asking," or "Your arrangement of the blocks does not match the model").

20. Direct the patient's attention to the original question and repeat his/her original response. Ask patient, "Is your response correct?" If the patient responds correctly, reinforce him/her (e.g., say "Great!"). If the patient gives an incorrect response, gently correct it.

If the patient begins to perseverate, interrupt him/her and say, "You are repeating yourself."

21. Use colored chips or symbols to give the patient feedback on the accuracy of his/her response (e.g., give patient a red checker immediately after a correct response, saying "That's right!" and a black checker after an incorrect one, saying "That's incorrect; let's try another one").

22. Ask the patient to audibly verbalize each step in a motor sequence. For example, while assembling a puzzle, say "This piece is red in the upper-left corner, red in the upper-right corner, white in the lower-left corner, and red in the lower-right corner." Assess for effectiveness in interrupting perseveration.

23. By pacing questions 10 seconds apart, encourage the patient to slow his/her response to inquiries. In the interval between questions, lead the patient through exercise to keep attention focused on neutral stimulus (e.g., "Take some slow, deep breaths. One . . . two. Here's the next item"); reinforce reductions in verbal perseveration.

24. Explain to the patient that you are going to become quiet, look away, and not

pay attention whenever he/she becomes repetitious.

25. As soon as a perseverative response begins, break eye contact and direct attention away from the patient (e.g., begin making notes on a sheet of paper, stand up to look out the window, etc.).

26. Immediately after the patient terminates the perseverative response and is reengaged in meaningful activity, show interest in what he/she is doing (e.g., "Oh, let's take a look at that!" or "Let me ask you a question about what you just said," or "Great! You just came up with a new word!").

27. Consult with the patient's treating physician about the potential of medications to reduce perseveration and to increase functional behaviors or accurate verbalizations.

28. Decide how the patient's medication will be administered, monitored, and managed.

29. Assist the patient (and family) in getting information about potential benefits and side effects of medication.

30. Monitor the patient's use of prescribed medication, its effectiveness, and address issues regarding compliance. Facilitate making physician aware of any side effects.

31. Assess family's need for education regarding the cause and nature of perseveration, and coordinate educational sessions with the therapists as needed.

32. Inform the family about the techniques that have been most helpful to the patient in interrupting perseveration and refocusing attention.

33. Observe family members as they manage the patient's perseveration, paying careful attention to family's and patient's emotional reactions as family attempts to structure the interaction.

34. Point out or describe patient's and family's emotional and behavioral reactions to management of perseverative behavior as they take place in the session, or shortly thereafter; allow for family members to ventilate their feelings.

35. Speak frankly about how frustrating it can be to communicate and interact with someone who is experiencing perseveration, and facilitate family members expressing their feelings.

36. Support the importance of respecting the patient's and family's emotional and cognitive limits, and facilitate family members expressing their feelings.

37. Strongly encourage the family to terminate redirec-

tion or confrontation when emotional or cognitive limits are reached.

38. Talk with the patient and family about patient's usual occupational responsibilities, hobbies, and other activities. Inquire carefully about activities having physical (e.g., driving, use of power tools or knives, contact with hot objects), financial (e.g., trading stocks on home computer), or other risk potential.

39. Consult with the patient's physician and treatment team regarding precautions or modifications that should be put in place until perseveration diminishes. Share this information with patient and family.

40. Determine that family is capable of restricting the patient from potentially harmful activities, should doing so be necessary.

41. Recommend that family restrict or eliminate the patient's access to potentially dangerous situations until perseveration diminishes.

42. Provide family with information about support groups or names of psychotherapists familiar with the problems faced by persons after brain impairment.

___. _____
    _____

___. _____
    _____

___. _____
    _____

DIAGNOSTIC SUGGESTIONS

Axis I: 290.xx   Dementia
          294.1   Dementia Due to (Axis III Condition)
          294.8   Dementia NOS
          294.9   Cognitive Disorder NOS
          295.xx   Schizophrenia
          295.70   Schizoaffective Disorder
          296.xx   Bipolar Disorder

          _____   _____

          _____   _____

Axis II: V71.09   No Diagnosis or Condition

          _____   _____

          _____   _____

POSTTRAUMATIC STRESS DISORDER

BEHAVIORAL DEFINITIONS

1. A traumatic event in which actual or threatened serious injury/death to other(s) or self was experienced or witnessed, resulting in feelings of intense fear, helplessness, or horror.
2. Recurrent, intrusive, distressing recollections of a traumatic event.
3. Repetitive dreams about the traumatic event.
4. Experiences of reliving the event through flashbacks, illusions, or hallucinations.
5. Intense emotional distress and/or physiological reactivity when exposed to reminders of the distressing event.
6. Avoidance of thoughts, activities, people, or other reminders of the threatening event.
7. Inability to recall an important aspect of the trauma.
8. Noticeably decreased interest or participation in significant activities.
9. Experience of being detached or estranged from others.
10. Restricted or blunted affect.
11. Sense of restricted or shortened future.
12. Difficulty falling or staying asleep.
13. Increased irritability or anger.
14. Difficulty concentrating.
15. Excessive vigilance.
16. Exaggerated startle response.
17. Substance abuse used as a means of escape from emotional pain related to trauma.

Note: A fuller description of the psychotherapeutic interventions described in this chapter can be found in Miller (1998).

—. _____

—. _____

—. _____

LONG-TERM GOALS

1. Emotions, behaviors, sleep, and concentration are similar to those experienced before the trauma.
2. Thoughts and reminders of the traumatic event trigger only moderate emotional and/or physical reactions.
3. Patient experiences satisfaction while participating in activities and relationships.
4. Patient plans for and anticipates enjoyment of future activities.

—. _____

—. _____

—. _____

SHORT-TERM OBJECTIVES

1. Identify emotions, physical reactions, thoughts, and avoidance behaviors associated with reminders of the traumatic event. (1, 2, 3)

2. Cooperate with psychological testing to identify concurrent psychological disorders. (1, 4, 5)

3. Verbalize understanding of posttraumatic stress disor-

THERAPEUTIC INTERVENTIONS

1. Using clinical interview and psychological testing, assess whether the patient's history and symptoms fit a diagnosis of a posttraumatic stress disorder.

2. If the patient is a poor historian, obtain permission from patient or legally responsible party to interview

der as a natural and fre-
quently occurring emotional
reaction to the experience of
trauma. (6, 7)

4. Tell the story of the traumatic experience. (8, 9, 10)

5. Report feeling safe and secure in current circum-
stances. (11, 12, 13)

6. Indicate willingness to deal
with more painful aspects of
trauma. (14, 15, 16)

7. Demonstrate skills in using
physical relaxation tech-
niques to lower physiologic
arousal levels.
(17, 18, 19, 20, 23)

8. Use imagery, memories,
and/or music to promote relaxation. (20, 21, 22, 23)

9. Trigger relaxation response
with cue. (23, 24, 25, 26)

10. Demonstrate the ability to
keep arousal at moderate
levels while bringing the
traumatic scene to mind.
(27, 28)

11. Identify negative, dysfunctional thoughts that are associated with the trauma.
(29)

12. Replace negative thoughts
regarding the trauma with
positive, realistic thoughts
that reduce anxiety and
other maladaptive emo-
tions. (30, 31)

13. Utilize thought-stopping
techniques to escape negative rumination. (32)

14. Maintain reasonable comfort in presence of physical

person(s) familiar with
his/her history.

3. Review medical records
and/or consult with the patient's physician to identify
medical conditions and
medications that might be
affecting his/her symptoms.

4. Arrange for or perform psychological testing to evaluate levels of anxiety,
depression, or other coexisting psychological disorders.

5. Give feedback to the patient
(and family), treatment
team, and other designated
persons regarding assess-
ment results and recom-
mendations.

6. Talk with the patient about
the causes, symptoms, clinical course, treatment, and
anticipated outcome of
stress disorders.

7. Refer the patient to books
about symptoms and man-
agement of stress disorders,
such as *I Can't Get Over It:
A Handbook for Trauma
Survivors* (Matsakis).

8. Actively build the level of
trust with the patient in individual sessions through
consistent eye contact, active listening, unconditional
positive regard, and warm
acceptance to help increase
his/her ability to identify
and express feelings.

9. Ask the patient to tell about
the traumatic event, and
listen empathically.

reminders of trauma. (33, 34, 35)

15. Cooperate with Eye Movement Desensitization and Reprocessing (EMDR) techniques to reduce PTSD symptoms. (36)

16. Report understanding of flashbacks, including probable triggers and ways to manage associated anxiety reactions. (37, 38, 39)

17. Describe disturbing dreams related to trauma and construct alternate scenes that demonstrate empowerment and successful resolution of the scene. (40, 41, 42)

18. Practice good sleep hygiene habits. (43, 44, 45, 46)

19. Complete evaluation for medications for acute symptom management. (47, 48)

20. Take medications as prescribed and report to appropriate professionals on effectiveness and side effects. (49)

21. Report awareness of "numbing" or "detachment" reactions and utilize a constructive behavioral technique to restore feelings and sense of connectedness. (50, 51, 52)

22. Verbalize an acceptance of anger as legitimate reaction to hurt or unfairness and communicate these feelings appropriately. (53, 54, 55)

23. Report success in overcoming symptoms and congrat-

10. Assist the patient in labeling his/her emotions as they are expressed.

11. Inquire into the patient's current experience regarding physical safety and security.

12. Identify actions that would help the patient feel safe, and support him/her in following through on implementing them.

13. If the patient lacks resources necessary to attain a sense of personal security, refer him/her (his/her family) to social worker, social service agencies, or other professionals.

14. As the patient describes the traumatic event, notice sudden shifts in emotional or physical reactions or abrupt changes in topic. Inquire into the patient's experience at the time of the reaction or topic shift.

15. Recommend that the patient bring photos, police reports, medical records, or other documents that show what occurred and how it affected the patient, and assist the patient in processing the feelings that are elicited as these objects are reviewed.

16. While maintaining rapport, assist the patient with reality testing and avoidance of catastrophizing or fortune-telling, using confrontation as necessary.

ulate self on progress. (56, 57)

24. Verbalize awareness of how the traumatic experience has influenced own beliefs about fairness, justice, and security. (58, 59, 60)

25. Identify and act on opportunities for new directions and growth in life. (61, 62)

26. Family members report understanding of how the patient's trauma has impacted family and are aware of steps family can take to gradually return to usual way of functioning. (63, 64)

__. _____
   _____
__. _____
   _____
__. _____
   _____

17. Instruct the patient in deep breathing techniques.

18. Train the patient in progressive muscle relaxation techniques.

19. Perform or arrange for biofeedback to develop relaxation skills.

20. Select or allow the patient to choose a chapter in *Relaxation and Stress Reduction Workbook* (Davis, Eshelman, and McKay), then work with the patient to implement the chosen technique.

21. Instruct the patient in guided imagery for relaxation.

22. Encourage the patient to identify and use music that promotes relaxation.

23. Facilitate the patient's obtaining audiotape(s) of favorite relaxation technique(s).

24. Assign the patient to practice a relaxation technique one to three times per day.

25. Have the patient select a verbal (e.g., "calm"), visual (e.g., beach scene), or other cue that can be brought to mind at the point of deepest relaxation.

26. Instruct the patient to bring the relaxation cue to mind during the session and have him/her notice how the cue is effective in creating a sense of relaxation.

27. Assist the patient in developing a hierarchy of images that are associated with the trauma.

28. Starting with the least threatening image, have the patient relax, and then bring the image to mind, maintaining a relaxed state. Progress to the more threatening images according to the patient's tolerance.

29. Explore the patient's negative automatic thoughts (e.g., catastrophizing, fortune-telling, filtering, feelings are facts, etc.).

30. Assist the patient in developing alternative, positive, realistic thoughts to replace dysfunctional thoughts that trigger anxiety, guilt, anger, or depression.

31. Use role-playing, modeling, and behavioral rehearsal to teach patient implementation of realistic, positive thoughts that generate a sense of peace or empowerment.

32. Teach the patient thought-stopping techniques (e.g., shouting STOP silently in the mind while imagining a stop sign, or snapping a rubber band around the wrist to interrupt thought) to utilize when ruminating about the trauma.

33. Assist the patient in identifying when he/she is emotionally ready to be in

the presence of physical reminders of trauma (e.g., can visit scene of accident, can talk with family of deceased person).

34. Rehearse the steps that the patient can take (e.g., use of relaxation techniques, thought-stopping, deep breathing, positive self-talk) to maintain reasonable sense of comfort and control while confronting reminders of trauma.

35. Identify actions that the patient can take to deal with overwhelming feelings, should they occur when exposure to physical reminders of the trauma is implemented (e.g., make arrangements to talk with a trusted person afterward or make written notes describing the experience to be processed in the next session).

36. Perform or refer for therapeutic intervention utilizing Eye Movement Desensitization and Reprocessing (EMDR).

37. Assist the patient in identifying events, thoughts, and other factors that trigger flashback experiences.

38. Work with the patient to evaluate the low probability of the traumatic event occurring again.

39. Assist the patient in identifying several strategies (e.g., wearing seat belts consis-

tently, purchasing a car with air bags and a strong frame, using divided highways rather than two-lane roads when available, carrying a chemical spray to ward off an assailant) that he/she could use to minimize chance of life-threatening situation developing should a similar event occur again.

40. Inquire about details of the patient's dreams, adjusting depth of questioning according to his/her ability to tolerate painful emotions.

41. Assign the patient to "rewrite" nightmares, suggesting that the patient write in scenes demonstrating his/her strength and ability to handle the situation successfully.

42. Discuss nightmares and assist the patient in revising the dream to reflect themes that would be empowering for him/her.

43. Inquire into behaviors that might negatively affect the patient's sleep quality, such as excessive napping, heavy eating, stimulating prebedtime activities, and remaining in bed too long after unwanted awakening.

44. Assist the patient in planning dietary intake to promote good sleep, identifying substances such as caffeine, nicotine, and alcohol that might impair sleep, as well as those (such as protein-

rich snacks) that might induce sleepiness.

45. Encourage the patient to use relaxing rituals such as hot bubble baths, soothing reading, music, or relaxation procedures to promote sense of restfulness before bedtime.

46. Instruct the patient to get out of bed and engage in some quiet activity during episodes of insomnia, until sleepy feeling returns.

47. Assess need for medications to improve sleep or to reduce anxiety or depression, and consult with the patient's treating physician about how medication will be prescribed, monitored, and managed.

48. Address the patient's (and family's) concerns about medications and assist them in getting answers to questions about medications and side effects.

49. Monitor the patient's use of prescribed medications and their effect on symptoms; address issues affecting compliance and side effects.

50. Inquire into the patient's experience of numbing and detachment (e.g., factual, expressionless description of close friend's death; statements such as "I don't feel anything," or "I feel like I'm watching a movie, like it didn't really happen to me");

point out those that occur during therapy session.

51. Identify destructive responses to the numbing, such as excessive anger, depression, self-injurious behavior, or substance abuse.

52. Assist the patient in identifying benign or helpful ways to respond to numbing, such as telephoning a friend, taking a hot shower, exercising, stroking a pet, snapping a rubber band on one's wrist, etc.

53. Listen empathically as the patient reports anger, and support it as an understandable and reasonable reaction to the hurt that he/she has experienced.

54. Identify those beliefs or philosophies that interfere with the patient voicing and accepting anger, and work with the patient to enable him/her to become comfortable with own anger.

55. Assist the patient in developing methods to vent anger (e.g., screaming when alone, writing angry feelings in a journal, striking a punching bag, or talking calmly with others about the anger) that will not jeopardize relationships.

56. Have the patient point out, or name for patient, success in overcoming painful emotions and regaining sense of control.

57. Direct the patient to acknowledge the strength demonstrated in his/her working through the trauma.

58. Be attentive to questions that the patient raises about existential issues and inquire into patient's previous beliefs and how these have been altered by this experience.

59. Recommend that the patient read books discussing responses to uncontrollable suffering, such as *Man's Search for Meaning* (Frankl and Allport) or *When Bad Things Happen to Good People* (Kushner).

60. Encourage the patient to resume participation in friendships and social, religious, and other communities where he/she will have opportunities to hear others' viewpoints about security, fairness, and justice in life.

61. Listen for ways in which new opportunities have been created (e.g., ways in which the patient's self-concept may have been expanded, a deepened commitment toward the accomplishment of life goals, etc.) and point these out to the patient.

62. Brainstorm about actions the patient might take, based on new realizations and stronger commitments to life goals.

63. Suggest that the patient and family read about coping with the effects of trauma on relationships, in books such as *Trust After Trauma: A Guide to Relationships for Survivors and Those Who Love Them* (Matsakis).

64. Conduct or refer for family therapy to assist family members in working through changes associated with the trauma experienced by the patient and to return to pretrauma level of family functioning.

__. _____

_____

__. _____

_____

__. _____

_____

DIAGNOSTIC SUGGESTIONS

Axis I: 309.81   Posttraumatic Stress Disorder
          308.3   Acute Stress Disorder
          _____   _____
          _____   _____

PROBLEM SOLVING/PLANNING/ JUDGMENT DEFICITS

BEHAVIORAL DEFINITIONS

1. Failure to initiate actions to resolve problem situations.
2. Incomplete or inaccurate listing of steps required for problem resolution.
3. Inability or reduced ability to formulate realistic alternative solutions.
4. Difficulty in sequencing steps necessary to complete a project.
5. Impaired ability to organize and complete basic daily tasks (e.g., planning and preparing meals, paying bills on time, arranging for someone to repair a malfunctioning appliance).
6. Failure to incorporate relevant information or feedback to guide task performance.
7. Failure to adjust behavior to changing circumstances.
8. Difficulty evaluating the quality of a completed product.
9. Poor prioritization of activities, leaving important actions incomplete.
10. Acting in ways that put self and/or family in jeopardy, by making commitments that are not in accord with family resources or priorities.
11. Making rash or hurtful comments without considering consequences.

—. _____
   _____
—. _____
   _____
—. _____
   _____

LONG-TERM GOALS

1. Initiate and persist in carrying out actions to resolve a problem situation.
2. Check the adequacy of the solution and persist until the goal is accomplished or abandoned.
3. Use compensatory strategies and assistive devices to enhance effectiveness in decision making and in managing responsibilities.
4. Solicit and utilize input from trustworthy family members or friends when faced with decisions having significant consequences.
5. Acknowledge tendency to act before considering consequences, and monitor own social behavior to minimize hurtful experiences.
6. Emotionally accept changes in problem-solving and judgment skills and consequences for lifestyle.
7. Adjust lifestyle to maximize performance in spite of problem-solving and judgment deficits.

—. _____

_____

—. _____

_____

—. _____

_____

SHORT-TERM OBJECTIVES

1. Cooperate with an evaluation of acute and chronic factors influencing current planning, judgment, and problem-solving skills. (1, 2, 3, 4, 13)

2. Provide information (and allow others to share information) about own typical level of planning and problem solving, giving specific examples of situations in which skills are now different. (2, 5, 6, 7)

THERAPEUTIC INTERVENTIONS

1. Review the patient's medical record to identify factors (e.g., developmental disorder, site of brain impairment, educational level) that might be influencing his/her current planning, judgment, and problem-solving skills.

2. Obtain a history of the onset and course of the patient's planning, problem-solving, and judgment problems from the patient

3. Cooperate with a neuropsychological evaluation. (8, 13)

4. Participate willingly in activities to assess planning and problem-solving strategies. (9, 10, 13)

5. Agree to assessment procedures to identify current and past psychiatric conditions. (11, 13)

6. Cooperate with efforts to identify specific deficits and other factors contributing to impaired planning, judgment, and problem solving skills. (12, 13)

7. Agree to medical interventions to improve thought processes. (14, 15)

8. Obtain treatment to address psychiatric disorders. (16)

9. Participate in treatment for impaired deficit awareness. (17)

10. Put good effort into activities designed to improve specific cognitive skills that contribute to normal judgment and problem solving. (18)

11. Participate in therapies designed to improve effectiveness in planning, judgment, and problem solving. (19)

12. Describe the positive motivating effects of working on challenging (but not overly difficult) problems and receiving specific feedback re-

as well as from someone who is familiar with him/her.

3. Consult with the patient's physician regarding medical factors (i.e., acute medical conditions, medications) that might be affecting the patient's planning, judgment, and problem-solving skills.

4. Inquire into the patient's past and current use of alcohol, street drugs, or other substances that could affect his/her planning, judgment, and problem-solving skills.

5. With the patient's permission, ask the patient's family, coworkers, employer, or others who are familiar with the patient how his/her judgment and ability to make decisions have changed since the illness/injury.

6. Consult with the patient's rehabilitation therapists about the patient's ability to plan ahead and solve problems in everyday situations (e.g., following a recipe, using a schedule to keep up with therapy appointments, calling the social worker to get information about Social Security disability benefits).

7. Ask the patient and others who know him/her well (e.g., family members, rehabilitation therapists) to identify the patient's ability to complete specific tasks,

garding progress toward goal attainment. (20, 21)

13. Participate in psychotherapy to address and manage emotional reactions resulting from the changed problem-solving abilities and interfering with effective problem solving. (22, 23)

14. Identify the problem situations that are frequently encountered in daily life. (24)

15. Implement a systematic approach toward planning and problem solving. (25, 26, 27)

16. Use self-verbalizations to focus and maintain attention during problem solving. (28, 29)

17. Implement environmental modifications to enhance performance and safety. (30, 31, 32)

18. Utilize procedures to reduce choices, to cue self to perform necessary actions, and to otherwise enhance problem-solving effectiveness. (33, 34, 35)

19. Establish routines linked to existing habits to improve the predictable and timely management of task. (36, 37)

20. Use computerized alarm systems to generate time-sensitive reminders of tasks to be accomplished. (38)

21. Carry out activities to promote generalization of problem-solving strategies

using measuring devices such as the Patient Competency Rating Scale (Roueche and Fordyce), the Profile of the Executive Control System (Sohlberg), or the Brock Adaptive Functioning Questionnaire (Dywan and Segalowitz).

8. Refer for or perform a neuropsychological evaluation to identify how specific information-processing skills (e.g., attention, memory, verbal reasoning) might be affecting the patient's planning, problem-solving, and judgment abilities.

9. Refer for or perform an evaluation of the patient's planning, problem-solving, and judgment abilities using unstructured techniques such as the Tower of London[DX]: Research Version (Culbertson and Zillmer), Tower of Hanoi (Glosser and Goodglass), Tinkertoy Test (Lezak), Executive Function Route-Finding Task (Boyd and Sautter), Six Elements Test (Shallice and Burgess), and Multiple Errands Test (Shallice and Burgess).

10. Recommend that the therapists fabricate situations to assess the patient's problem-solving skills (e.g., planning a menu on a budget and shopping for the ingredients, developing a schedule for workers to staff round-the-

to situations other than those worked on in therapy. (39, 40)

22. Family demonstrate effective use of general and specific verbal cues to encourage the patient's initiation of behavior. (41)

23. Participate in leisure activities requiring reasoning. (42, 43)

24. Coordinate a referral for an evaluation of the patient's safety in carrying out specific household and community activities. (44, 45)

25. Accept the recommendations of rehabilitation professionals regarding necessary modifications in daily activities to ensure personal safety and welfare. (46, 47)

26. Agree to consult with a vocational rehabilitation counselor. (48)

27. Describe accommodations that are necessary in order to perform best at school or at work and take actions toward implementing them. (49)

28. Verbalize knowledge of relevant laws regarding the right to accommodations and the procedures to follow to have them implemented. (50)

29. Acknowledge the painful emotions associated with one's changed role and work

clock shifts for a one-month period, etc.).

11. Perform or refer for a psychodiagnostic evaluation to identify psychiatric conditions (e.g., depression, psychotic disorders, personality disorders, substance abuse disorders) that may be affecting the patient's judgment and problem-solving abilities.

12. Consult with the patient's rehabilitation therapists, or coordinate a team meeting to share information in order to identify points at which planning and problem-solving behaviors (e.g., basic cognitive processes, reasoning, executive functions) are breaking down.

13. Give feedback to the patient (patient's family), physician, rehabilitation team, and other designated persons regarding assessment results and recommendations.

14. Consult with the patient's physician, or coordinate a referral for evaluation and treatment of medical conditions (e.g., delirium, hypothyroidism, etc.) acutely impairing cognition.

15. Consult with the patient's physician regarding adjustments in medications that might enhance his/her cognition (i.e., discontinuing medications that interfere with cognition or adding medica-

to resolve them and to accept one's new life. (51)

30. Complete (or have family complete) applications for disability benefits or other financial assistance if there will be a significant delay in returning to work. (52)

31. Responsible individual agrees to assist with decision making, if the patient is deemed incompetent to make medical, financial, and/or personal decisions. (53, 54, 55)

32. Cooperate with others' efforts to terminate abusive treatment. (56)

33. Demonstrate skill in circumventing or interrupting socially inappropriate behaviors. (57, 58, 59)

34. Family demonstrate skill in using management of antecedents, time-out, contingency management, and other behavioral techniques to reduce occurrences of and reinforcement of the patient's socially inappropriate behavior. (60)

35. Exercise independence in circumscribed decision making. (61)

36. Family members describe their emotional acceptance of the patient's problem-solving and judgment changes and the ways in which their family life have been altered. (62, 63)

tions to enhance the patient's cognitive functioning).

16. Initiate or arrange for treatment for depression, substance abuse, or other psychiatric conditions that might be impairing the patient's judgment and problem-solving abilities. (See Depression/Grief, Substance Abuse, or other relevant chapters in this Planner.)

17. Initiate or refer for treatment for impaired deficit awareness. (See Denial and Impaired Awareness chapter in this Planner.)

18. Initiate or refer for treatment for impairments in specific cognitive processes (e.g., language functioning, attention, memory). (See Speech Problems [Aphasia], Impulsivity, Attention and Concentration Impairment, and Memory Impairment chapters in this Planner.)

19. Coordinate a referral for or initiate cognitive rehabilitation therapy targeted towards planning, judgment, and problem-solving deficits.

20. Recommend that therapists adjust item difficulty level to keep the patient's error rate at 10 to 20 percent.

21. Recommend that the therapists graph the patient's progress toward specific goals.

—. _____

_____

—. _____

_____

—. _____

_____

22. Initiate or refer for psychotherapy to assist the patient in working through grief, frustration, anger, and other emotional reactions associated with the patient's awareness of his/her planning and problem-solving deficits.

23. Point out instances in which the patient's problem-solving and judgment abilities are negatively impacted by emotions (e.g., frustration). Instruct the patient in ways (e.g., relaxation techniques) to interrupt distracting emotional reactions; monitor effectiveness.

24. Ask the patient to generate a list of the kinds of problems he/she routinely manages in his/her life (e.g., planning meals, arranging transportation schedules for children's after-school events, scheduling staff to cover shifts through the week).

25. Encourage the patient to select three problems that he/she normally has to manage, and then assign him/her to work through each problem in writing in a systematic way, identifying the goal, necessary actions, sequence of steps, and comparing the obtained result to the stated goal.

26. In collaboration with the patient's cognitive rehabilitation therapist, assign the

patient to apply a specific problem-solving strategy to a task in his/her life and to report back on the results, using notes to reinforce memory, if needed.

27. Recommend that the treatment team assign the patient to develop his/her own daily schedule, taking into consideration the mandatory activities and specific details of the therapists' schedules (e.g., physical therapist leaves at noon on Mondays, pool therapy is only available from 1:00 to 2:00 P.M., etc.).

28. Suggest that the patient verbalize as he/she works through a problem, in order to maintain focus, and then inquire into the effectiveness of this technique.

29. When the patient has completed a task using overt self-guidance, recommend that he/she verbalize internally (silently) as he/she works through a task. Inquire into the effectiveness of covert cuing.

30. Talk with the patient (and family) about ways to simplify the environment to reduce distractions (e.g., arranging closet and dresser drawers to hold only the clothes for a few seasonal outfits; asking to be eliminated from junk mail lists; cleaning off desk area where one processes mail).

31. Encourage the patient and/or patient's family to modify the patient's environment to reduce potentially dangerous situations (e.g., purchase heat-generating appliances such as coffeepots and irons that automatically turn off after a specific period; obtain a microwave oven to use for cooking [instead of a range] when alone in the home).

32. Talk with the patient about how the environment can be arranged to reduce the need to organize information mentally, and to make it easier to accomplish the task (e.g., putting bills in a folder specifying the week of the month in which they must be paid; creating a filing system for important documents; creating forms to cue the patient about what must be documented, and routinizing as much of the documentation as possible).

33. Discuss procedures that would ease the patient's accomplishment of tasks (e.g., open mail in area where files are located so that items can be sorted immediately into designated files; document information on a form reflecting the types and order of information required for the final report, rather than taking notes and organizing them after the fact).

34. Structure tasks in such a way as to reduce the number of choices that the patient must make (e.g., write menu for meals and associated shopping list on file cards to simplify meal planning and grocery shopping; put all receipts necessary for income tax return in one file, rather than separating them by type of deduction).

35. Work with the patient to develop checklists that will cue the patient to tasks to be performed as well as help him/her monitor task progress and completion.

36. For recurring tasks, work with the patient to develop a routine that he/she can follow to accomplish the task in the same way every time, using written notes as necessary to compensate for memory deficits.

37. Use "chaining" to link the first step of a routine to an environmental cue, to increase the patient's independence in problem solving and to decrease the amount of judgment required for him/her to initiate the problem-solving sequence.

38. Evaluate the potential benefit of computerized systems (e.g., watch alarms, computerized calendars, computerized cuing systems) to remind the patient to initiate necessary activi-

ties (e.g., taking medications, paying the rent, etc.). Assist the patient in selecting a system that is user-friendly and suits his/her needs.

39. Ask the patient to select a particular problem, and then encourage him/her to generate two or three different ways to solve it. Evaluate the probable effectiveness of each solution.

40. Ask the patient to select a particular problem-solving strategy, and have him/her identify three situations to which this strategy could be applied in his/her life

41. Instruct the family in ways to use general cues (e.g., "What should you check after you leave the house?") followed, if necessary, by specific cues (e.g., "Check to make sure that the door is locked") if the patient fails to initiate a problem-solving activity.

42. Recommend that the patient and family participate in recreational activities in which reasoning is required (e.g., Battleship® game; card games such as bridge, pinochle, or rummy; chess, checkers; etc.) for successful competition.

43. Coordinate a referral to a recreational therapist for recommendations regarding leisure activities that would help stimulate the patient's

reasoning, strategy forma-
tion, and self-monitoring.

44. Refer the patient for an occupational therapy evaluation to assess the impact of
the patient's problem-
solving or judgment deficit
on his/her ability to safely
perform instrumental activities of daily living (e.g.,
cooking, taking medications,
locking the house, paying
bills, caring for children).

45. Refer the patient for a driving evaluation to determine
whether he/she can safely
drive, given the current
problem-solving or judg-
ment deficits.

46. In consultation with the
treatment team, identify
those activities that the patient should not perform at
all due to safety concerns,
should perform with over-
sight, or could perform independently.

47. Reinforce the patient for
implementing the treat-
ment team's recommenda-
tions, reminding him/her
that utilizing input from
trustworthy persons and respecting limitations are
signs of effective problem
solving and emotional
strength.

48. Refer the patient for a vocational evaluation to determine how problem-solving
and judgment deficits will
affect his/her ability to return to school or to work,

and to identify modifications necessary for successful reentry.

49. Assist the patient in identifying accommodations that could be made at school or in the workplace to help the patient perform at his/her best (e.g., developing worksheets that the patient will use to identify and record the main thesis and supporting arguments of articles or book chapters; developing a checklist to monitor that a project has been completed; arranging for a job coach to cue the patient to use problem-solving strategies, and to give the patient feedback on the result). Facilitate implementation of such accommodations.

50. Teach the patient the general implications of the Americans with Disabilities Act (ADA) and subsequent related legislation and judicial rulings on his/her entitlement to reasonable accommodations. For specific questions or problems, refer the patient to an attorney familiar with this area of the law.

51. Work with the patient to deal with loss, frustration, anxiety, and other emotional reactions in the event that he/she is unable to resume important roles and activities.

52. Refer the patient (patient's family) to a social worker, community social service agency, or personnel office to determine what benefits he/she might be eligible for during the period when he/she is unable to resume work.

53. Taking into account the provisions of state law, clarify whether the patient is competent to make imminent medical, personal, or financial decisions.

54. Following the provisions of state law and the policies of the institution, identify the person who is legally authorized to make specific decisions for the patient. Obtain legal counsel, if necessary. Document this information in the patient's medical record.

55. In accord with state laws and the policies of the institution, talk with the patient's family (and/or partner) about the patient's presumed incompetence. Assist them in identifying who would be eligible and appropriate to assume decision making for the patient, and inform them about steps to pursue guardianship.

56. If there is evidence to suggest that an incompetent patient is being abused physically, financially, or in other ways, coordinate a referral to social services or to

the state's adult protective services agency, following the institutional guidelines and the requirements of state law.

57. Ask the patient to name those behaviors that others have seemingly reacted to with embarrassment, discomfort, or disapproval (e.g., making suggestive comments to the classmate of one's teenage daughter; asking a person about private matters at a dinner party; making loud rude comments to the umpire at son's baseball game).

58. Enlist the patient's cooperation in keeping records about incidents in which others have seemed embarrassed, noting specifically what the patient said and did, as well as antecedents and consequences of the behavior.

59. Assist the patient in developing and testing actions to circumvent or interrupt disinhibited behavior (e.g., taking a deep breath when feeling worked up; trying to imagine what one's spouse would say if action were carried out; having partner squeeze one's hand to signal that a behavior should be terminated).

60. Instruct the family in basic behavioral principles and develop a plan that family members feel comfortable

implementing when the patient says or does embarrassing things in their presence.

61. Brainstorm about ways to protect the patient's and family's welfare while maintaining as much independent decision making as possible for the patient (e.g., open a charge account for the patient with a credit limit that is low enough to prevent financial harm should he/she make impulsive purchases; determine recreational activities that are safe for the patient to participate in, and inquire about his/her preferences among those activities; give the patient a small portion of the family's savings to invest and manage, etc.).

62. Educate the family about the patient's residual deficits in problem solving and judgment, recommended activity modifications, compensatory techniques, and accommodations, using examples that relate specifically to the patient's and family's life.

63. Refer family members to resources (family therapy, support groups, advocacy groups, reading material, etc.) to assist them in understanding and addressing the patient's needs and in coming to terms emotion-

ally with the changes in
their family life.

__. _____
   _____

__. _____
   _____

__. _____
   _____

DIAGNOSTIC SUGGESTIONS

Axis I: 290.xx   Dementia
            294.1   Dementia Due to (Axis III condition)
            294.8   Dementia NOS
            294.9   Cognitive Disorder NOS

            _____   _____

            _____   _____

Axis II: V71.09   No Diagnosis or Condition
            799.9   Diagnosis Deferred

            _____   _____

            _____   _____

RECREATIONAL AND SOCIAL LIFE PROBLEMS

BEHAVIORAL DEFINITIONS

1. Noticeable decrease in time spent in leisure or social activities in comparison to preinjury/preillness pattern.
2. Inability to pursue leisure activities in a way that produces pleasure.
3. Changes in functioning make it difficult or impossible to safely continue preferred recreational pursuits.
4. Participation in recreational activities limited by paralysis, weakness, or other neuromuscular changes.
5. Cognitive or perceptual changes affect safety, accuracy, and/or enjoyment of intellectually challenging activities.
6. Physical barriers interfere with pursuit of recreational or social activities.
7. Decreased interest in social activities due to brain-injury/illness-related changes in emotions or personality.
8. Friends rarely talk with or spend time with the patient.
9. Friends and family report that it is burdensome to socialize with the patient.

__. _____

_____

__. _____

_____

__. _____

_____

LONG-TERM GOALS

1. Allocate time on a regular basis for leisure and/or social activities.
2. Participate in recreational activities that provide pleasure, satisfaction, and/or stress reduction and are suited to physical and cognitive skills.
3. Terminate recreational activities that are hazardous due to residual impairments.
4. Use adapted equipment or adapted procedures to facilitate participation in leisure activities.
5. Obtain and utilize information about the accessibility of various public facilities.
6. Request accommodations in an assertive and timely way.
7. Maintain contact with friends and engage in activities suited to new abilities.
8. Continue to develop new friendships with others who share interests.

—. _____

_____

—. _____

_____

—. _____

_____

SHORT-TERM OBJECTIVES

1. Describe how free time was spent prior to the illness/injury and how each activity was satisfying. (1, 2)

2. Describe social life prior to the injury/illness and note specific ways in which it was enjoyable. (3, 4)

3. Voice concerns about the potential impact of the illness/injury on ability to resume recreational and social activities. (5)

THERAPEUTIC INTERVENTIONS

1. Ask the patient (and family) to talk about what he/she previously enjoyed doing in free time (e.g., jogging, making furniture, reading novels).

2. Inquire into how each leisure-time activity was satisfying and enjoyable (e.g., provided relaxation, sense of accomplishment, intellectual stimulation).

4. List leisure and social activities that one intends to resume. (6)

5. Accept a referral to a recreational therapist. (7)

6. Cooperate with a psychological evaluation to identify emotional, chemical dependency, or other psychiatric problems interfering with one's recreational and social life. (8)

7. Cooperate with an assessment of neuropsychological functioning. (9, 10)

8. Verbalize the ways in which abilities to resume leisure and social activities have been impacted by the medical event. (11)

9. Describe the modifications that will be needed in recreational and social activities in order to protect own safety and that of others. (12, 13)

10. Agree to refrain from participation in risky activities while rehabilitation team judges that residual deficits or medical conditions jeopardize safety. (14)

11. Family members (or others close to patient) list actions they will take to prevent him/her from participating in potentially dangerous leisure activity. (15)

12. Cooperate with therapies to increase awareness of deficits and ability to effec-

3. Ask the patient to describe those social activities in which he/she previously participated (e.g., having extended family over for a barbecue, participating in Toastmasters, attending home football games with fraternity brothers).

4. Inquire into the ways in which each social activity provided enjoyment (e.g., strengthened family ties, collegial support while challenging self, relaxation and opportunity to be playful).

5. Inquire into the patient's point of view about how his/her ability to pursue favorite recreational activities may be affected by his/her injury or illness (e.g., difficult to dig holes for plants due to hemiparesis; embarrassed by aphasia and prefers to avoid social situations; pain and overall "not feeling well" interfere with desire to travel).

6. Ask the patient to list those activities that he/she hopes to resume; process the list for appropriateness and possible additions.

7. Refer the patient to a recreational therapist to assist in identifying leisure activities that the patient could resume in the near future and to identify modifications or equipment that would enhance his/her performance.

tively compensate for them. (16)

13. Participate in psychotherapy to facilitate coming to terms emotionally with the changes in life and activities. (17, 18)

14. Verbalize the importance of recreational and social activities and identify new interests that one might be willing to pursue. (19, 20, 21, 22)

15. Identify concerns about resuming contact with friends and describe specific ways to make the interaction more comfortable. (23, 24, 25)

16. Describe the damaging effects of depression on recovery and relationships. (26)

17. List the symptoms of depression that suggest the need to obtain professional consultation. (27)

18. Work with a speech therapist to improve communication skills. (28)

19. Utilize communication technology to supplement oral messages. (29)

20. Make use of large-print books and/or books on tape to continue enjoying literature. (30)

21. Accept referral to a speech therapist to improve effectiveness in conversations. (31)

22. Communicate emotions through speech intonation

8. Perform, refer for, or evaluate the findings of a psychodiagnostic evaluation to identify depression, anxiety, chemical dependency, or other factors that could negatively impact the patient's resumption of social and recreational activities.

9. With the patient's (or legally designated representative's) permission, obtain results from recent neuropsychological testing.

10. Perform or refer for neuropsychological testing to determine how cognitive deficits may impact the patient's ability to successfully resume specific leisure and social activities.

11. Coordinate a meeting with, or get input from, members of the patient's rehabilitation team to determine how cognitive, perceptual, emotional, neuromuscular, and other factors will likely affect his/her ability to resume leisure activities, and what interventions might be helpful in accomplishing a return to enjoyable recreational pursuits.

12. Talk with the patient about factors (e.g., visual field cut, distractibility, left neglect) that would make it risky for him/her to resume certain activities (e.g., hunting, woodworking, cooking) at this time.

and facial expressions.
(32, 33, 34)

23. Agree to treatment for depression, anxiety, substance abuse, or other psychiatric disorders. (35)

24. Implement pain management strategies on a consistent basis. (36)

25. Budget time and energy to allow for social and recreational activities. (37)

26. Describe ways to meet transportation needs for recreational activities. (38)

27. Demonstrate skill in identifying accessible accommodations, public transportation, and recreational facilities, and in making arrangements for specific needs. (39, 40, 41)

28. Outline a plan for the use of a gender-specific public restroom. (42)

29. Describe ways to more easily manage eating in a restaurant. (43)

30. Select vacation locations and leisure activities compatible with own tolerance for stimulation. (44)

31. Demonstrate effective use of alternative communication methods to request assistance in getting urgent needs met by strangers. (45)

32. Participate in a community outing and process the experience and the feelings generated by it. (46)

13. Determine the degree to which the patient has insight into the risk that the deficits present by inquiring about the patient's opinion regarding his/her ability to safely resume specific hobbies.

14. Taking into account state laws concerning confidentiality of psychological information, consult with the rehabilitation team regarding how recommendations that patient refrain from dangerous hobbies will be implemented (e.g., patient agrees not to use power tools until physician approves; ask family to take guns out of the home; suggest family notify friends with whom patient normally goes scuba diving about his/her memory problems).

15. Assist the family in handling practical and emotional issues surrounding actions they will take to protect the patient's safety during the period in which he/she is unaware of deficits.

16. Perform, or refer the patient for therapies to decrease deficit denial. (See Denial and Impaired Awareness chapter in this Planner.)

17. Perform or refer for psychotherapy to help the patient deal with feelings of grief, loss, frustration, and anger associated with the injury/illness and its effect

33. Family members make use of counseling to deal with emotions and adjustments to family social life caused by the patient's injury/illness. (47)

34. Family members network with other families having a member with a brain injury/illness to gain support and ideas about recreational and social life issues. (48)

__. _____
_____

__. _____
_____

__. _____
_____

on participation in favorite activities.

18. Assist the patient in verbalizing anger, disappointment, and other feelings associated with the unexpected and upsetting behaviors of those who have previously been close (e.g., best friend rarely makes contact, fiancé breaks engagement, boss does not call to check on progress).

19. Talk with the patient about the importance of including recreational and social activities in his/her life.

20. Inquire into those activities that the patient had thought about pursuing (but had not) prior to the injury/illness (e.g., learning about bluegrass music, learning to play golf, volunteering with the Red Cross) and brainstorm about the possibility of following up on those or similar interests at this time.

21. Talk with the patient about changes the patient might like to make in his/her social life now that there is an opportunity to begin anew (e.g., volunteer to help at hospital, purchase season tickets to football games for self and spouse, attend children's sports activities).

22. Explore the patient's reservations about pursuing certain recreational, avocational, or social opportunities and assist the patient in

overcoming his/her reluc-
tance to try new things.

23. Assist the patient in verbalizing concerns about how
others will react to his/her
changed condition.

24. Challenge the patient to
consider which is the
greater loss: to experience
friends' sympathy or other
reactions that make the patient uncomfortable, or to
forego contact with friends.

25. Brainstorm about ways in
which the patient can de-
flect attention away from
his/her medical condition
and restore reciprocity to
the interaction (e.g., asking
about the other person's
life; initiating conversation
about nonmedical topics
such as recent sporting
events; showing confidence
in one's ability to manage
residual deficits).

26. Educate the patient (and
the family) about the negative long-term consequences
of depression.

27. Talk with the patient (and
family) about the symptoms
of depression, and how they
would know (e.g., persistent
depressed mood rather than
"a bad day") that the pa-
tient should consult with a
professional for treatment
of depression.

28. Coordinate a referral to a
speech therapist to increase
patient's effective compen-

sation for residual symptoms of aphasia.

29. Encourage the patient to use a Text Telephone (TTY) device, e-mail, or other systems to communicate if oral speech is laborious or unintelligible.

30. Refer the patient to books on tape, large-print books, or other resources for persons having visual perceptual or other difficulties interfering with reading standard material.

31. Refer the patient for therapies designed to improve speech pragmatics (e.g., poor turn taking, hyperverbosity, tangential speech). (See the Speech Problems [Aphasia] chapter in this Planner.)

32. Refer for treatment with a speech therapist to improve patient's intonation in speech.

33. Recommend that the patient enhance emotional intonation in voice by putting conscious effort into pitch and volume (e.g., communicating an emotion while singing, doing a dramatic reading, audiotaping self while reading phrases with emotional inflection and then reviewing the audiotape).

34. Recommend that the patient enhance the communication value of facial expressions by conscious

practice (e.g., making faces in front of a mirror to reflect specific emotions, working with a partner in which one person makes an emotional facial expression while the other guesses which emotion is being displayed).

35. Coordinate treatment for depression, anxiety, substance abuse, or other factors affecting interest in and success at social and recreational activities. (See Depression/Grief, Anxiety/Fear, Substance Abuse, and other relevant chapters in this Planner.)

36. Reinforce the patient's follow-through on pain management techniques in order to reduce the negative impact of chronic pain on mood, motivation, and energy level. (See Chronic Pain chapter in this Planner.)

37. Inquire into the possibility of the patient limiting hours spent on work in order to have energy left for recreational and social activities.

38. Talk with the patient (and family) about ways that he/she will arrange to meet friends or attend social events if he/she is unable to drive. (See Driving Deficiencies chapter in this Planner.)

39. Refer the patient (and family) to information (e.g., American Automobile Asso-

ciation publications, American Association of Retired Persons Web site, travel agents, specific Web sites) concerning accessible accommodations and tips for travelers with a disability.

40. Identify specific questions that the patient (family) should ask to determine whether restaurants, theaters, or other public places are accessible for his/her particular need.

41. In a role-play situation, ask the patient to rehearse requesting accommodations in a clear, assertive manner.

42. If the patient requires assistance with toileting, talk with the patient and his/her spouse (family) about how they prefer to handle the use of public restrooms (e.g., spouse asks someone to enter the restroom to see if others are inside and ask their permission to enter; spouse asks someone to stand by the door and let others know there is a person of the opposite gender inside; utilize women's restroom in which all stalls are private).

43. Encourage the patient (and family) to think about ways in which the patient could more easily and independently manage eating in a restaurant (e.g., ordering foods that can easily be picked up in one hand; re-

questing that kitchen staff cut food into bite-sized pieces before the plate is brought to the table; calling in advance to request a table with enough space for a wheelchair).

44. Plan vacations, recreational activities, and social events so as to reduce the risk of overstimulation (e.g., spend week in a cabin on a lake instead of in Las Vegas; have friends over for a small dinner party rather than for a large barbecue).

45. Work with the patient and consult with his/her speech therapist to identify strategies (e.g., use of pictograms, communication board, augmentive communication device) by which the patient can communicate basic needs (e.g., need to use the bathroom, separated from friends and need to relocate them, experiencing pain) if verbal communication is impaired.

46. Recommend that the patient plan an outing into the community. Set specific goals, identify potential problems, brainstorm about potential solutions, and report on successes and problems afterwards.

47. Conduct, or refer for, family sessions to deal with family discomfort and embarrassment regarding the change in the patient's social skills.

48. Refer the patient and family members to advocacy or self-help groups in which they can problem-solve with others in similar circumstances regarding resumption of social and recreational activities.

—. _____

_____

—. _____

_____

—. _____

_____

DIAGNOSTIC SUGGESTIONS

Axis I: 309.0   Adjustment Disorder With Depressed Mood
                309.24   Adjustment Disorder With Anxiety
                309.28   Adjustment Disorder With Mixed Anxiety and Depressed Mood
                309.3   Adjustment Disorder With Disturbance of Conduct
                309.4   Adjustment Disorder With Mixed Disturbance of Emotions and Conduct
                309.9   Adjustment Disorder, Unspecified
                300.0   Anxiety Disorder NOS
                V61.9   Relational Problem Related to a Mental Disorder or General Medical Condition

                _____   _____

                _____   _____

Axis II: V71.09   No Diagnosis or Condition

                _____   _____

                _____   _____

REHABILITATION NONCOMPLIANCE

BEHAVIORAL DEFINITIONS

1. Observed behaviors differ from clearly defined medical recommendations.
2. Other patients, family, or staff report that patient is failing to carry out rehabilitation instructions.
3. Falsely states that recommendations are being followed.
4. Medical condition fails to improve as expected.
5. States intention to ignore rehabilitation team's recommendations, without offering a clearly defined alternate plan to achieve recovery.

—. _____

_____

—. _____

_____

—. _____

_____

LONG-TERM GOALS

1. Behave in ways consistent with rehabilitation team's recommendations most of the time.
2. Carry out medical recommendations whether or not others are observing.
3. Educate self about treatment options, take responsibility for choice of which to pursue, and consistently follow treatment guidelines.
4. Participate in treatment designed to address chronic factors (e.g., addictions) that may affect adherence to rehabilitation recommendations.

5. Give straightforward, honest account of own actions that relate to medical recommendations.

—. _____
    _____

—. _____
    _____

—. _____
    _____

SHORT-TERM OBJECTIVES

1. Willingly provide information to identify whether activities are aligned with long-term rehabilitation and medical goals. (1, 2, 3, 4)

2. Consider others' viewpoints concerning how effectively recommendations are being followed. (5, 6)

3. Describe factors affecting motivation to carry out recommendations. (7)

4. Identify positive and negative reinforcers of current behavior practices. (7, 8, 9)

5. Describe how availability of resources is affecting ability and willingness to follow medical advice. (10)

6. Develop and implement plan to acquire resources necessary for meeting medical and rehabilitational needs. (11, 12)

7. Discuss beliefs concerning what brings about recovery and wellness and how these

THERAPEUTIC INTERVENTIONS

1. Consult with the patient, patient's physician, therapists, family, and caregivers to identify the activities that the patient is performing (or failing to perform) that are interfering with rehabilitation progress and ongoing health maintenance. Identify what, when, where, in whose presence, and how often.

2. Consult with the patient, family, physician, and rehabilitation team to identify the current consequences of nonadherence to rehabilitation recommendations, as well as potential long-term damaging effects.

3. Inquire into the patient's goals for recovery. Ask him/her how current behavior relates to long-term goals.

4. Talk with the patient about the targeted noncompliance behavior. Inquire into whether the patient believes that he/she is follow-

beliefs might be influencing current behaviors. (13)

8. Cooperate with psychodiagnostic procedures to identify psychiatric disorders that might be affecting decision making and lack of cooperation with treatment program. (14, 15, 17, 24)

9. Participate willingly in neuropsychological testing to identify cognitive factors that might be affecting judgment of current situation and ability to follow through on plan. (16, 17, 24)

10. Accept referral for treatment of psychiatric conditions. (18, 19)

11. Take psychotropic medications regularly as prescribed and report on effectiveness and side effects. (20, 21)

12. Verbalize accurate understanding of medical condition, treatment options, and anticipated outcomes. (22, 23, 24)

13. Responsible individual agrees to assist with decision making if patient is deemed incompetent to make medical and/or personal decisions. (24, 25, 26, 27)

14. Verbalize understanding of and willingness to accept consequences of decisions regarding medical care. (28, 29, 30, 31)

15. Cooperate with efforts to assure basic safety and well-being if selected course of

ing recommendations, factors affecting current behavior, and the patient's understanding of short- and long-term implications of current behavior.

5. If the patient denies consistent nonadherence, sensitively inform him/her about others' reports concerning behavior that is presumed to undermine treatment effectiveness.

6. Encourage the patient to vocalize anger or other feelings following confrontation, and inquire into the patient's perspective on how others' observations could differ from those of the patient.

7. Identify the patient's "motivation quotient": clarify how much work (pain, discomfort, etc.) the target behavior requires in comparison to the value of the expected outcome as well as the patient's perceived probability of achieving that outcome.

8. Talk with the patient, family, caregivers, and therapists about the identified noncompliant behavior. Clarify antecedent and consequent events in order to define reinforcement contingencies affecting the patient's adherence to treatment recommendations.

9. In a family therapy session, inquire about the targeted noncompliance behavior and observe emotions and

action is one that treating professionals cannot justify or support. (32, 33, 34, 35)

16. Give honest answers to questions about treatment options and therapeutic activities that would be acceptable, potentially tolerable, or totally unacceptable. (36, 37)

17. Identify beliefs and thoughts that interfere with seeing purpose and value in therapeutic activities. (38)

18. Implement positive self-talk that fosters motivation and encourages follow-through on therapeutic recommendations. (39, 40, 41)

19. Describe preliminary rehabilitation treatment plan that is consistent with personal and therapy goals. (42, 43)

20. Evaluate effectiveness of rehabilitation plan on a regular basis, and modify as needed. (44, 45, 46)

21. Therapists, family, and others significant to the patient provide frequent reinforcement for cooperation with the treatment plan during the initial weeks of implementation. (47, 48)

22. Identify ways to increase short-term rewards for recommended therapeutic activities. (49, 50, 51)

23. Report on progress toward accomplishment of long-term goals. (52, 53)

behaviors displayed by the patient and family members. Pay attention to repeating patterns (e.g., one member making excuses for the patient, the patient attempting to aggravate particular family member, etc.).

10. Assess whether the patient has the financial or social resources to follow through on recommendations (e.g., can afford to pay for medications, has someone who will assist with portion of home exercise program that the patient cannot do independently, etc.).

11. Coordinate referral to social services or community agencies that can assist the patient in acquiring financial or other resources necessary for successful rehabilitation.

12. Address the patient's reluctance to seek assistance from community agencies, reminding the patient that in all probability his/her taxpayer contributions have helped others in similar situations in earlier years.

13. Inquire into the patient's health, religious, cultural, or other beliefs (e.g., healing should occur without use of medications; people get stronger by resting as much as possible; it is not necessary to adapt to physical changes because God will perform a miraculous cure) that might have relevance to

24. Acknowledge the possibility that some disability may persist for the foreseeable future, and allow self to grieve. (53, 54, 55)

25. Talk with others experiencing similar disability challenges or situations. (56)

26. Identify ways that interests and goals might be pursued even if disability persists. (57, 58)

27. Family vocalize understanding of patient's condition, therapy needs, and implications of condition for future activities. (59)

28. Family, caretakers, therapists, and others who are significant to the patient reinforce his/her behavior in ways to increase the likelihood of its long-term persistence. (48, 60)

29. Family acknowledge that the goals of all members must be taken into account in family decision making and resource allocation in order to promote healthy functioning over the long term. (61, 62)

—. _____
_____

—. _____
_____

—. _____
_____

the patient's lack of follow-through on particular medical recommendations.

14. Conduct or arrange for a psychodiagnostic interview to identify factors such as denial, depression, anxiety, addictions, personality disorders, or other psychiatric conditions that might be affecting the patient's cooperation with the rehabilitation treatment.

15. Conduct or refer for psychological testing to clarify psychiatric diagnostic issues.

16. Conduct or refer for neuropsychological testing to identify cognitive problems affecting insight, judgment, memory, or other cognitive skills necessary to grasp the significance of recommendations and to follow through on them.

17. Give feedback to the patient (family), physician, rehabilitation team, and other designated parties regarding assessment results and recommendations.

18. Refer for or initiate treatment to address psychiatric disorders that may be causing, coexisting with, or maintaining problems in following medical recommendations.

19. Address the patient's (and family's) questions and concerns about diagnosis and planned treatment for psychiatric disorders.

20. Consult with the patient's treating physician about how medication for psychiatric conditions will be prescribed, monitored, and managed.

21. Assist the patient (and family) in getting answers to questions they might have about medications and side effects.

22. Coordinate efforts to provide additional information to the patient regarding medical condition in words that are compatible with his/her cognitive skills and stage of emotional acceptance.

23. Ask the patient to explain own medical condition, treatment options, and likely outcomes; clarify any misinformation.

24. Determine whether the patient's decision-making competence has been compromised to the degree that decisions must be made by a legally designated representative.

25. Document in the medical record the opinion that the patient is not competent to make a specific decision, including the facts supporting the opinion.

26. Inquire about whether the patient has made legal arrangements for someone to serve as the decision maker in the event of patient's incapacity.

27. Follow procedures outlined in applicable laws to determine who should act as decision maker for patient and how this decision-making ability is to be conferred and implemented.

28. Outline the patient's options (e.g., patient can remain in rehabilitation program only if he/she attends therapies and attempts exercises; patient can be discharged from rehabilitation center, but must go to nursing home or hire attendants to assist in own home; to respect religious beliefs, patient may refuse medications if the patient or his/her legal representative sign statement that this action is against medical recommendations and may lead to a worsening of the patient's health) regarding rehabilitation interventions and probable consequences for each. Ask the patient to repeat options, using own words.

29. Ask the patient or designated decision maker to choose among available options for how, whether, or where rehabilitation care will be provided.

30. Communicate the patient's (decision maker's) choice regarding rehabilitation plan to treating professionals and other designated persons. Coordinate plan to implement choice.

31. Inform the patient and/or responsible person if selected choice of rehabilitation plan is one that treating professionals cannot implement, considering medical, legal, ethical, or other factors (e.g., the patient refuses recommended physical therapy exercises and insists that the only thing he will do is "walk" in parallel bars; patient who had recent seizure and is distractible following brain injury continues to drive despite laws prohibiting same). Clarify consequences such as discharge from therapy program or physician notifying driver's license bureau of the patient's medical condition.

32. If treatment is to be terminated prematurely, speak with legal counsel if necessary to determine that professionals have met their responsibilities.

33. Consult with treatment team regarding the patient's need for assistance due to physical, emotional, or cognitive limitations.

34. Refer to social services, state department of adult protective services, or other professionals to assist in identifying resources needed to assure the patient's safety after discharge.

35. Request that the patient (or legally responsible person)

sign statement outlining the decision that has been made, the discharge arrangements, and the professionals' anticipations of the consequences.

36. Inquire into the patient's degree of willingness to implement each of the therapeutic recommendations, and assist patient in verbalizing factors underlying reluctance or refusal.

37. Point out inconsistencies in what the patient says he/she would be willing to do and what he/she has been doing recently, and inquire into what has changed such that the patient now expects to carry out these actions.

38. Assist the patient in identifying negative beliefs (e.g., "What is the point in doing leg exercises if I won't be able to walk?"; "I don't believe in putting chemicals into my body") that appear to be limiting him/her in getting full benefit from the rehabilitation program.

39. Teach the patient positive alternative beliefs (e.g., "These exercises keep my legs from getting stiff, making it easier for met to get in and out of the car; therefore, my friends will be more willing to pick me up to go to parties" or "Taking this medication will restore 'normal' brain chemistry")

that would support the patient's following through on recommendations and maintaining health.

40. Create a system that will assist the patient in remembering realistic beliefs to counter negative, distorted ones (e.g., section in daily planner or memory book labeled "Thoughts About Recovery," with columns listing negative thoughts and more positive, motivating thoughts; notes on wall listing purpose of rehabilitation).

41. During psychotherapy or other therapeutic meetings with the patient, ask, "What are you thinking about your exercises (diet, etc.)?" Ask the patient whether this thought is helpful or not, and have him/her suggest (and perhaps write down) a more useful, though still realistic, thought.

42. Discuss the therapeutic recommendations with the patient and ask him/her to suggest modifications that would make them acceptable and practical.

43. Coordinate communication among the patient, family, physician, therapists, and other relevant individuals to develop a treatment plan that is acceptable to all.

44. Consult with the patient, (family), (caregivers), and

therapists to develop a system to document at consistent, frequent intervals the patient's accomplishment of therapeutic rehabilitation activities, progress toward interim therapy goals, and problems with the treatment plan.

45. Review records of activities and goal accomplishment during meetings with the patient and inquire into his/her thoughts and feelings associated with rehabilitation program and results.

46. Coordinate follow-up communication with relevant family members, caregivers, and professionals to address problems with treatment plan and to agree upon adjustments.

47. Educate the patient, family, caregivers, and therapists about types (positive, negative, extinction, punishment) and schedules (fixed/random, interval/ratio) of reinforcements and their impact on behavior.

48. Recommend that therapists, family, and caregivers use positive reinforcement after *every* occurrence of the desired behavior during the initial weeks of the effort.

49. Inquire into techniques that the patient thinks might help sustain motivation, and follow through on rec-

ommendations (e.g., listing each therapy and crossing it out as it is completed; keeping a graph of walking distance; videotaping favorite television show and watching it during exercise session; going out to lunch with attendant at end of week if all the exercises for that week are complete).

50. Ask if the patient experiences any short-term benefit as a result of following recommendations (e.g., decreased pain level, decreased stress level, pride in accomplishing something difficult, increased physical conditioning).

51. Explore the possibility of accomplishing therapeutic activity in a more interesting, enjoyable way (e.g., exercising at a health club rather than at home; participating in aquatic exercises; collecting new recipes that are consistent with dietary needs and putting them in an attractive folder or box; using exercise bicycle on deck overlooking garden rather than using it in basement).

52. Periodically discuss the patient's long-term goals and inquire into patient's point of view about whether he/she is progressing toward them. Ask the patient to give specific evidence for stated opinions.

53. Listen for statements suggesting that the patient believes long-term goals will not be achieved. With great sensitivity, help the patient to verbalize this belief.

54. Inquire into the patient's opinions and feelings about what life would be like if patient were to be left with a level of disability greater than what he/she had expected.

55. Schedule psychotherapy to assist the patient in dealing with grief and other emotional reactions following realization that functional recovery may be less than 100 percent. (See Depression/Grief chapter in this Planner.)

56. Discuss with the patient the potential advantages of networking with others having a similar disability (e.g., attending support groups, sending e-mail, reading Internet Web pages from advocacy organizations, subscribing to publications for persons having disabilities, or joining patient-focused self-help organizations).

57. Gently challenge the patient to identify alternative ways that he/she might be able to achieve important goals, even if some degree of disability remains (e.g., enjoy watching sports if unable to play; participating in social

groups or volunteer activities to increase opportunities to meet someone to date).

58. Refer the patient to resources (e.g., recreation therapist, occupational therapist, vocational counselor) to assist him/her in achieving greater community integration, given persistent disability.

59. Arrange for family (caregiver) education so that family and caregivers understand long-term therapy plan and the implications for failure to implement it.

60. Emphasize to family (caregivers) the importance of using positive reinforcement periodically once the patient has been following therapy recommendations for several weeks.

61. Encourage family members to verbalize their own needs, and support each of them in meeting those needs.

62. Schedule family meeting (including the patient) to discuss the needs of the entire family system and the importance of prioritizing the needs of each member from time to time in order to promote healthy long-term family functioning.

__. _____

_____

_____.   _____
          _____
_____.   _____
          _____

DIAGNOSTIC SUGGESTIONS

Axis I: 309.3   Adjustment Disorder With Disturbance of
                       Conduct
              309.4   Adjustment Disorder With Mixed Disturbance
                       of Emotions and Conduct
              309.9   Adjustment Disorder, Unspecified
              316   Psychological Factor (Specify) Affecting
                       (General Medical Condition)
              V15.81   Noncompliance With Treatment
              V62.4   Acculturation Problem

              _____   _____

Axis II: 301.83   Borderline Personality Disorder
              301.9   Personality Disorder NOS
              799.9   Diagnosis Deferred
              V71.09   No Diagnosis

              _____   _____
              _____   _____

SEXUAL ACTING OUT

BEHAVIORAL DEFINITIONS

1. Occupies public or semipublic area with private body parts or underclothing exposed (e.g., female patient lies in bed with blouse unbuttoned and opened; male patient sits in wheelchair with trousers' zipper open).
2. Masturbates in public or semipublic area, without attempting to establish privacy (e.g., before masturbating does not ask nurse to pull curtain or close door to room, masturbates while sitting in wheelchair beside nurses' station, puts hands down pants when therapist arrives to help dress patient).
3. Asks for more assistance than is judged necessary in cleansing or dressing genital area.
4. Touches or attempts to touch therapist's breasts, thighs, or genital region.
5. Attempts to kiss staff person when staff person is performing tasks that put him/her within patient's personal space.
6. Makes sexually suggestive comments (e.g., "Give me a kiss honey!" or "I wish you were in bed with me!").
7. Makes flirtatious remarks that generate uncomfortable feelings for therapists (e.g., "I could look at your beautiful blue eyes all day"; "You sure have great muscles; I'd like to see more of them"; "You sure are cute—why aren't you married yet?").
8. Invites staff to have romantically-based relationship (e.g., "I want your phone number so I can call you for a date"; "Would you spend a week with me at the beach next month?"; "I know a romantic restaurant that I would love to introduce you to").
9. Asks third party about another staff person's intimate relationships or sexual life (e.g., "Are Dr. Smith and her husband having trouble conceiving?"; "Is Joanne lesbian?"; "Carl seems like he's not getting enough at home, if you know what I mean").
10. Repeatedly tells off-color, sexually provocative jokes.

11. Talks indiscriminately about sexual life and activities.
12. Leaves sexually arousing printed material or overtly sexual objects within view of staff persons or visitors.
13. Makes undesired sexual advances toward partner, especially when others may be observing.

—. _____

_____

—. _____

_____

—. _____

_____

LONG-TERM GOALS

1. Behave in ways that are congruent with cultural, legal, and societal expectations regarding nudity, privacy, and sexual activity.
2. Respect the professional nature of the therapist-patient relationship by refraining from sexually suggestive actions or words.

Note: The authors acknowledge that ethical guidelines regarding the establishment of personal relationships with patients vary among professional disciplines. The philosophical underpinnings of interventions in this chapter are based on the *Ethical Principles of Psychologists and Code of Conduct* (American Psychological Association, 1992). These principles prohibit a psychologist from engaging "in sexual intimacies with a former therapy patient or client for at least two years after cessation or termination of professional services" (American Psychological Association, 1992, §4.07a). If relationships are established after two years have elapsed, the burden falls on the therapist to demonstrate that there has been no exploitation of the former patient. Multiple relationships with current patients (e.g., contracting with a patient to serve as one's real estate agent, taking advantage of a patient's offer to buy products his/her company sells at a discount, etc.) are also discouraged; the therapist is cautioned to consider whether these relationships might compromise the psychologist's judgment or effectiveness.

It is the authors' bias that, even when professional ethical guidelines allow for dual and/or romantic relationships with a patient, the therapist is responsible for putting the patient's long-term physical, medical, and psychological welfare above the convenience or pleasure anticipated from the relationship. Serious consideration should be given to potential negative consequences to the patient before entering into such a relationship. Therapists would be wise to consult with a neutral colleague before agreeing to participate in dual or romantic relationships with a patient.

3. Communicate feelings about another's attractiveness in a way that is enjoyable to the other person and not embarrassing, humiliating, or sexually provocative.
4. Express anger, frustration, and dissatisfaction directly rather than by acting out sexually in ways that humiliate or embarrass others.
5. Acknowledge concerns about sexuality and sexual relationships in a direct way that can be addressed by honest communication.
6. Negotiate a sexual relationship with a partner in a way that respectfully considers the needs and expressiveness style of the partner.

___. _____

_____

___. _____

_____

___. _____

_____

SHORT-TERM OBJECTIVES

1. Cooperate with efforts to identify the circumstances surrounding episodes of sexually inappropriate behavior. (1, 2, 3)
2. Verbalize the degree to which the sexually inappropriate behavior is volitional, and the perceived degree of discomfort that others appear to have with this behavior. (4, 5)
3. Describe preinjury/preillness style of sexual expression. (6)
4. Significant others contrast patient's current pattern of sexual behavior with preinjury/preillness style of sexual expression. (7, 8)

THERAPEUTIC INTERVENTIONS

1. Interview staff, family, or relevant persons to specifically determine what the patient is doing that seems inappropriate and the ways in which the behavior is troublesome to various persons. Clarify when, where, and how often the behavior occurs, being attentive to antecedent and consequent events.
2. Observe the patient in those conditions in which the reported inappropriate sexual behavior occurs. Notice what is happening before the onset of the behavior. Note how the patient and others respond to

5. Identify fears about the effect of the medical condition on one's sexual life. (9, 10)

6. Cooperate with psychodiagnostic procedures to identify coexisting psychiatric conditions that might be affecting behavior and coping. (11, 12, 14)

7. Cooperate with neuropsychological assessment. (13, 14)

8. Participate in therapy activities that are structured to reduce opportunities for inappropriate physical contact. (15)

9. Listen attentively to therapist's explanation of imminent actions and follow directive given. (16)

10. Agree to guidelines describing appropriate expression of sexuality in the rehabilitation setting. (17, 18)

11. Accept feedback from therapists and family about their reactions to sexual behavior and about acceptable ways of interacting. (19, 20, 21)

12. Participate in behavioral intervention to reduce unacceptable sexual behaviors and/or institute those that are comfortable to self and others. (22, 23, 24)

13. Demonstrate ability to express sexual feelings and concerns in ways that are socially acceptable, straightforward, and respectful. (25, 26, 27, 28)

the behavior, being attentive to potential reinforcement contingencies.

3. Explore with the patient, therapists, family, and other relevant persons the typical consequences of patient's sexual behavior (e.g., therapist stops painful stretching exercise; therapist blushes and smiles; family talks with patient at length about why he/she must not behave this way). Assess the patient's awareness of and reaction to these consequences, noting what he/she says as well as his/her facial expression and body language.

4. Explore the patient's awareness of the inappropriateness of his/her sexual behavior and the negative impact of this behavior on others.

5. Listen calmly as the patient explains why he/she is behaving in a sexually inappropriate manner, and try to understand the meaning and purpose of the identified behavior to the patient.

6. Ask the patient about pertinent aspects of his/her sexual history, including sexual preference, availability of partner(s), frequency of sexual encounters, and modes of sexual expression.

7. Ask the patient's sexual partner about how the patient's current behavior differs from that observed prior to the injury or illness.

14. Acknowledge success in managing sexual feelings in ways that are acceptable to self, staff, partner, and family. (29, 30)

15. Identify and resolve anger, powerlessness, or other emotions that underlie sexual acting out. (31, 32, 33)

16. Describe perception of body image, relationship role, and other issues that negatively affect sexual identity and self-esteem. (34, 35)

17. Patient (partner, family) obtain information about ways in which changes in brain functioning may be affecting sexual desire, sexual responsiveness, sexual performance, emotional responses, or social judgment. (36, 37, 38)

18. Participate in therapy sessions with sexual partner to address sexual relationship issues. (39, 40, 41)

19. Educate self about ways to compensate for injury-related/illness-related limitations during sexual activities. (42)

20. Sexual partner (and family) demonstrate ability to give patient feedback about inappropriate behavior. (19, 20, 21, 43, 44)

21. Sexual partner (and family) describe emotional response(s) to patient's inappropriate sexual behavior and demonstrate ability to

8. Ask the patient's partner, family, and/or friends to describe how the patient's current sexual allusions (off-color jokes, open flirting with therapists, keeping magazines with nude photos) differ from his/her sexualized behaviors prior to the injury/illness.

9. While putting the patient at ease, inquire into questions and concerns about the impact of his/her medical condition on sexual attractiveness and performance.

10. Review the patient's medical record and/or consult with referring physician to identify site of brain lesion(s), medications, illnesses, injuries, or other medical factors that might be affecting level of sexual desire, ability to perform sexually, and ability to control impulses.

11. Refer for or perform psychodiagnostic interview to identify depression, substance abuse, or other psychiatric conditions that might be influencing the patient's sexual acting out.

12. Administer or refer for psychological tests to identify depression, substance abuse, personality disorder, or other conditions affecting patient's actions and coping abilities.

13. Refer for or administer neuropsychological testing to

work through these emotions in a constructive way. (45, 46)

—. _____
    _____

—. _____
    _____

—. _____
    _____

identify cognitive deficits (e.g., disinhibition, impulsivity, memory) that might explain why patient fails to inhibit sexual comments, gestures, or activities, or might affect the manner in which the therapist intervenes to address sexual behavior problems.

14. Give feedback to the patient (family), treatment team, referring physician, and other designated parties regarding assessment results and recommendations.

15. Recommend that therapists structure their interactions with the patient so as to reduce opportunities for the patient to make physical contact (e.g., therapist extend arms fully while working and keeps face, chest, etc. beyond easy reach of the patient; ask the patient to grasp a towel or hold siderails on bed while positioning him/her for transfer; sit far enough from the patient that he/she cannot easily make physical contact) during therapeutic activity.

16. Advise therapist to make short, clear statement of what activity they are about to begin (e.g., "I am going to look in your mouth to see that you have swallowed your medication"; "I am going to show you how you can put your pants on") in order to focus the patient's

attention on therapeutic activity.

17. Discuss the expectations for the patient's behavior while in rehabilitation (e.g., arrange for privacy before engaging in sexual activity, perform self-care tasks with only the therapeutically prescribed amount of assistance, do not kiss therapists, etc.), mentioning only those guidelines that apply to the problem(s) the patient has demonstrated.

18. Using language and/or pictograms suited to the patient's level of understanding, write down guidelines regarding patient's sexually offensive behavior. Put guidelines in a place that will be easily accessed by patient (but not easily seen by visitors, if the patient [or family] prefer), and communicate them to his/her rehabilitation team (and family).

19. Instruct therapists (and family) to point out inappropriate behavior while it is occurring or immediately afterward (e.g., "Take your hand off my breast!"; "It is *not* okay to say that [i.e., explicit sexual comment] to me"; "That is a very personal question about [another rehabilitation professional] and it is not appropriate for you to be asking anyone about that").

20. Suggest that therapist (and family) inform the patient about feelings that his/her sexual behavior creates (e.g., "I feel uncomfortable when you keep telling me how pretty my eyes are"; "I am frustrated that you continue to ask me for my home phone number when I have told you that I am not available to go out with you"; "I am embarrassed when you say in front of my family that you can't wait to get in bed with me").

21. Recommend that therapists (and family) suggest socially appropriate ways for the patient to manage his/her sexual feelings (e.g., "It is fine for you to let me know that you enjoy working with me"; "Would you like us to arrange for you to have some private time with your husband?"; "We can kiss after our visitors have left!").

22. Develop unambiguous, observable definitions for the offensive, sexual, target behavior(s), and measure the baseline frequency and/or intensity of the target behavior.

23. Develop a behavioral plan that specifies what staff or family should say or do when they observe the offensive, sexual, target behavior(s), and how they should record the occur-

rence of the target behavior. Communicate this plan, along with its implementation date, to the patient, patient's partner, patient's family, and rehabilitation therapists.

24. Monitor the consistency of implementation of the behavioral plan and its effectiveness in impacting the target sexual behavior. Modify as needed, keeping the rehabilitation team, patient, partner, and family informed about changes.

25. Assist the patient in verbalizing what he/she intended to occur as a result of the inappropriate sexual behavior.

26. Ask the patient to identify several ways, other than sexual acting out (e.g., agree to talk about fears that no one will ever date him/her again; invite the patient's partner to join the patient's psychotherapy session to discuss the failed effort at sexual intercourse the previous weekend; thank therapist for the way he/she reduces fear and instills confidence), to achieve his/her desired goal for the sexual behaviors.

27. Role-play with the patient several scenarios that could lead to accomplishment of the goal of the sexual behavior, and discuss the feelings that would likely be elicited by all involved.

28. Assign the patient to "try out" one of the alternate, socially acceptable behaviors in a real-life situation and report on the results.

29. Point out the patient's success in changing sexual behaviors that were upsetting to others and in managing behavior in a way that is comfortable to all.

30. Ask the patient to describe satisfaction and other positive mood states associated with expressing feelings of attractiveness, liking, or closeness in ways that respect professional boundaries or privacy needs.

31. Assist the patient in exploring those emotions that are associated with sexually explicit or provocative behavior. Be sensitive to indications that the provocative behavior is a way of expressing anger or resolving powerlessness (or other emotions), and discuss this possibility with the patient.

32. Assist the patient in identifying healthy, more direct ways of dealing with anger, helplessness, or other emotions underlying sexual acting out.

33. Assist the patient in working through the painful emotions that underlie sexual acting out.

34. Inquire into the ways in which the patient feels that

his/her sexual attractiveness might have been diminished by changes in his/her body, appearance, or abilities.

35. Assist the patient in identifying ways in which he/she might regain a sense of sexual attractiveness (e.g., choice of flattering clothing and accessories, experiencing pride in accomplishments, complimenting partner).

36. Coordinate educational session with the patient (partner, family), physicians, neuropsychologist, psychologist, or other professionals to discuss how medical and/or cognitive factors are affecting desire for sexual contact, expression of desire, and ability to participate in intimate sexual encounters.

37. Refer the patient (partner, family) to support groups or advocacy organizations specific to patient's condition.

38. Refer the patient (and partner) to peer counselor who can normalize concerns and emotions about sexual problems and indicate that others have dealt with similar problems.

39. Conduct or refer for conjoint therapy to address the impact of the patient's illness/injury and its physical, emotional, and behavioral sequelae on intimate relating.

40. In a conjoint session, encourage the patient and his/her partner to openly discuss role changes and the impact these have on the relationship dynamics and sense of sexual attraction.

41. Conduct or refer for sexual counseling or sex therapy that will focus on resolution of sexual dysfunction problems.

42. Coordinate educational sessions between the patient (patient's partner) and physical therapist, occupational therapist, rehabilitation nurse, or other professional(s) to address ways in which the patient and his/her partner might reduce the impact of physical limitations (e.g., hemiparesis) or medical devices (e.g., catheter) on sexual activity. (See Sexual Dysfunction chapter in this Planner.)

43. Meet with the patient's sexual partner (and family) to develop a plan for describing constructive, therapeutic responses to inappropriate sexual behavior.

44. Identify and address partner's (family's) reservations that might interfere with the partner (family) carrying out a plan of constructive responses to the patient's inappropriate sexual behavior.

45. Encourage the patient's partner (family) to verbalize

what they feel and think when patient engages in off-putting or offensive sexual activity. Assist the partner (family) to recognize that these are normal feelings.

46. Assist the patient's partner (family) in working through anger, frustration, and embarrassment that follow patient's sexual acting out, and identify ways in which they can share these feelings in a constructive way with him/her.

__. _____
   _____

__. _____
   _____

__. _____
   _____

DIAGNOSTIC SUGGESTIONS

Axis I:

294.9	Cognitive Disorder NOS
310.1	Personality Change Due to (General Medical Condition)
625.8	Other Female Sexual Dysfunction Due to (General Medical Condition)
608.89	Other Male Sexual Dysfunction Due to (General Medical Condition)
309.3	Adjustment Disorder With Disturbance of Conduct
_____	_____
_____	_____

SEXUAL DYSFUNCTION

BEHAVIORAL DEFINITIONS

1. Decreased satisfaction in sexual relationship since injury/illness.
2. Concerns about ability to form intimate partnerships.
3. Significant change in interest in and frequency of sexual activity, leading to relational difficulties.
4. Erectile dysfunction.
5. Orgasmic dysfunction.
6. Paralysis, weakness, or pain interfere with sexual activity.
7. Decreased sensation interferes with enjoyment of sexual activity.
8. Fatigue interferes with sexual relationship.
9. Unsafe use of contraception.
10. Failure to protect self and partner from sexually-transmitted diseases.

__. _____
    _____
__. _____
    _____
__. _____
    _____

LONG-TERM GOALS

1. Obtain satisfaction with partner in a variety of physical expressions of affection and attraction.
2. Display confidence in ability to meet people and form intimate relationships despite medical changes.
3. Accommodate to changed sensory and motor functioning affecting sexual activities.

4. Work cooperatively with physician and rehabilitation team in planning contraception.
5. Practice safe-sex methods.

___. _____

_____

___. _____

_____

___. _____

_____

SHORT-TERM OBJECTIVES

1. Provide information about anticipated or actual problems in enjoying sexual activities since the injury/illness. (1, 2, 3, 4)

2. Describe the impact of sensory or motor changes on sexual activity. (5)

3. Identify the effects of physical and mental changes on one's body image and perceived sexual attractiveness. (6)

4. Cooperate with an evaluation of medical factors affecting sexual interest and activity. (7, 8, 11)

5. Willingly provide information about neuropsychological functioning. (9, 11)

6. Participate in an evaluation of depression, anxiety, chemical dependency problems, or other psychiatric problems interfering with sexual functioning. (10, 11)

THERAPEUTIC INTERVENTIONS

1. Identify specific problems in the patient's level of sexual desire and performance.

2. Explore the patient's experiences in dating and sexual activity. Ask about patient's concerns regarding the potential negative effects of the injury/illness on his/her dating life and ability to find a partner.

3. Interview the patient and/or partner regarding their usual pattern of sexual relating and how their sexual relationship has been changed since the injury/illness.

4. Refer for, or perform, an evaluation of the patient's satisfaction with his/her sexual functioning using structured assessment techniques (e.g., the Derogatis Interview for Sexual Function [Derogatis]).

7. Partner describe the impact that patient's illness-related/injury-related deficits have on partner's feelings of attraction and closeness to him/her. (12)

8. Identify the contribution of fatigue and stress on sexual interest and satisfaction. (13, 14, 15)

9. Describe preexisting sources of relationship stress that have been reactivated with the illness/injury. (16)

10. Agree to participate in treatment to address psychiatric disorders. (17)

11. Partner acknowledge own emotional needs and seek support to help with the stress associated with managing the patient's injury/illness. (18)

12. Couple accept referral to conjoint/marital therapy to resolve preexisting relationship issues that are interfering with adaptation to circumstances changed by the patient's illness/injury. (19)

13. Implement actions to improve self-esteem and sense of attractiveness, and report on results. (20)

14. Frankly discuss thoughts and feelings regarding the loss of, or lack of, a relationship partner. (21)

15. Describe tentative plans to address sexual feelings during the time that a relation-

5. Inquire about the degree to which physical conditions (e.g., hemiparesis, decreased sensation in parts of body, pain) are affecting the patient's ability to obtain enjoyment from sexual activities.

6. Assess how the patient's body image and perceived sexual attractiveness have changed since the illness/injury, asking the patient to give specific examples of factors influencing his/her opinion.

7. Review the patient's medical record and/or consult with his/her physician to identify medical factors (e.g., diabetes, vascular disease, alcoholism) that might be influencing the patient's sexual functioning.

8. Talk with the patient's physician or consult with a pharmacist about the possible effects of medications on the patient's sexual arousal and performance.

9. Review recent neuropsychological or cognitive test results, or refer for (perform) neuropsychological testing to identify the degree to which cognitive impairments are contributing to the patient's changed social behaviors (e.g., apathy, disinhibition) and to identify cognitive resources that may be effective in compensation efforts.

ship partner is unavailable. (22)

16. Identify problems anticipated when resuming dating and practice ways to handle awkward situations. (23, 24)

17. Describe the time framework for the development of sexual problems after a brain event and verbalize an understanding that improvement may be gradual or incomplete. (25, 26)

18. Describe perception of what constitutes sexual behavior. (27)

19. Talk honestly with partner about concerns associated with resuming sexual activity; listen carefully to partner's concerns as well. (28, 29)

20. Discuss concerns with physician about the potential negative medical consequences of sexual activity. (30)

21. Consult with physician about the contraceptive options that are available; select the most appropriate method and implement it according to instructions. (31)

22. Verbalize how role and responsibility changes can affect the feelings of sexual attraction in the relationship. (32, 33)

23. Work cooperatively with therapists to increase the ability to perform hygiene,

10. Refer for or perform a psychodiagnostic interview to evaluate depression, anxiety, chemical dependency, or other psychiatric disorders negatively impacting the patient's sexual relationship.

11. Give feedback to the patient (partner), physician, rehabilitation team, and other designated persons about assessment results and recommendations.

12. Encourage the patient's partner to describe disability-related changes (e.g., drooling, aphasia, hemiparesis) affecting his/her level of sexual attraction to the patient; address those problems that perhaps can be better managed by referring partner to particular rehabilitation therapist.

13. Inquire into the effect of fatigue on sexual desire and enjoyment by asking the patient and partner to identify circumstances surrounding the times when their sexual experiences have been most satisfying.

14. Facilitate a discussion of stressors (e.g., financial pressure, child whose grades are failing, no time to relax because of extra time needed for dressing and grooming) brought on by the injury/illness that may affect sexual functioning.

dressing, and other basic tasks with less assistance. (34)

24. Partner delegate assistance with patient's toileting, bathing, and basic hygiene to attendant, adult child, or other individual, if possible. (35)

25. Identify own and partner's preferences for sensual touch. (36)

26. Try out rehabilitation therapist's recommended ways to compensate during sexual activity for changes in mobility resulting from the medical event. (37)

27. Talk with partner about degree of enjoyment using various physical positions for intercourse; agree to eliminate those that are unpleasant for either partner. (38)

28. Consult with the patient's physician about adjustments that could be made in medications to reduce those side effects interfering with sexual functioning. (39, 40)

29. Plan timing of sexual activity to optimize enjoyment. (41, 42)

30. Consider that tactile sensitivity may be reduced on one side of the genital area; focus on stimulating the nonaffected side. (43)

31. Incorporate actions to increase the intensity of sexual stimulation in lovemaking

15. Assess other stressful situations (e.g., caring for a parent with dementia, raising a child with Down's syndrome, launching a new business) that the couple is facing in addition to those associated with this medical event.

16. Ask about issues that had caused relationship conflict prior to the illness/injury (e.g., patient's excessive drinking, extramarital affair, poor money management) and inquire about how these issues may be affecting the couple's emotional reaction to the patient's disability (e.g., patient involved in automobile accident while intoxicated; partner resents having to care for the patient when she was ignored earlier; couple has limited savings and no disability insurance because one partner insisted on expensive car and clothes).

17. Initiate or refer the patient for treatment of depression, anxiety, substance abuse, or other psychiatric disorders affecting sexual desire and performance. (See Depression/Grief, Anxiety/Fear, Posttraumatic Stress Disorder, Substance Abuse, or other relevant chapters in this Planner.)

18. Recommend that the patient's partner seek evaluation of his/her need for

activities, if both partners agree. (44)

32. Agree to a referral to a sexual counselor to assist with working through emotional and relationship barriers to adjusting sexual life to the new circumstances. (45)

33. Accept a referral to a medical specialist to diagnose and treat medical conditions interfering with sexual relationship. (46, 47, 48)

34. Implement physician's recommendations to enhance one's enjoyment of sexual activity; report back to physician on effectiveness and complications. (49)

35. Report comfort in managing urinary catheters during sexual activity. (50)

36. Describe and implement procedures to minimize risk of bladder or bowel incontinence during sex. (51)

37. Partner demonstrate skill in giving prompt objective feedback when patient acts in embarrassing, socially inappropriate ways. (52)

38. Report accurate knowledge about ways to reduce the risk of transmission of sexually transmitted diseases and the risk of conception; describe consistent adherence to "safe sex" practices. (53, 54)

__. _____

_____

psychotherapy and/or a support group to deal with the emotions and stress associated with caregiving.

19. Refer for or perform conjoint/marital therapy to deal with couple's unresolved relationship problems.

20. Ask the patient to name specific actions (e.g., getting dressed every morning in attractive outfit, having a weekly manicure) that he/she would be willing to implement to improve own sense of physical attractiveness. Encourage the patient to try at least two actions and report on the effects in the next therapy session.

21. Identify the patient's feelings about the loss of, or lack of, a sexual partner. Process associated feelings and their impact on the patient's self-esteem.

22. Inquire into options the patient is considering in order to deal with the lack of a partner (e.g., waiting until one "meets the right person" and gets married, use of a dating service to facilitate meeting people, meet people through support group, masturbation) and facilitate the patient's exploration of the positive and negative aspects of each activity.

—. _____

_____

—. _____

_____

23. Brainstorm with the patient about ways that he/she might resume social life (e.g., attend brain injury support group social activities; participate in Sunday school class at church; go to gym to swim during hours when other single people will likely be there).

24. Help the patient identify potentially embarrassing situations that might occur in dating (e.g., having difficulty thinking of specific words; being unable to drive to pick up date; excusing self from noisy situations); role-play ways to handle these situations.

25. Educate the patient (and partner) that problems in sexual functioning may emerge months after the occurrence of the injury; recommend they contact a physician or rehabilitation professional should problems in sexual functioning develop.

26. Educate the patient (and partner) that it takes time to recover from the emotional impact of having experienced an illness or injury affecting the brain; encourage them to be patient and to set realistic expectations for themselves and the resumption of their sexual life.

27. Explore the patient's (couple's) beliefs about sexuality

(e.g., sexuality includes all the ways couples feel about each other; sexuality is hugging, kissing, and flirting; sexuality is intercourse) and the ways that he/she/they enjoy feeling close (e.g., touching, massaging, lying next to each other, intercourse).

28. Facilitate a conjoint session, or recommend that the patient talk frankly with his/her sexual partner about how each feels about the changes brought on by the injury/illness (e.g., perceptions of attractiveness, awkwardness, and self-consciousness in altering lovemaking activities) and their impact on feelings of closeness in the relationship.

29. In a conjoint session, or in a conversation with the patient's sexual partner, discuss fears and concerns regarding resumption of sexual activity (fear of causing partner pain, fear of being unable to perform, fear of having another stroke) affecting sexual relationship.

30. Recommend that the patient (and partner) consult with patient's physician to address concerns about potential negative effects of sexual activity (e.g., causing another stroke, interfering with recovery from shunt

surgery), and to clarify any restrictions on sexual activity (e.g., refrain from intercourse for specific period) related to the patient's medical condition.

31. Recommend that the patient talk with his/her physician about contraceptive techniques that are safe (e.g., do not increase risk of stroke) and practical (e.g., can be inserted or applied using one hand or through assistance of sexual partner), given current medical and physical condition.

32. Talk with the patient and his/her sexual partner about how changes in roles (e.g., husband is on disability and doesn't feel like the "breadwinner"; wife is unable to manage household and feels helpless and resentful) and responsibilities (e.g., wife taking care of patient, children, home, and yard while maintaining full-time employment) may impact sexual desire. (See Family Stress Reactions chapter in this Planner.)

33. Talk with the patient and partner about the negative effects that caretaking—especially for hygiene and basic physical tasks—can have on sexual attraction and sexual relationship satisfaction.

34. Consult with the patient's rehabilitation team about

the patient's potential to increase independence in toileting, hygiene, and basic self-care tasks through additional therapy and use of adapted equipment; coordinate referral, if appropriate.

35. Explore the possibilities of hiring an attendant or using an adult child or other person to assist the patient with toileting, bathing, personal hygiene, and basic self-care tasks in order to minimize the partner's involvement in care of patient's body areas that are also associated with sexual activity.

36. Recommend that the couple spend time acquainting themselves with what areas of the body and types of touch each enjoys.

37. Coordinate a referral to, or recommend that the patient consult with a physical or occupational therapist regarding modifications that could be implemented (e.g., use of pillows, positional changes, higher footboards, handles on headboards) to assist in positioning during sexual activities to compensate for muscle weakness, pain, or other physical limitations.

38. Suggest that the couple experiment with positions for sexual intercourse suited to the patient's physical abilities and talk with one an-

other about what was enjoyable (or not) about each.

39. Recommend that the patient (and partner) consult with the patient's physician about the risks and benefits associated with using medications having fewer negative side effects on sexual functioning in place of those that interfere with sexual arousal and/or performance.

40. Suggest that the patient (and partner) talk with the patient's physician about ways to lower the occurrence of side effects (e.g., timing sleeping pills to reduce morning sedation, taking antihypertensives after sexual activity rather than before).

41. Recommend that the patient and partner plan sexual activity for times when each will be better rested and relaxed (e.g., in the morning or afternoon rather than late at night).

42. Suggest that the patient and partner plan sexual activity for times when they will not be rushed, to allow extra time for slowed physical responses.

43. Remind the patient and partner that feeling may be decreased or lost on one side of the patient's genital area, and that he/she will probably respond more to stimulation on the unaffected side.

44. Suggest that the patient and partner consider the use of alternative ways to enhance sexual stimulation (e.g., self-stimulation during lovemaking, oral sex, use of vibrator) to compensate for changed sensory motor functioning.

45. Refer for or perform sexual counseling to address emotional reactions and other factors interfering with the patient's ability to resume a satisfying sexual life.

46. Talk with the patient's physician or suggest that the patient consider a consultation with an endocrinologist to rule out neuroendocrine problems as a basis for decreased sexual interest.

47. Recommend or coordinate the patient's referral to a gynecologist or other physician specializing in the evaluation and treatment of arousal and orgasmic dysfunction.

48. Recommend or coordinate the patient's referral to a urologist, psychiatrist, or other physician specializing in the assessment and treatment of erectile or ejaculatory dysfunction.

49. Inquire about and reinforce the patient's implementation of physician's recommendations; inquire about the effectiveness of the recommended actions and any problems.

50. Refer the patient (and partner) to the patient's physician or rehabilitation nurse to learn how to manage the patient's urinary catheter during sexual intercourse (e.g., fold catheter back over penis and cover with a condom, tape catheter tubing to abdomen or thigh, remove catheter prior to sexual activity and reinsert it later); inquire into the couple's comfort and confidence in implementing these steps.

51. Refer the patient (and partner) to his/her physician and/or rehabilitation nurse to learn ways to decrease the chances of urinary or bowel accidents during sexual intercourse (e.g., avoid consuming liquids two hours prior to intercourse; empty bladder immediately before intercourse; plan intercourse to occur within eight hours following a bowel movement).

52. Talk with the patient's partner (and the patient) about ways to manage the patient's socially inappropriate sexual behaviors (e.g., give patient clear feedback immediately after the behavior; reduce the patient's opportunities to enter situations in which the behavior is more likely to occur; reward patient for socially appropriate behaviors). (See Sexual Acting Out chapter in this Planner.)

53. Inquire into the patient's adherence to safe sexual practices and contraceptive procedures.

54. Taking into account state laws and judicial rulings governing confidentiality of psychological information, and consulting with colleagues and legal counsel as needed, make a decision regarding whether to warn the patient's sexual partner about the patient's reported sexually transmitted diseases if the patient is unwilling or unable to do so. Document this decision and the rationale in the medical record.

__. _____

_____

__. _____

_____

__. _____

_____

DIAGNOSTIC SUGGESTIONS

Axis I: 625.8   Female Hypoactive Sexual Desire Disorder Due to (General Medical Condition)

608.89   Male Hypoactive Sexual Desire Disorder Due to (General Medical Condition)

607.84   Male Erectile Disorder Due to (General Medical Condition)

625.0   Female Dyspareunia Due to (General Medical Condition)

608.89   Male Dyspareunia Due to (General Medical Condition)

	625.8	Other Female Sexual Dysfunction Due to (General Medical Condition)
	608.89	Other Male Sexual Dysfunction Due to (General Medical Condition)
	291.89	Alcohol-Induced Sexual Dysfunction
	292.89	Substance-Induced Sexual Dysfunction (Specify Substance)
	V61.10	Partner Relational Problem
	_____	_____
	_____	_____
Axis II:	V71.09	No Diagnosis
	799.9	Diagnosis Deferred
	_____	_____
	_____	_____

SPEECH PROBLEMS (APHASIA)

BEHAVIORAL DEFINITIONS

1. Inability or reduced ability to comprehend oral or written language, numerals, or arithmetic signs.
2. Fluent speech that is nonsensical or mostly unrelated to conversation.
3. Inability or difficulty in thinking of or stating specific words.
4. Inability or reduced ability to communicate thoughts or intentions in oral or written form.
5. Impaired ability to perform arithmetic operations.
6. Reduced skill in understanding or expressing meaning as conveyed through tone of voice, pauses, and other nonverbal cues.
7. Difficulty in adhering to conversation etiquette such as turn-taking.

__. _____
   _____

__. _____
   _____

__. _____
   _____

LONG-TERM GOALS

1. Develop an awareness of difficulty in language-related comprehension, and adapt activities to minimize impact on daily functioning.
2. Understand basic, everyday communication.
3. Communicate effectively in routine situations and in family and social relationships.
4. Use strategies to facilitate or compensate for residual expressive language problems.

5. Process arithmetic tasks accurately, compensating for residual deficits as needed.
6. Comprehend and communicate through inflections and pauses, compensating for residual deficits in these abilities.
7. Attend to the "rules of conversation" and nonverbal information affecting communication with minimal or no reminders from others.
8. Accept communication limitations and demonstrate a reduction in frustration and depression related to these limitations.

—. _____

_____

_____

—. _____

_____

_____

—. _____

_____

SHORT-TERM OBJECTIVES

1. Cooperate with an evaluation of cause, type, and severity of language-related deficits. (1, 2, 3, 8)

2. Participate willingly in evaluation to identify other cognitive changes that may coexist with aphasia. (4, 8)

3. Provide information about symptoms of depression, frustration, or other emotional or psychiatric syndromes. (5, 6, 7, 8)

4. Accept referral for treatment of psychological or psychiatric conditions. (9, 10)

5. Take medications regularly as prescribed and provide information to best of ability regarding effectiveness and side effects. (11, 12, 13)

THERAPEUTIC INTERVENTIONS

1. Review the patient's medical record and consult with speech pathologist to identify nature, severity, and etiology of language dysfunction; coordinate referral for neurological evaluation if necessary.

2. Observe the patient in informal conversational speech to identify his/her skill in adhering to rules of conversation and detecting intonations or facial expressions that would affect the meaning of the communication.

3. Administer or refer for language screening test or more detailed aphasia battery to further clarify language deficit.

6. Participate actively in rehabilitation activities designed to improve language
   and communication skills.
   (14, 15, 16)

7. Demonstrate communica-
   tion of "yes" and "no" responses. (17, 18, 19)

8. Increase attention to
   speaker in a quiet environment to facilitate comprehension. (20, 21)

9. Tolerate exercises designed
   to increase skills in maintaining focus on communication in the presence of
   normal background noise
   and communication. (22, 23)

10. Participate in conversations
    that are structured to pro-
    mote comprehension.
    (24, 25, 26, 27, 28)

11. Express needs, experiences,
    and concerns in simple,
    basic terms. (29, 30, 33)

12. Use aids to compensate for
    difficulties in verbal expres-
    sion. (31, 32, 33)

13. Persist in attempts to com-
    municate using words, ges-
    tures, symbols, and/or
    speech aids despite frustra-
    tion. (34, 35)

14. Report awareness of
    changed mathematical
    skills and demonstrate will-
    ingness to make adapta-
    tions. (36, 37, 38)

15. To the best of one's ability,
    communicate emotional re-
    actions to the changes intro-

4. Administer or refer for neuropsychological testing to
   identify the patient's pattern
   of language and other cognitive deficits for diagnostic,
   prognostic, and treatment
   planning purposes.

5. Inquire into the patient's
   psychiatric history and into
   current symptoms that
   would suggest depression,
   anxiety, or other psychiatric
   disorders.

6. Consult with the patient's
   therapists and family about
   behaviors such as sleep, appetite, cooperation with sessions, energy level,
   frustration tolerance, and
   change from usual personality that might lend insight into patient's
   emotional status.

7. If aphasia or other factors
   preclude obtaining valid
   history from the patient, obtain permission from patient or legally responsible
   party to obtain information
   from person(s) familiar with
   his/her history.

8. Give feedback to the patient
   (and family), treatment
   team, and other designated
   person(s) regarding assessment results and recommendations.

9. Refer for or initiate treatment for psychological/
   psychiatric disorders that
   are coexisting with the
   aphasia and affecting pa-

duced by speech problems. (35, 39, 40)

16. Indicate understanding of the impact of emotions, fatigue, minor illness, and other factors on the success of communication and demonstrate skill in managing communication under these conditions. (41, 42)

17. Accept feedback that verbalizations lack meaning or are unrelated to the conversation. (34, 43, 45, 46, 47)

18. Increase the use of "pragmatic" language skills (e.g., turn-taking). (44, 45, 46, 47)

19. Participate in activities designed to improve awareness of nonverbal aspects of communication (e.g., others' facial expressions, sarcasm, pauses, or inflections) and respond to nonverbal components as well as to verbal content. (44, 45)

20. Willingly participate in exercises to improve tonal range and inflections in speech. (46, 47, 48, 49)

21. Family members report understanding of patient's language skills and how to manage different communication problems. (50, 51, 52, 53)

22. Family members acknowledge own difficulty in coping with patient's changed communication abilities and indicate willingness to

tient's participation in treatment.

10. Address the patient's (and family's) questions and concerns about diagnosis and planned treatment for psychiatric disorders.

11. Consult with the patient's treating physician regarding use of medication to reduce patient's emotional symptoms and/or to enhance his/her ability to attend and participate in treatment; clarify how medication will be prescribed, monitored, and managed.

12. Address the patient's (and family's) concerns about medications and assist them in getting answers to questions about medications and side effects.

13. Monitor the patient's use of prescribed medications and their effect on symptoms; address issues regarding compliance and side effects.

14. Coordinate the patient's referral for speech therapy.

15. Consult with speech therapist or review the patient's medical chart to identify strategies that are currently being used to facilitate communication. Utilize those strategies in meetings with patient to maintain consistency, and reinforce the importance of the therapeutic work.

utilize support networks and resources. (54, 55)

23. Accept assistance designed to protect self from potential harm due to inability to comprehend language and/or to express self clearly. (56, 57, 58)

24. Family or other responsible person demonstrate willingness to assist in personal, medical, or financial decision making during time when aphasia interferes with making competent, informed decisions. (56, 57, 59, 60)

—. _____

  _____

—. _____

  _____

—. _____

  _____

16. Point out the patient's progress, giving specific examples, and congratulate him/her on accomplishments.

17. Inform the patient that you will be asking some simple, sometimes silly questions in order to learn how you can communicate best with him/her.

18. Ask the patient to show how he or she will indicate "yes" and "no" (e.g., saying "yes, no," nodding/shaking head, thumb up/down).

19. Ask the patient a series of simple questions about common objects that can be answered "yes" or "no," such as "Am I a man," or "Is this a book?" Note the patient's response. Cue the patient to respond, if necessary. Vary the questions so that the correct answer will sometimes be "yes" and other times "no." Give the patient feedback regarding accuracy of "yes/no" responses.

20. Decrease or eliminate background noise (e.g., turn television off when speaking to the patient; work in quiet private room).

21. If more than one person is with the patient, have individuals take turns speaking with the patient, avoiding interruptions or simultaneous conversations.

22. When the patient can reliably attend to communica-

tion in a quiet environment, introduce distractions gradually while asking the patient to continue focusing on task.

23. Point out the patient's progress in maintaining focus under distracting conditions.

24. Use brief, grammatically simple (e.g., subject, predicate, and object) sentences when speaking with the patient.

25. Select positive statements to promote comprehension (e.g., "We must wait for the nurse," instead of "We cannot go to lunch until the nurse arrives").

26. While maintaining normal inflection and volume, slow rate of speech to facilitate processing and comprehension by the patient.

27. To facilitate comprehension, freely utilize gestures as you speak (e.g., point to the door while saying "We are going to group therapy now," or mimick brushing one's teeth while asking, "Would you like to brush your teeth?").

28. Maintain rapport and working relationship with the patient by avoiding casual jokes that patient may take literally and find offensive.

29. Encourage the patient to communicate, providing structure such as asking closed questions (i.e., ques-

tions that can be answered yes or no), inquiring about photos or other personal belongings in the patient's room, and demonstrating willingness to wait while the patient searches for word.

30. Ask the patient if he/she would like you to supply the word or phrase that he/she is searching for; avoid automatically providing words for the patient.

31. Reinforce the patient's use of a communication board (i.e., a board having an assortment of pictograms to communicate, for example, that the patient is experiencing pain or has a need to void, or a board having letters of the alphabet to which the patient can point) that has been approved by the patient's speech therapist.

32. Encourage the patient's use of an artificial communication device (e.g., voice synthesizer) that has been recommended by his/her speech pathologist.

33. If the patient can write, and if several attempts to communicate via spoken language have proven unsuccessful, request that the patient write a word or a sentence.

34. If the patient is too fatigued to communicate, do not pretend to understand what he/she is attempting to say (e.g., by nodding your head,

smiling, and saying "uh-huh"). Instead, suggest that you and the patient try again later after some rest.

35. Reinforce the patient's attempts to communicate ideas and intentions by stating that you are glad to know some of what he/she is thinking and you are confident that the communication will get easier with time.

36. Engage the patient in exercises requiring basic arithmetic skills, such as balancing a checkbook. Confront the patient's rationalizations about the existence of an arithmetic deficit by pointing out that he/she performed this skill successfully prior to the illness or injury. (See the Denial and Impaired Awareness chapter in this Planner.)

37. Assess the patient's ability to use strategies (e.g., calculators, double- or triple-checking work, matching the shapes of numerals rather than thinking of their names) to improve accuracy in arithmetic operations.

38. Inquire into the patient's preference for managing financial business (such as paying bills and preparing income taxes) while arithmetic skills are impaired, and facilitate his/her acting on this decision.

39. Normalize the patient's emotions associated with

communication difficulties by reporting that many people feel awkward and frustrated when they cannot clearly understand each other.

40. Inquire into the patient's experience about communication difficulties by using closed-ended questions (e.g., "Are you feeling frustrated/ isolated/frightened, etc.?") as necessary to compensate for any word-finding difficulties.

41. Educate the patient that communication will be more difficult and unreliable when he/she is stressed, upset, tired, or not well physically. Point out occasions when these factors are present and affecting the quality of communication. For example, if the patient has many word-finding problems during a late afternoon session but was more fluent in the morning, point this out and suggest that fatigue may be a factor.

42. Strongly urge the patient to take a break from communicating when frustration or fatigue interfere, and try again later.

43. Use a short statement (e.g., "I don't understand you") and/or a signal (e.g., raising a hand as if to indicate "stop") when the patient verbalizes sounds or words that are meaningless or totally unrelated to context.

44. When the patient begins to dominate a conversation, interrupt him/her, apologizing for doing so (if necessary), and remind the patient that you are working on the skill of turn-taking.

45. Recommend that therapists who are treating the patient in a group format be attentive to the patient's problem in monitoring vocal output and attending to nonverbal components of communication, and that they point out these problems as they occur. Comment on instances in which the patient demonstrates improved pragmatic skills.

46. Using videotape or audiotape, record the patient's speech and play it back to him/her.

47. Halt playback of the patient's speech periodically to sensitively point out communication errors to the patient, monitoring his/her ability to grasp the problem.

48. Assess effectiveness of having the patient "sing" a phrase or sentence, adjusting the volume and tone to impart emotion.

49. Recommend that the patient act as if playing a role in a drama, and urge him/her to communicate the emotion associated with a line or sentence.

50. Observe the patient's family while interacting with the patient, and identify family's inaccurate assumptions about the patient's language difficulties and how they should be managed.

51. Address the family's basic questions and misunderstandings about communication (e.g., family mistakenly interpreting the patient making a common response such as nodding as representing genuine understanding; family wondering why patient has begun to use profanity when this is out of character; family bringing elementary school textbooks to patient in an attempt to "teach" him/her to read or do arithmetic).

52. Encourage the family to maintain a communication style that acknowledges the patient's dignity (e.g., speaking "to" patient and not "about" him/her; choosing topics discussed in patient's presence based on the assumption that he/she might understand any part of what is being said).

53. Identify the family's need for additional education, and facilitate meeting with the patient's speech therapist.

54. Encourage family members to discuss how they are being affected by the patient's aphasia, as well as

how they perceive family relationships and roles being affected.

55. Coordinate referral to peer counselors, support groups, psychotherapists, chaplains, or others who might provide emotional and practical support in dealing with the challenges that the patient's aphasia presents to the family.

56. Taking into account the provisions of state law, clarify whether the patient is competent to make imminent medical, personal, or financial decisions.

57. Inquire whether the patient has made provisions for a designated person to assist in specific decision making.

58. If the patient appears at risk for being taken advantage of financially or in other ways, coordinate referral to social services or to state's adult protective services agency.

59. If there is a question about who may legally make a pending decision on the patient's behalf, obtain or refer for legal counsel.

60. Refer family members to professionals who can advise them about guardianship, if necessary.

—. _____

_____

—. _____

_____

DIAGNOSTIC SUGGESTIONS

Axis I:	290.xx	Dementia
	294.1	Dementia Due to (Axis III Condition)
	294.8	Dementia NOS
	294.9	Cognitive Disorder NOS
	315.31	Expressive Language Disorder
	315.32	Mixed Receptive-Expressive Language Disorder
	315.39	Phonological Disorder
	307.9	Communication Disorder NOS
	_____	_____
	_____	_____
Axis II:	V71.09	No Diagnosis or Condition
	_____	_____
	_____	_____

STIMULUS NEGLECT

BEHAVIORAL DEFINITIONS

1. Predominant failure to notice or interact with stimuli on one side of body (most frequently the left side).
2. In spite of intact sensory functioning, does not acknowledge sounds, visual stimuli, and/or tactile stimuli presented to one side of body.
3. Acknowledges and interacts with visitors and therapists only when they are standing or sitting on nonaffected side.
4. Notices or interacts with only the top or bottom portions of an object.
5. Failure to acknowledge limb(s) on affected side as belonging to self; regards limb as an object rather than as part of one's body (e.g., states "I would have more room in bed if this thing [arm] wasn't in here with me").
6. Failure to perform activities of daily living or other tasks on affected side (e.g., eats food on right side of plate while leaving food on left side of plate untouched; dresses right side of body but makes no effort to put clothing on left side; brushes teeth on one side of mouth while ignoring remaining teeth).

Note: This chapter will deal with the behavioral manifestations of three disorders of neglect: hemi-inattention, hemispatial neglect, and simultagnosia. See *A Guide to Adult Neuropsychological Diagnosis* (Stringer) for a discussion of the subtypes of neglect. See Weinberg and Diller's chapter in *Psychotherapeutic Interventions for Adults with Brain Injury or Stroke: A Clinician's Treatment Resource* (Langer, Laatsch, and Lewis) regarding therapeutic interventions for cognitive and emotional aspects of stimulus neglect.

Examples in this chapter assume that the left side is the affected side, because this is the most common presentation. In cases in which other spatial areas are affected, interventions should be adjusted accordingly.

7.   Completes tasks using or paying attention to only one side of the area given to complete the task (e.g., draws clock with all 12 numbers crowded into one-half of the clock face; plants flowers in only one-half of the container; ignores first few words from left margin when reading a page of text).

8.   Makes significantly greater number of errors on one side of space in comparison with the other (e.g., omits 10 of 15 targets on left side of page in a letter cancellation task while omitting 1 of 15 on right side).

9.   Frequently bumps into same side of hallway or door frame when ambulating.

10.   Frequently bruises or injures limb on affected side (e.g., gets affected arm caught between wheelchair and door frame, lets affected arm dangle with fingers in spokes of wheel, allows affected foot to get caught under wheelchair while attempting to move forward).

11.   Able to perceive only one aspect of a visual scene at a time.

12.   Rationalizes or gives excuse for failing to successfully accomplish task in the "ignored" part of spatial field (e.g., "I can't read that article because I forgot my glasses"; "I didn't do well on those drawings because I was tired when the psychologist gave them to me"; "I always use a calculator so there was no point in doing those multiplication problems").

__. _____

_____

__. _____

_____

__. _____

_____

LONG-TERM GOALS

1.   Acknowledge stimulus neglect as the main problem underlying difficulties in performing tasks in which attention must be directed to all sections of visual space.

2.   Become aware of and responsive to stimuli in all sections of visual space most of the time.

3.   Use compensatory strategies independently or after cuing to pay attention to and interact with area that is prone to be ignored.

4.   Use strategies to increase safety while interacting with environment in the neglected spatial area.

5. Make lifestyle changes required to live safely with residual stimulus neglect problems.
6. Emotionally accept need for lifestyle adaptations and use of compensatory strategies to overcome stimulus neglect problems.

—. _____
   _____

—. _____
   _____

—. _____
   _____

SHORT-TERM OBJECTIVES

1. Cooperate with an evaluation of sensory and motor functioning. (1, 2, 4)
2. Participate willingly in neuropsychological testing. (3, 4)
3. Family and patient verbalize an understanding of the cause, prognosis, and planned treatment for the stimulus neglect problem. (4, 5, 6)
4. Family interact with the patient in a manner that is effective in eliciting best performance, reducing frustration, or facilitating recovery from stimulus neglect. (7, 8, 23)
5. Show normal initiation in obtaining and using objects placed on nonaffected side. (9)
6. Put effort into searching for and interacting with objects on affected side. (10)

THERAPEUTIC INTERVENTIONS

1. Review medical records and/or consult with the patient's physician and rehabilitation therapists to rule out any sensory or motor impairments (e.g., decreased visual acuity, restricted visual fields, impaired auditory acuity, impaired sensory-motor functioning) affecting the patient's ability to perceive or interact with portions of the environment.
2. Identify the patient's point of view about why he/she is not performing activities successfully, by listening to the way in which he/she explains, denies, rationalizes, or excuses the problems.
3. Refer for or perform a neuropsychological evaluation to identify the mechanism(s) underlying the patient's difficulty in perceiving and in-

7. Participate actively in occupational therapy exercises and activities designed to increase independence in dressing, grooming, and other self-care activities. (11)

8. Participate willingly in speech therapy exercises designed to improve accuracy in reading, writing, and calculations. (12)

9. Acknowledge the presence of a stimulus-neglect-related deficit. (13)

10. Verbalize one's perspective on why the stimulus-neglect problem is occurring and the significance of the deficit. (14)

11. Acknowledge that performance is not adequate due to the stimulus neglect but that it could be improved. (15, 16, 17)

12. Give best effort to improving performance; monitor results with the therapist. (18, 19)

13. Correctly state the ways in which the stimulus neglect presents and the kinds of things that can be done to improve performance. (20, 21, 22)

14. Participate in visual scanning exercises. (23, 24)

15. Utilize feedback from therapists and family to improve effectiveness of visual processing. (8, 25, 26, 34, 41)

16. Implement strategies to focus attention on all of the

teracting with the environment and to assess other cognitive and emotional factors affecting rehabilitation planning.

4. Give feedback to the patient (patient's family), physician, treatment team, and other designated persons regarding assessment results and recommendations.

5. Educate the patient and the family that stimulus neglect is caused by brain-related problems of focusing attention on a certain portion of space rather than because of difficulties with vision, hearing, or perception.

6. Discuss the patient's prognosis and the treatment strategies with the family (and the patient).

7. Show the family ways to elicit good performance or avoid frustration when the patient cannot effectively direct attention to the affected area, by positioning articles or themselves on the nonaffected side (e.g., conversing with the patient from the nonaffected side; positioning financial statements right of midline and pointing to significant information; placing Kleenex, water, and so forth on table on the patient's right side).

8. Demonstrate ways in which the family can facilitate the patient's recovery from stimulus neglect by encour-

written information and to restore more normal scanning patterns. (27, 28, 29, 30)

17. Practice effective scanning techniques while reading or searching for words. (31)

18. Tolerate having auditory information presented at a louder volume on the affected side, and consciously direct attention to auditory information. (32)

19. Continue conscious efforts to accurately process information presented to affected side as cues are faded and withdrawn. (33, 34)

20. Verbalize an awareness of the need to use compensatory strategies on a long-term basis when accurate performance is required. (35, 47)

21. Select crafts, games, or other recreational activities that will encourage the development of effective visual scanning and stimulus processing. (36, 37, 38)

22. Consciously attempt to make eye contact during conversations and to pay attention to others' facial expressions. (39, 40)

23. Family and therapists adopt consistent strategy in responding to the patient's neglect-related problems. (41)

24. Cooperate with an evaluation for medications in-

aging him/her to direct attention to the "ignored" side (e.g., sitting on the patient's affected side while visiting; cuing the patient to look farther left to find the television control; when bringing the patient's pet to visit, putting the pet on the patient's affected side and saying, "Look at [pet's name]!").

9. If the patient is unable to attend to the affected side, or requires significant cuing to do so, position items that he/she needs for safety, health, or recovery (e.g., nurses' call button, urinal, water pitcher, calendar, orientation information) on the nonaffected side.

10. Position articles that are of potential interest to the patient (e.g., telephone, window, door to hallway, television control) on the affected side to facilitate the patient's awareness of this portion of space.

11. Coordinate referral of the patient to an occupational therapist to increase patient's ability to effectively accomplish dressing, grooming, and other daily tasks.

12. Coordinate referral of the patient to a speech therapist for strategy training to improve reading, calculation, and other skills affected by stimulus neglect.

13. Engage the patient in a task that will demonstrate

tended to enhance attention to relevant stimuli. (42, 43)

25. Participate in vocational rehabilitation counseling to assess return-to-work potential. (44)

26. Follow the physician's recommendations regarding ability to drive, operate power tools, cook, or engage in other potentially dangerous activities. (45, 46, 47)

27. Talk with a psychotherapist, counselor, minister, or other trained professional to work through the emotional issues associated with neglect-related losses. (48)

___. _____
_____

___. _____
_____

___. _____
_____

the nature of the deficit (e.g., multiplying a 3-digit number by another 3-digit number; making change with coins laid out on a table; crossing out target words in a page of print). Point out and discuss the errors with the patient.

14. Ask the patient why he/she is having difficulty completing these tasks. While listening to the patient's explanation, identify his/her level of resistance to acknowledging the brain-related cause of the neglect (active resistance, passive indifference, rationalizations, verbal acknowledgement of problem but without corrective efforts).

15. If the patient is resistant or indifferent to the neglect, frequently point out problems and errors that are caused by the neglect (e.g., "Feel your face; you have not finished shaving," or "There are still some pieces left; you must use all the pieces to complete the puzzle," or "Look at your left arm; it is caught between the wheelchair and the door frame").

16. Counter the patient's rationalization of the error by pointing out behaviors that are inconsistent with the rationalization (e.g., if the patient says "I need my glasses to read that," say

"You read the words on this side of the page just fine, even without your glasses," or if he/she says "I didn't give you exact change because pennies aren't worth bothering with," say "But you shortchanged me by a quarter!").

17. Provide an accurate explanation of the reason for the problem and explain how the patient can use a strategy to perform the task accurately (e.g., "You are not paying attention to all the things on your left; look for the edge of the table and then start scanning to your right," or "You are having trouble noticing things in your left visual field; turn your head as far to the left as you can and then begin looking").

18. Increase the patient's awareness of the stimulus neglect and use of compensatory strategies by challenging him/her to implement actions to successfully overcome the neglect (e.g., "Remember to look carefully to your left," or "See if you can find all the As on this page," or "Try to go all the way down this hallway without bumping into anything on your left side," or "Pick up enough coins to make 37 cents").

19. Give the patient specific feedback about improve-

ments in performance as he/she puts effort into overcoming stimulus neglect (e.g., number of targets identified, number of multiplication problems completed correctly, ability to avoid obstacles).

20. Inform the patient that he/she is expected to be able to describe the types of cognitive and perceptual problems that he/she is experiencing and to explain the purpose of therapeutic activities used to treat them.

21. Make periodic inquiries about the patient's deficits and the rationale for the therapeutic program.

22. Reinforce the patient's correct explanation (e.g., "You described that very well") of his or her deficit(s) and treatment plan. Correct any inaccuracies (e.g., "Your vision is fine; you are having difficulty paying attention to things on your left side").

23. Recommend that the patient practice visual tracking (e.g., have the patient visually track the therapist's finger back and forth; ask the patient to call out colors of papers taped to the wall in a left-to-right fashion; read and discuss comic strips).

24. Ask the patient to describe what is happening in a

photograph or painting
showing multiple activities
(e.g., a mother reading to a
child while a cat plays with
yarn on the floor). If the patient names single figures
(a lady, a child, a cat) or ignores figures on the left,
ask questions to help the
patient appreciate the scene
as a whole ("Oh, what is
happening over here [point-
ing to figure on the left]?" or
"Yes, that is a lady; what is
she doing?" or "What story
does this picture tell?").

25. Direct the patient to focus
his/her attention on a person or object in the ne-
glected spatial area (e.g.,
while sitting on the affected
side, say "Look over to your
left, at me," or say "Would
you like to try the apple pie
that is to the left of your
dinner plate?").

26. Provide cuing to the patient
as needed to demonstrate a
correct response to a visual
stimulus (e.g., "The first
drawing shows Charlie
Brown mailing a Valentine.
The next drawing shows
him looking in his mailbox,"
or "A mother is reading to
her child while a cat plays
by her feet").

27. Introduce a visual anchor
(e.g., a broad red line down
the left side of a page of
text) and instruct the patient to find the anchor before beginning to read.

28. Increase the stimulus intensity that is presented to the patient by increasing the size of the print.

29. Overlay the page of print with a mask (i.e., a solid sheet of paper with an opening cut to reveal a limited amount of material) to reduce the amount of material in the patient's visual field and to cue the patient where to direct attention.

30. Instruct the patient to scan visual material more slowly than usual, reminding himself/herself of the tendency to ignore part of the visual field.

31. Prescribe or carry out with the patient visual scanning exercises (e.g., letter or word cancellation tasks, circling words embedded in a matrix of letters, reading and summarizing short articles), using sensory cues or adaptations (e.g., visual anchors, masking, increased print size) as necessary to facilitate success.

32. Increase the volume of auditory information presented on the patient's affected side.

33. Gradually fade the stimulus cue (e.g., make the anchor dimmer or narrower, decrease font size, increase the size of the mask opening to include more information, decrease auditory volume) while maintaining

the patient's accuracy at an acceptable level.

34. Reinforce the patient's success in gradually overcoming stimulus neglect (e.g., "You read all the words in this line without using the screen," or "You noticed the potted plant on the left side of the page!" or "You looked to the left without any reminders from me").

35. Educate the patient about the need to use intentional visual scanning strategies to compensate for changes in visual attention; assist him/her in identifying those situations where accurate processing is crucial (e.g., driving a vehicle, crossing a street, cooking on a stove).

36. Engage the patient in familiar games requiring structured visual scanning and tracking (e.g., bingo, solitaire, crossword puzzles, Parcheesi).

37. Refer the patient to a recreational therapist for recommended leisure activities that will help build attention on the neglected side.

38. Encourage the patient to work on craft projects that will require attention to all areas of space (e.g., creating a tile trivet, painting a stained glass design, painting a birdhouse), but that will not put the patient at risk of injury due to stimulus neglect.

39. Remind the patient that it is important to look at the other person's face during a conversation.

40. Cue the patient to make eye contact while conversing (e.g., "Look at me").

41. Develop a behavioral plan describing what therapists, family members, and others who interact regularly with the patient are to do when specific symptoms of stimulus neglect occur (e.g., when the patient's affected arm hangs limply against the wheel of the wheelchair, say, "You need to protect your left arm; put it on the lap tray"; when the patient gazes off in space, say "Look at my face while we are talking"; when the patient eats only from the right side of his/her plate, say "Look at this food you haven't tried yet").

42. Consult with the patient's physician regarding the patient's potential to benefit from medications to increase attention to the affected side, and decide how these medications will be prescribed, monitored, and managed.

43. Monitor the patient's compliance with prescribed medications, and their effectiveness and side effects, and report to the prescribing physician.

44. Refer the patient for vocational counseling to assist with return-to-work planning and to identify reasonable accommodations that may be necessary.

45. Recommend an evaluation of the patient's ability to safely operate power tools, cook on a stove, cut with a knife, or perform other potentially dangerous activities.

46. Coordinate referral of the patient for a driving evaluation to determine whether he/she can effectively compensate for residual symptoms of neglect while operating a motor vehicle.

47. Inform the patient about those residual neglect symptoms that are expected to be chronic. Remind the patient that the ability to perform a task safely while using strategies does not mean that the neglect has been "cured" (e.g., if the patient has been driving safely using intentional scanning, he/she remains at significant risk for an accident if the strategy is not applied).

48. Refer for or perform psychotherapy to deal with emotional issues affecting the patient's ability to accept stimulus-neglect-related changes and the need to implement compensatory strategies.

—.   _____
      _____
—.   _____
      _____
—.   _____
      _____

DIAGNOSTIC SUGGESTIONS

Axis I: 294.9   Cognitive Disorder NOS

____   _____

____   _____

Axis II: V71.09   No Diagnosis or Condition

____   _____

____   _____

SUBSTANCE ABUSE

BEHAVIORAL DEFINITIONS

1. Consistent use of alcohol or other mood-altering substances until high, intoxicated, or passed out.
2. Inability to stop or cut down use of mood-altering substance once started, despite the verbalized desire to do so and the negative consequences continued use brings.
3. Sometimes experience amnesiac blackouts when abusing alcohol.
4. Blood work that reflects a pattern of heavy substance use (e.g., elevated liver enzymes).
5. Blood work that reflects significant use of a substance at the time of the accident, injury, or medical event (e.g., high blood alcohol levels at time of motor vehicle accident).
6. Denial that chemical dependence is a problem despite direct feedback from spouse, relatives, friends, or employers that the use of the substance is negatively affecting them and others.
7. Continued drug and/or alcohol use despite experiencing persistent or recurring physical, legal, financial, vocational, social, or relationship problems that are directly caused by the use of the substance.
8. Suspension of important social, recreational, or occupational activities because they interfere with abuse.

Note: For more information about many of the therapeutic interventions described in this chapter, please refer to *Substance Use and Abuse after Brain Injury: A Programmer's Guide,* published by the Ohio Valley Center for Brain Injury Prevention and Rehabilitation, 1997. Portions of the content of this chapter were drawn from Jongsma, A. and Peterson, L.M., *The Complete Adult Psychotherapy Treatment Planner,* second edition (New York: John Wiley & Sons, Inc., 1999) © 1999 by Arthur E. Jongsma, Jr., and L. Mark Peterson. Reprinted with permission.

9. Large investment of time or money to obtain the substance, to use it, or to recover from its effects.
10. Increased tolerance for the drug, reflected in the need to use more to become intoxicated or to attain the desired effect.
11. Consumption of substance in greater amounts and for longer periods than initially intended.
12. Physical or emotional symptoms (e.g., shaking, seizures, nausea, headaches, sweating, anxiety, insomnia, and/or depression) when the substance is withdrawn.
13. Continued use of mood-altering chemical after being told by a physician that it is causing health problems or interfering with rehabilitation progress.

__. _____

   _____

   _____

__. _____

   _____

   _____

__. _____

   _____

LONG-TERM GOALS

1. Accept own chemical dependence and actively participate in a recovery program.
2. Cooperate with family and/or caregivers in their efforts to promote abstinence.
3. Establish and maintain total abstinence while increasing knowledge of the disease and the process of recovery.
4. Establish a sustained recovery, free from the use of all injurious mood-altering substances.
5. Acquire the necessary skills to maintain long-term sobriety from all injurious mood-altering substances.
6. Understand the factors predisposing one to substance abuse (e.g., parents who were alcoholics) and/or triggering episodes of abuse (e.g., work-related stress, grief over relationship loss).
7. Develop and utilize a support system (e.g., Alcoholics Anonymous, Narcotics Anonymous, psychotherapist) to assist in maintaining abstinence, promoting self-esteem, and building healthy attitudes and relationships.
8. Utilize relapses as opportunities to learn about high-risk triggers and the importance of sobriety in maintaining physical and emotional health.

9. Improve quality of life by maintaining abstinence from injurious substances and attending to physical and emotional health.
10. Achieve optimal cognitive recovery and reduce risk of subsequent brain injury or neurological event by maintaining sobriety.
11. Family members participate in support groups (e.g., Al-Anon, Ala-teen, Nar-Anon, Families Anonymous) or in psychotherapy to reduce negative impact of addiction on the family environment.
12. Family interact with patient in a way that supports ongoing abstinence and clarifies patient responsibility for own actions.

—. _____
_____

—. _____
_____

—. _____
_____

SHORT-TERM OBJECTIVES

1. Family, friends, or medical personnel provide information to identify the existence of a substance abuse/dependence problem. (1, 2, 3)

2. Acknowledge a history of drug/alcohol use that is problematic. (4)

3. Agree to interventions to manage physiologic withdrawal symptoms. (5, 6, 7)

4. Display willingness to talk with psychologist, psychiatrist, physician, or other designated professional regarding own substance use. (8)

5. Accurately describe the amount, frequency, and his-

THERAPEUTIC INTERVENTIONS

1. Review the patient's medical records to identify symptoms of substance abuse (e.g., elevated blood alcohol level at time of accident) and listen to family's and friends' concerns about the patient's use of substances.

2. With the patient's (or responsible person's) permission, ask family or other designated persons about the patient's use of alcohol and mood-altering substances.

3. Consult with the patient's treating physician regarding laboratory tests (e.g., elevated liver enzymes, positive results on drug screen, brain CT showing degenerative changes) that

tory of substance abuse. (9, 10)

6. Cooperate with psychodiagnostic procedures to identify coexisting psychiatric conditions. (11, 37)

7. Identify both positive experiences and negative consequences associated with drug and/or alcohol abuse. (12, 13, 24, 25)

8. Describe the anticipated benefits of terminating the addictive behavior. (14, 15)

9. Work through initial resistance associated with giving up the addictive behavior. (16, 17)

10. Verbalize an understanding of personal, social, family, and genetic factors contributing to chemical dependence. (11, 18, 19, 20)

11. Verbalize acceptance of having an addiction to mood-altering substance and acknowledge its negative impact on life. (21, 22, 23)

12. Listen to and agree with others' perception of the negative consequences that own substance abuse has had on self and others. (24, 25)

13. Continue focusing on the probable positive outcomes associated with sobriety, enlisting support and input from friends and family. (14, 15, 26, 27)

14. Identify alternate ways to achieve the pleasant experi-

may indicate sustained or recent substance use, or physical damage due to substance abuse.

4. Ask the patient about history of drug and/or alcohol use and whether the patient has ever considered his/her use of substances to be problematic.

5. Interview the patient (responsible person) about current symptoms (tremor, excessive anxiety) that may indicate acute withdrawal symptoms.

6. Consult with the patient's treating physician to develop a plan to manage acute withdrawal symptoms (e.g., consult a psychiatrist, introduce chemically similar substance and gradually wean, use medications and other interventions to reduce symptoms to safe and tolerable levels, refer the patient for inpatient psychiatric care).

7. Adjusting vocabulary and statement length to the patient's cognitive abilities, explain to the patient (and family) why he/she is having withdrawal symptoms and what will be done to help him/her through the withdrawal.

8. Put effort into building trusting relationship and ask permission to inquire about the patient's use of drugs and/or alcohol.

ences that patient associates with substance use. (28, 29)

15. Family and friends indicate that they consider patient responsible for the consequences of his/her actions while abusing substances. (30, 31)

16. Family use strategies and resources to protect own well-being while holding patient responsible for substance use. (32, 33, 34)

17. Cooperate with cognitive evaluation. (35, 36, 37)

18. Family or interested person take steps to legally assume decision-making responsibilities if patient has insufficient ability to make judgments about medical care, finances, or personal matters. (37, 38, 39)

19. Family and friends frequently recommend that patient change addictive behavior, and reinforce his/her efforts to do so. (40, 41)

20. Patient and family describe how a brain injury can affect the use and effects of substance. (42, 43, 44, 48)

21. Patient and family state the negative impact that continued substance use can have on rehabilitation, recovery, and health. (3, 45, 46, 47, 48)

22. Compare the advantages of substance use with the ad-

9. Gather a complete drug/alcohol history from the patient (or responsible party if patient is not a good historian), including amount, pattern, signs, and symptoms of use.

10. Utilize assessment instruments to obtain psychosocial history and information about substance use (e.g., the Addiction Severity Index [ASI] [McLellan, Kushner, Metzger, Peters, Smith, Grissom, Pettinati, and Argeriou], the Substance Abuse Subtle Screening Instrument [SASSI] [Miller], or the Michigan Alcoholism Screening Test [MAST] [Selzer]) and review the results and recommendations with the patient.

11. Conduct or refer for psychodiagnostic interview and/or psychological testing to identify mood, anxiety, or personality disorders that may be coexisting with or contributing to the patient's substance abuse problem.

12. Ask the patient to identify how substance use has affected mood or behavior in ways that he/she has enjoyed.

13. Inquire into ways in which substance abuse has negatively impacted the patient's life.

14. Explore the patient's past attempts to stop using sub-

vantages of abstinence, considering both the number of advantages for each as well as the duration of the effects (short- or long-term). (12, 15, 25, 49)

23. Identify obstacles that will most likely affect own efforts to achieve abstinence. (50)

24. Name at least two ways to deal with each potential personal trigger. (51)

25. Agree to a referral to an intensive program to address substance abuse issues. (52, 53)

26. Use psychoactive medications as prescribed to reduce desire for substance and to manage any coexisting psychiatric conditions. (54, 55)

27. Name support systems or activities that might be helpful in maintaining sobriety. (56)

28. Family demonstrate skill in managing conversations and actions to encourage and support sobriety. (57, 58, 59)

29. Family identify problems they expect to experience while supporting patient in achieving sobriety, and describe at least two ways they might resolve each problem. (60, 61)

30. Patient and family report understanding that re-

stances, asking what led to those decisions to quit.

15. Encourage the patient to consider and verbalize ways in which life might be better if he/she no longer used drugs and/or alcohol.

16. Explore the patient's thoughts about the anticipated negative consequences associated with giving up substances. Point out ways in which the patient might be exaggerating the magnitude or frequency of each of the negative consequences.

17. Challenge the patient to arrive at a more realistic appraisal of the consequences of giving up substances.

18. Investigate situational stress factors (e.g., receiving past-due notices for bills; teenager arguing with the patient and/or spouse; loneliness) or daily rituals (e.g., predinner cocktail hour; drinking beer while watching football games; wine before, during, and following dinner) that may foster the patient's chemical dependence.

19. Probe the patient's family history for chemical dependence patterns and relate these modeling and genetic factors to patient's use.

20. Explore extended family chemical dependence history and relate this to a genetic vulnerability for

lapses are part of the process of behavior change, not indications that patient will fail in changing addictive behavior. (62, 63)

31. Family and friends gather data during relapses to point out specific problems related to substance use and share this information in a therapeutic setting. (25, 64)

32. Develop plan to decline alcohol or drugs when they are offered. (65, 66)

33. Family demonstrate ability to assess the patient's insight into own cognitive deficits. (67, 68)

34. Family support patient in managing triggers, utilizing strategies that are appropriate to patient's level of insight. (69, 70, 71, 72)

35. Family reinforce patient's successful actions to maintain sobriety in social situations. (73, 74)

36. State changes that will be made in social relationships, recreational pursuits, social activities, and places in which leisure time is spent that will replace substance-abuse-related activities. (75, 76, 77)

37. Identify constructive projects, suited to physical and cognitive skills, that will be accomplished now that more time and energy are available in sobriety. (77, 78)

patient to develop chemical dependence also.

21. Work with the patient to complete a First-Step paper and then process it, giving the patient feedback. If possible, ask patient to go over this paper with group and/or sponsor as well.

22. Require the patient to attend didactic lectures related to chemical dependence and the process of recovery. Ask the patient to write down several points from each lecture; discuss these in the next therapy session.

23. Model and reinforce statements that reflect acceptance of chemical dependence and its destructive consequences for self and others (e.g., "I" statements demonstrating acceptance of chemical dependence and personal responsibility for negative consequences).

24. Assign the patient to ask two or three people who are close to him/her to write a letter in which they identify how they saw the patient's chemical dependence negatively impacting his/her life.

25. Coordinate a meeting to include the patient, family, friends, and other significant persons to process the information with the patient about the specific ways in

38. List the actions that will be taken to make amends to significant others who have been hurt by the life dominated by substance abuse. (79)

39. Verbalize how living situation contributes to chemical dependence and acts as a hindrance to recovery. (18, 80, 81)

40. State the need for a more stable, healthy living situation that will support recovery. (81, 82)

41. Make arrangements to terminate current living situation and move to a place more conducive to recovery and suited to physical and cognitive abilities. (82, 83)

42. Write a good-bye letter to drug of choice. (84)

43. Sign an abstinence contract. (85)

44. Develop a written aftercare plan to avoid relapse and to support maintenance of long-term sobriety. (86)

45. Attend support groups and organizations regularly to support recovery and maintenance of sobriety. (87, 88)

46. Continue to educate self about addiction and ways to manage situations that might lead to relapse. (87, 88, 89)

—. _____

_____

which their lives have been negatively affected by his/her substance use.

26. Encourage the patient to review and expand upon the previously developed list of advantages of sobriety.

27. Recommend that the patient talk with friends and family about how they think his/her life might be better if he/she were to achieve long-lasting sobriety.

28. Ask the patient to identify ways in which he/she feels better when using a substance (e.g., increased relaxation, heightened self-confidence, escape from troubles). Request that the patient record these responses in a memory book under the title *Reasons Why I Use* ____.

29. Encourage the patient to brainstorm about ways other than using drugs or alcohol to achieve positive experiences (e.g., relaxation training, yoga, tai chi, working out, monitoring negative thoughts and replacing them with constructive ones, participating in vocational counseling to get a better job). Assign the patient to implement one or more of these activities and report on results.

30. Assist the family in identifying ways in which they can have the patient bear re-

—. _____

_____

—. _____

_____

sponsibility for actions (e.g., refuse to cancel psychotherapy appointment pretending the patient is "sick" when he/she is actually intoxicated; insist the patient enter residential treatment if he/she continues to abuse substances while living with family; make the patient sign note for money borrowed from relative).

31. Encourage the family members to state, in their own words, why it is important for the patient to experience the consequences of own behavior (e.g., lets him/her know there are consequences in life, will learn how to get along, can have a sense of pride in accomplishments).

32. Work through the concerns the family has about their reactions if they do not "bail patient out" (e.g., reactions if the patient was thrown out of apartment; if they encountered their family member sleeping on the street; if the patient lost his/her job, etc.).

33. Assist the family members in developing plans to reduce their own suffering during times they are holding the patient accountable for actions (e.g., insist the patient not talk with them about the homeless shelter where he/she spent the previous night; identify public or charitable financial as-

sistance that can be accessed if patient loses job).

34. Refer family members to social services and/or community agencies to assist them in identifying and accessing resources to protect family's welfare.

35. Conduct or refer for neuropsychological evaluation to identify cognitive problems affecting the patient's insight, judgment, impulse control, and ability to remember and implement behavior-changing strategies.

36. Conduct or refer for evaluation or clinical interview to define the patient's current capacity for making informed decisions.

37. Give feedback regarding the evaluation results and recommendations to the patient, (family), physician, rehabilitation team, and other designated persons.

38. If the patient is not currently competent, communicate with the patient's rehabilitation team and family (if appropriate) to develop plan for identifying and designating a decision maker and for implementing this plan, being guided by state law and institution's policies.

39. Refer family or person who will be designated decision maker to social services and/or legal counsel for information about the options

for and steps associated with assuming decision-making responsibilities.

40. Instruct family and friends about the value of encouraging the patient to give up substances, focusing on specific benefits (e.g., "We would like to stop worrying that you'll be sent to prison for buying drugs"; "Our daughter would like you to watch her basketball games"; "We worry that substance use will cause you to die early").

41. Recommend that family reinforce the patient for any efforts that might lead to recovery (e.g., "I appreciated your going to the AA meeting this afternoon"; "I was happy to see you give away the beer you had stored in the basement").

42. Inform the patient and family of reasons (e.g., problems with self-esteem following loss of job and friends, attempts to quickly mask depression and loneliness, greater difficulty managing emotions and using good judgment) that persons may develop substance abuse problems for the very first time after a brain injury.

43. Educate the patient and family that people are at much higher risk for a second brain injury if they continue to abuse substances after the first injury.

44. Explain to the patient and family why the results of a second injury are typically much more severe and harder to recover from than the symptoms of the first.

45. Talk with the patient and family about the harmful effects of drug or alcohol use on the brain's ability to recover from the damage.

46. Coordinate educational sessions for the patient and family to address medical complications that might occur with substance use (e.g., seizures), or ways in which the substance might alter the effectiveness of the patient's medication(s).

47. Have the patient and family describe the current cognitive difficulties the patient is having and how these interfere with his/her life. Ask them to consider and describe the likely problems the patient would experience if he/she were also under the influence of a substance.

48. Inform the patient and family that a person is typically more sensitive to the effects of alcohol or other drugs after the brain has been injured; that is, the patient will have a lower tolerance for the substance.

49. Encourage the patient to list the advantages of substance use and the advantages of

abstinence, including the approximate duration of each effect. Inquire into the patient's thoughts and reactions to this exercise.

50. Suggest that the patient put into words what he/she thinks about why people resume using harmful substances. Ask the patient to identify which of these factors would most likely cause him/her to relapse and to record these relapse triggers in a notebook or journal for future reference.

51. Help the patient expand awareness of relapse triggers and alternative ways of effectively handling own relapse triggers (e.g., call someone when lonely; sign up for volunteer work to fill daytime hours; invite friends to watch football game at home rather than meeting them in a sports bar). Record these in a notebook.

52. Coordinate referral of the patient for intensive substance abuse treatment.

53. Answer the patient's and family's questions and address their concerns about the recommended treatment.

54. Coordinate referral of the patient to physician specializing in substance abuse treatment for evaluation to determine whether the patient might benefit from medications to reduce crav-

ing for alcohol or drugs, or to manage emotions that might increase risk of relapse.

55. Monitor the patient's use of prescribed medications and their effectiveness; address issues affecting compliance and side effects.

56. Ask the patient to identify specific resources (e.g., Alcoholics Anonymous, psychotherapist, friend) or activities (e.g., prayer, meditation, exercise) that might be helpful in maintaining sobriety. Record these, if desired, in notebook or journal.

57. Educate the patient's family about codependency and reinforcement principles as they affect persistence of substance abuse problems.

58. Ask the family to identify some specific ways in which they might have played into or inadvertently encouraged the patient's substance use (e.g., spouse who normally feels inadequate feels strong and capable when patient is incapacitated). Work with family to identify responses that would not support continuing use of substances (e.g., spouse gets additional training to earn job advancement).

59. Facilitate referral to Al-Anon, Nar-Anon, Families Anonymous, or other support group for family members of addicted person.

60. Meet with family members and encourage them to verbalize their concerns about their ability to support the patient in process of achieving sobriety (e.g., patient states, "What I do with my life is my own business"; family members are angry with the patient for the suffering they have already experienced; family members prefer to distance selves from the patient).

61. Request that family members generate at least two ideas about ways that they could manage each obstacle to effective support (e.g., "What you do with your life affects us all, too"; "Explain to me how being drunk is what you want to do with your life"; "We have already invested a lot in _____'s recovery, perhaps we should not give up now"; _____ was a very special person in the family before drugs interfered").

62. Educate the patient and family about the fact that achieving sobriety is a process that typically includes some relapses.

63. Help the family and patient understand that some relapses, rather than signifying inability to recover, can be attempts by the patient to determine whether it is essential to make lifestyle changes.

64. Help family members identify ways in which they can make careful observations during periods of relapse, so that this experience might be used therapeutically to aid in the patient's recovery from substance abuse (e.g., noticing that the patient drank immediately after his girlfriend stormed out of the house; videotaping or audiotaping behavior while the patient is under the influence of substance, to demonstrate how dysfunctional he/she becomes; writing a letter during or soon after the relapse, describing what they experienced while the patient was intoxicated).

65. Assist the patient in developing a standard response that he/she is willing to use when exposed to an opportunity to use mood-altering substance (e.g., "No thanks"; "Thanks, but I'm not drinking since my injury"; "No more drugs for me!").

66. With the patient's permission, inform family and caregivers about the patient's preferred response when offered alcohol or drugs; suggest they remind the patient to say this if the occasion arises.

67. Teach family members to assess the patient's awareness of deficits by asking, "Has your ability to think changed since you had your

brain injury?" If the patient is aware of changes, ask him/her what difference they make in everyday life.

68. Suggest that family rate patient's awareness of cognitive deficits as follows: Stage One—unaware of any changes, perceives cognition to be entirely normal; Stage Two—vaguely aware of changes, but unable to name significance; Stage Three—able to name change in cognition, able to identify effect of cognitive deficit as problem is occurring; Stage Four—names cognitive deficit and anticipates impact on imminent activity.

69. For patient at Stage One level of insight, instruct the family to reduce or eliminate the patient's exposure triggers (e.g., avoid serving wine with dinner; decline invitation to party in which it is certain that alcohol will be served; do not allow the patient to socialize alone with friend who is known to use cocaine).

70. During Stage Two insight level, family should remind the patient verbally or with cue card why it is necessary to avoid substance (e.g., "Alcohol could cause a seizure"; "Your memory will get worse if you drink"; "You might have another stroke if you use cocaine").

71. When the patient is at Stage Three insight level, family should remind the patient, prior to entering situation in which substance will be available, to use agreed upon strategy (e.g., saying to oneself, "Stop, think, act," or "I'll protect my brain").

72. When the patient has reached Stage Four insight, family should encourage him/her to take responsibility for managing situation in which substance is available. Family should unobtrusively monitor the patient's behavior when in the presence of substances, and cue the patient to use strategy only if he/she attempts to obtain substance.

73. Encourage family to compliment the patient on successful follow-through on recommendation to avoid situations in which substances might be available.

74. Encourage family to reinforce the patient for successfully managing behavior in situation in which substance was available and the patient declined or avoided use.

75. Review the negative influence of continuing old alcohol- or drug-related friendships ("drinking buddies") and assist the patient in making a plan to develop new sober friendships.

76. Assist the patient in developing insight into life

changes (e.g., moving to a neighborhood in which drugs are not readily available; making time for AA, NA, or other activities to nourish emotional and spiritual growth; terminating dating relationship with person who is addicted) that are needed in order to maintain long-term sobriety.

77. Assist the patient in planning social and recreational activities that are appropriate to current skills and are free from association with substance abuse; refer to recreational therapist, if necessary.

78. Plan projects that are appropriate to the patient's physical and cognitive abilities that can be accomplished to build self-esteem now that sobriety affords time and energy for such constructive activity.

79. Discuss the negative effects that substance abuse has had on family life, friends, and work relationships (e.g., the patient ignored his/her children because he/she was drinking instead; the patient borrowed money from friends for "emergencies" and then spent it on drugs; the patient missed work frequently, putting greater workload on coworkers and creating problems for supervisor) and encourage a plan to make amends for such

hurt (e.g., committing time regularly to spend with family; admitting to friend how money had been used and paying back the money that was borrowed; apologizing to coworkers and supervisor).

80. Evaluate the role of the patient's living situation in fostering a pattern of chemical dependence.

81. Assign the patient to write a list of negative influences for chemical dependence inherent in his/her living situation.

82. Encourage a plan for a change in living situation that is suitable for the patient's physical and cognitive abilities and that will foster recovery.

83. Reinforce a positive change in the patient's living situation.

84. Direct the patient to write a good-bye letter (assisting, if needed) to drug of choice; process related feelings during a therapy session.

85. Develop an abstinence contract with the patient regarding the use of his/her drug of choice. Process the emotional impact of this contract during a therapy session.

86. Assist the patient in developing a written aftercare plan that includes specifics regarding ongoing therapy, support groups, sponsors,

trigger and relapse prevention, and so forth.

87. Recommend that the patient attend Alcoholics Anonymous (AA) or Narcotics Anonymous (NA) meetings and discuss the impact of the meetings with the therapist.

88. Encourage the patient to select and maintain frequent communication with "buddy" or sponsor from AA or NA.

89. Recommend that the patient read books (e.g., *The Addiction Workbook* by Fanning and O'Neill, *Staying Sober: A Guide to Relapse Prevention* by Gorski and Miller, and *The Staying Sober Workbook* by Gorski).

__. _____

_____

__. _____

_____

__. _____

_____

DIAGNOSTIC SUGGESTIONS

Axis I: 303.90   Alcohol Dependence
305.00   Alcohol Abuse
304.30   Cannabis Dependence
305.20   Cannabis Abuse
304.20   Cocaine Dependence
305.60   Cocaine Abuse
304.00   Opioid Dependence
305.50   Opioid Abuse
304.10   Sedative, Hypnotic, or Anxiolytic Dependence

	305.40	Sedative, Hypnotic, or Anxiolytic Abuse
	304.80	Polysubstance Dependence
	_____	_____
	_____	_____
Axis II:	301.83	Borderline Personality Disorder
	799.9	Diagnosis Deferred
	V71.09	No Diagnosis
	_____	_____
	_____	_____

VOCATIONAL/EDUCATIONAL PROBLEMS

BEHAVIORAL DEFINITIONS

1. Receives negative feedback regarding performance upon return to usual employment/school position, when performance previously had been satisfactory.
2. Unable to complete assignments with sufficient accuracy, speed, or quality.
3. Lacks concern for quality of work.
4. Excessive number of days late or absent.
5. Frequent conflicts with colleagues, supervisors, instructors, or others.
6. Responds to frustrating situations by blaming others, dropping class, changing schools, quitting job, or other avoidance behaviors rather than attempting to resolve the problem.
7. Spends significantly more time studying, writing papers, or doing homework for classes in comparison to preinjury/preillness behavior.
8. Unable to keep up with academic assignments, given classload of similar difficulty to that taken before injury/illness.
9. Teachers/professors contact patient's family to report concern about change in behavior at school from preinjury/preillness level of functioning.
10. Reports high levels of stress while at work/school and after returning home, when stress level previously had been manageable.
11. Acts withdrawn, angry, or irritable.
12. Excessively fatigued at end of workday or school day.
13. Excessive number of headaches, gastrointestinal problems, insomnia episodes, or other stress-related physical symptoms.
14. Reports no satisfaction from effort invested in work/academic activities.

15. Gives up usual social and recreational activities in order to try to meet job or school demands.

__. _____

_____

__. _____

_____

__. _____

_____

LONG-TERM GOALS

1. Perform specified responsibilities according to agreed-upon standards.
2. Display good attendance and appear promptly for scheduled activities.
3. Complete assignments on time and according to directions.
4. Manage disagreements effectively by resolving problem or terminating exchange before it escalates.
5. Maintain normal mood while managing academic/job demands.
6. Use exercise and relaxation techniques to manage stress effectively.
7. Report satisfaction and sense of accomplishment from work.
8. Engage in recreational and social activities in free time.

__. _____

_____

__. _____

_____

__. _____

_____

SHORT-TERM OBJECTIVES	THERAPEUTIC INTERVENTIONS
1. Describe goals for returning to school or to work. (1)	1. Talk with the patient to determine what goals he/she has concerning return to school or to work (e.g., re-
2. Provide information about specific academic/job re-	

quirements and previous level of achievement. (2, 3)

3. Verbalize how medical conditions, medications, and the brain-related changes in function might affect the performance of specific job/academic functions. (4)

4. Describe the financial resources that are available to meet obligations while one is unable to work. (5)

5. List and process the factors that are pressing for the resumption of academic/career responsibilities. (6)

6. Describe the negative consequences of a premature and unsuccessful job/academic reentry. (7, 8)

7. Agree to consult with a vocational rehabilitation counselor. (9, 10)

8. Cooperate with therapies designed to increase awareness of deficits and ability to compensate for them. (11)

9. Cooperate with a neuropsychological evaluation. (12, 14)

10. Participate in an evaluation of personality and emotional functioning. (13, 14)

11. Participate in an evaluation of physical strength and motor skills. (15)

12. Implement recommended steps to evaluate and improve vision and hearing. (16)

sume same job/academic program; change to a different job; take early retirement; stay home with his/her children).

2. With the patient's (or legally responsible person's) permission, contact the patient's employer and/or school to inquire about parameters of his/her responsibilities and the level and types of abilities necessary to complete this work.

3. With the patient's (or legally responsible person's) permission, request copies of performance reviews, transcripts, or other records that would provide information about the patient's preinjury/preillness level of functioning.

4. Discuss with the patient in detail the requirements of his/her academic or work setting, and how he/she perceives that medical conditions (e.g., high blood pressure, seizures, diabetes), medications (e.g., anticonvulsants, anticoagulants), and the changes brought on by the brain condition might affect his/her ability to meet these responsibilities. Correct any misperceptions.

5. Recommend that the patient (family) determine the types of financial benefits the patient has through his/her work (e.g., signifi-

13. Obtain treatment to address depression, anxiety, or other psychiatric disorders. (17)

14. Cooperate with treatments to improve concentration, memory, and other cognitive skills. (18)

15. Work cooperatively with physician(s) and rehabilitation therapists to enhance health, language skills, motor strength, coordination, and/or dexterity. (19)

16. Verbalize the ways in which altered abilities will affect the return to work/school, and agree to implement accommodations to increase effectiveness. (4, 20, 21)

17. Identify the issues of concern associated with returning to work or to school. (22)

18. Verbalize realistic and distorted aspects of concerns about school/work reentry and identify strategies to address anticipated problems. (23, 24)

19. Identify schools that have facilities and programs suited to new needs. (25)

20. Consult with the school's disability services officer (or other designated person) to determine the actions that are necessary in order to have the recommended accommodations approved and implemented by the institution. (26, 27)

21. Outline the options that appear to be available regard-

cant period of long-term sick leave; disability insurance; eligibility for early retirement), the specific means of accessing each (e.g., physician's letter; documented inability to perform specific occupation/any work; forms requiring completion), and the financial implications of each option (paid at 100 percent; receives 60 percent of gross income adjusted annually for cost-of-living; receives pension and medical insurance until age 65).

6. Ask the patient how soon he/she hopes to resume academic or work-related activities and what factors are influencing the date he/she has selected (e.g., wants to graduate with his/her class; has exhausted sick leave, receives no income, and is behind on the mortgage; is sole proprietor and is afraid customers will go elsewhere if business is not reopened soon). Process the reality basis for each of these factors.

7. Inquire into the likely effects of an unsuccessful work/academic reentry (e.g., the patient may be fired and lose disability benefits and health insurance; may lose customers by not handling their accounts well; may flunk out of academic program). Encourage a re-

ing return to work and the implications of each for one's emotional, medical, and financial well-being. (5, 28, 29, 30)

22. Describe a plan for returning to work or to school that takes one's goals and abilities into account. (31)

23. Report on the agreement that has been reached with employer/school regarding workload/courseload, ways in which performance will be evaluated, and the implementation of recommended accommodations. (32)

24. Maintain good communication between school/ employer and rehabilitation professionals regarding the success of the return to school/work and the need for additional modifications. (33)

25. Participate in psychotherapy to facilitate coming to terms emotionally with changed cognitive and/or motor skills and the presumed impact of these changes on one's hopes for the future. (34)

26. Make notations in journal, day timer, or other written record about the criteria by which one will determine his/her own success. (35, 36)

27. Reward self for accomplishment of academic, vocational, or other specific goals. (37)

consideration of patient's return decision.

8. Ask the patient to consider how his/her confidence, self-esteem, and emotions will likely be affected if he/she is not successful at returning to work/school; suggest a gradual or delayed return to responsibilities.

9. Refer, or recommend a referral to a vocational counselor.

10. Inform the patient (and family) how to access vocational rehabilitation resources in the community.

11. Perform or refer for therapy to increase the patient's realistic awareness of deficits. (See Denial and Impaired Awareness chapter in this Planner.)

12. Perform or refer for neuropsychological testing to identify cognitive deficits and cognitive strengths that should be taken into account in planning the patient's return to work or school.

13. Perform or refer for a psychodiagnostic evaluation to identify depression, anxiety, chemical dependency, or other psychiatric conditions that might affect the patient's recovery and academic/career reentry.

14. Give feedback to the patient (patient's family), physician, rehabilitation team, and

28. Identify the sources and signs of stress. (38)

29. Utilize relaxation techniques to reduce stress levels. (39, 40, 41)

30. Report on stressful situations that have been encountered at work/school. (42, 43)

31. Identify alternative, more effective ways of handling those situations that previously have led to conflict. (44)

32. Demonstrate the ability to resolve frustrating situations successfully and report satisfaction with the outcome. (45)

33. Report the positive emotional reactions and effects on self-esteem associated with investing time in a satisfying avocational activity. (46, 47)

34. Complete applications for Social Security Disability Income (SSDI) or other sources of financial assistance. (5, 48, 49)

35. Describe the positive impact of participation in volunteer work, hobbies, or other goal-directed activities during the time one is unable to participate in school or paid employment. (50, 51)

36. Verbalize acceptance of limitations, satisfaction with adjustment, and affirmation of self. (52)

other designated persons regarding assessment results and recommendations.

15. Consult with the patient's physician regarding a referral for an evaluation of strength, speed, and coordination (e.g., a Functional Capacity Evaluation).

16. Consult with the patient's physician regarding how visual and auditory problems will be evaluated and corrected.

17. Perform or refer the patient for treatment for depression, anxiety, chemical dependency, or other psychiatric disorders affecting successful work reentry. (See Depression/Grief, Anxiety/Fear, Substance Abuse, or other relevant chapters in this Planner.)

18. Perform, or refer the patient for therapy designed to enhance cognitive skills (e.g., attention, concentration, memory) and to compensate for residual deficits affecting academic/vocational reentry. (See Attention and Concentration Impairment, Memory Impairment, Problem Solving/Planning/Judgment Deficits, or other relevant chapters in this Planner.)

19. Reinforce the patient's adherence to physician's recommendations and participation in speech, physical, occupational, or

___.   _____
       _____

___.   _____
       _____

___.   _____
       _____

other therapies; comment periodically about his/her progress.

20. Coordinate a conference with the patient, (patient's family), and rehabilitation team to identify key factors affecting the patient's work/academic reentry, including strengths, brain-condition-related changes, and accommodations (e.g., adapted equipment, environmental modifications, procedural accommodations) that should be implemented to compensate for residual disabilities.

21. Teach the patient (and family) the general implications of the Americans with Disabilities Act (ADA) and subsequent related legislation and judicial rulings for his/her entitlement to accommodations. Refer the patient (and family) to an attorney familiar with this area of the law for specific questions and problems.

22. Inquire into the patient's (and family's) feelings and issues of concern about returning to work/school (e.g., job security, employer's willingness to be flexible and supportive during patient's job reentry, reactions of coworkers/other students).

23. Assist the patient in identifying which of his/her issues of concern about returning to work/school are realistic

and which may be somewhat inflated due to anxiety, depression, or other emotional factors.

24. Recommend that the patient identify two specific actions that he/she could take to address each anticipated problem situation associated with return to school/work.

25. Recommend that the patient (and family) do research into the availability of schools that are more easily managed by persons with disabilities (e.g., campus that is relatively flat; campus designed for persons with disabilities; special athletic programs for students with disabilities).

26. Ask the patient (family) to identify and contact the disability services office (or similar office) at the patient's school and have them learn what steps are necessary for accommodations to be implemented.

27. With the patient's (or legally responsible person's) permission, provide documentation of specific accommodations needed by the patient because of his/her disability.

28. Recommend that the patient, in collaboration with his/her vocational rehabilitation counselor, discuss with his/her employer the options that are available in

returning to work (e.g., return to same job with modifications; return to different job; return to work on part-time basis).

29. Ask the patient to list negative medical or psychological consequences (e.g., stress might increase blood pressure and risk of another stroke; excessive hours at work might exhaust cognitive resources, making it impossible for patient to interact with family; work-related stress and fatigue might lead to frequent angry outbursts) that might result if the patient exceeds his/her limitations upon returning to work.

30. Recommend that the patient (or family) determine how the patient's return to work will affect income from Social Security Disability and disability insurance policies.

31. Assign the patient to develop a comprehensive job/school reentry plan that includes when he/she will resume work/school, whether this will be done on a full- or part-time basis, what accommodations will be implemented, and how the effectiveness of this plan will be evaluated.

32. Recommend that the patient, in collaboration with his/her vocational rehabilitation counselor, meet with

the patient's employer/ school administrator to develop a specific plan for job/ school reentry, criteria by which performance will be evaluated, and method to implement accommodations.

33. Obtain the patient's permission for communication to occur between designated rehabilitation professionals and a designated person at the school/worksite to monitor the success of the patient's return to school/work.

34. Refer for or perform psychotherapy to assist the patient in verbalizing and working through feelings associated with the loss of academic and/or career skills and presumed lost opportunities.

35. Assign the patient to identify what he/she would be willing to consider a successful outcome for his/her new level of functioning (e.g., taking two courses and completing them within the semester with a passing grade; earning a 2.8 grade point average; managing five rather than eight accounts accurately), and recommend that he/she record these criteria for future reference. Process the reasonableness of these goals.

36. Recommend that the patient collaborate with his/her psychologist, other rehabilitation professional,

or other trusted person to review his/her written goals, to note which have been achieved, and to update criteria for success at regular intervals.

37. Encourage the patient to build in rewards for achieving new goals (e.g., a party at the successful completion of a school term, a special dinner with one's spouse after completing the first three months at work successfully); assist him/her in listing potential rewards.

38. Ask the patient to identify sources of stress (e.g., students inquiring about why he/she has extra time to complete assignments; coworkers making jokes about the patient "having it easy" by working a shorter day) and the signs that he/she is stressed (e.g., irritability, insomnia, wanting to avoid work/school).

39. Teach the patient to use deep breathing, progressive muscle relaxation, biofeedback, exercise, and other physical methods to reduce stress levels. (See the Anxiety/Fear chapter in this Planner.)

40. Instruct the patient in the use of guided imagery, pleasant memories, relaxing music, or other methods to reduce stress levels. (See the Anxiety/Fear chapter in this Planner.)

41. Select or allow the patient to choose a chapter in *The Relaxation and Stress Reduction Workbook* (Davis, Eshelman, and McKay) that describes a stress reduction strategy; then work with the patient to implement the chosen technique.

42. Inquire into situations at work or school that have ended in conflict, in significant emotional distress, or with the patient wanting to leave the situation permanently.

43. Request that the patient identify what he/she was feeling before, during, and after the upsetting event, thereby helping the patient to identify the point at which he/she experienced vulnerability, helplessness, or other emotional pain.

44. Brainstorm with the patient about alternative ways that the stressful situations at work/school could have been responded to more effectively.

45. In a psychotherapy session, role-play alternative responses to the problem situation, and ask the patient to describe his/her feelings at the end of each scenario; review the patient's implementation of new, healthy responses in daily living situations.

46. Ask the patient to identify a hobby or other non-work-

related activity that provides pleasure, satisfaction, and a sense of fulfillment or making a contribution.

47. Recommend that the patient plan time to spend on a satisfying avocational or social activity weekly; monitor implementation and reinforce success.

48. Refer the patient (or family) to a social worker or community agency to identify financial resources that the patient (or family) might be eligible to access during the time that he/she is unable to work.

49. Recommend that the patient (or family) initiate an application for Social Security Disability Income (SSDI) or other disability benefits if it appears that he/she will be unable to be employed for a significant time.

50. Talk with the patient about the advantages (e.g., distraction from self-focus, sense of fulfillment, affirmation of abilities, contribution to other's welfare) of engaging in avocational activities (e.g., volunteer work, hobbies) during the time that he/she is unable to resume school or paid employment.

51. Refer the patient to a recreational therapist, vocational rehabilitation counselor, or other professional who can assist in the identification

of volunteer or other avocational activities suited to the patient's abilities and interests.

52. Refer for or perform psychotherapy to assist the patient in dealing with emotional issues and decision making during transition back to work/school, or transition to disability retirement.

__. _____

_____

__. _____

_____

__. _____

_____

DIAGNOSTIC SUGGESTIONS

Axis I:	309.0	Adjustment Disorder With Depressed Mood
	309.24	Adjustment Disorder With Anxiety
	309.28	Adjustment Disorder With Mixed Anxiety and Depressed Mood
	309.3	Adjustment Disorder With Disturbance of Conduct
	309.4	Adjustment Disorder With Mixed Disturbance of Emotions and Conduct
	309.9	Adjustment Disorder, Unspecified
	V62.2	Occupational Problem
	294.9	Cognitive Disorder, NOS
	_____	_____
Axis II:	V71.09	No Diagnosis
	799.9	Diagnosis Deferred
	_____	_____
	_____	_____

Appendix A

BIBLIOTHERAPY SUGGESTIONS

Agitation, Aggression, and Violence

McKay, M., P. Rogers, and J. McKay. (1989). *When Anger Hurts*. Oakland, CA: New Harbinger Publications.
Rubin, T. I. (1998). *The Angry Book*. New York: Macmillan.
Weisinger, H. (1985). *Dr. Weisinger's Anger Work Out Book*. New York: Quill.

Anxiety/Fear

Beck, A., G. Emery, and R. Greenberg. (1990). *Anxiety Disorders and Phobias*. New York: Basic Books.
Bourne, E. (1997). *The Anxiety and Phobia Workbook*. Second edition. New York: Fine Communications.
Burns, D. (1993). *Ten Days to Self-Esteem*. New York: Morrow, Williams, and Co.
Davis M., E. R. Eshelman, and M. McKay. (2000). *The Relaxation and Stress Reduction Workbook*. Fifth edition. Oakland, CA: New Harbinger Publications.
Friedman, E. (1990). *Friedman's Fables*. New York: Guilford Press.
Leith, L. (1998). *Exercising Your Way to Better Mental Health*. Morgantown, WV: Fitness Information Technology.
McKay M., P. Davis, and P. Fanning. (1998). *Thoughts and Feelings: Taking Control of Your Moods and Your Life*. Second edition. Oakland, CA: New Harbinger Publications.
Zuercher-White, E. (2000). *An End to Panic: Breakthrough Techniques for Overcoming Panic Disorder*. New York: Fine Communications.

Attention and Concentration Impairment

Staff of the Tampa General Rehabilitation Center. (1996). *Brain Injury: A Home Based Cognitive Rehabilitation Program*. Tampa, FL: HDI Publications.

Chronic Pain

Catalano, E., and K. Hardin. (1996). *The Chronic Pain Control Workbook.* Second edition. Oakland, CA: New Harbinger Publications.

Caudill, M. A. (1995). *Managing Pain Before It Manages You.* New York: Guilford.

Davis M., E. R. Eshelman, and M. McKay. (2000). *The Relaxation and Stress Reduction Workbook.* Fifth edition. Oakland, CA: New Harbinger Publications.

Jamison, R. (1996). *Learning to Master Your Chronic Pain.* Sarasota, FL: Professional Resources Press.

McKay M., P. Davis, and P. Fanning. (1998). *Thoughts and Feelings: Taking Control of Your Moods and Your Life.* Second edition. Oakland, CA: New Harbinger Publications.

Depression/Grief

Burns, D. (1999). *Feeling Good.* New York: Morrow, Williams, and Co.

Caplan, L. R., M. L. Dyken, and J. D. Easton. (1994). *American Heart Association Family Guide to Stroke Treatment, Recovery, and Prevention.* New York: Times Books.

Copeland, M. E. (1992). *The Depression Workbook.* Oakland, CA: New Harbinger Publications.

Lewinsohn, P., R. Muñoz, M. Youngren, and A. Zeiss. (1992). *Control Your Depression.* New York: Simon and Schuster.

McKay, M., P. Davis, and P. Fanning. (1998). *Thoughts and Feelings: Taking Control of Your Moods and Your Life.* Second edition. Oakland, CA: New Harbinger Publications.

Medina, J. (1998). *Depression: How It Happens, How It's Healed.* Oakland, CA: New Harbinger Publications.

National Stroke Association. (1986). *The Road Ahead: A Stroke Recovery Guide.* Denver, CO: The National Stroke Association.

National Resource Center for TBI (unknown). *Getting Better and Better After Brain Injury: A Guide for Survivors.* Richmond, VA: The National Resource Center for TBI.

Pellegreno, M. W. (1999). *I Don't Have an Uncle Phil Anymore.* Washington, DC: Magination Press.

Emotional Lability

Davis M., E. R. Eshelman, and M. McKay. (2000). *The Relaxation and Stress Reduction Workbook.* Fifth edition. Oakland, CA: New Harbinger Publications.

Family Stress Reactions

Caplan, L. R., M. L. Dyken, and J. D. Easton. (1994). *American Heart Association Family Guide to Stroke Treatment, Recovery, and Prevention*. New York: Times Books.

Dell Orto, A. E., and P. W. Power. (1994). *Head Injury and the Family: A Life and Living Perspective*. Winter Park, FL: PMD Publishers Group, Inc.

Gronwall, D., P. Wrightson, and P. Waddell. (1998). *Head Injury: The Facts: A Guide for Families and Care-Givers*. New York: Oxford University Press.

Holmes, M. M. (2000). *A Terrible Thing Happened: A Story for Children Who Have Witnessed Violence or Trauma*. Washington, DC: Magination Press.

Larkin, M. (1995). *When Someone You Love Has A Stroke*. New York: Dell Publishing.

Lash, M. (1993). *When a Parent Has a Brain Injury*. Boston: Massachusetts Head Injury Associations.

National Resource Center for TBI. (unknown). *Getting Better and Better After Brain Injury: A Guide for Family, Friends, and Caregivers*. Richmond, VA: The National Resource Center for TBI.

National Stroke Association. (1986). *The Road Ahead: A Stroke Recovery Guide*. Denver, CO: The National Stroke Association.

Pellegreno, M. W. (1999). *I Don't Have an Uncle Phil Anymore*. Washington, DC: Magination Press.

Useman, S., and E. Useman. (1999). *Tibby Tried It*. Washington, DC: Magination Press.

Ziegler, R. G. (1992). *Homemade Books to Help Kids Cope: An Easy-to-Learn Technique for Parents and Professionals*. Washington, DC: Magination Press.

Memory Impairment

Lorayne, H., and J. Lucas. (2000). *The Memory Book*. New York: Ballantine Books.

Staff of the Tampa General Rehabilitation Center. (1996). *Brain Injury: A Home Based Cognitive Rehabilitation Program*. Tampa, FL: HDI Publications.

Posttraumatic Stress Disorder

Davis M., E. R. Eshelman, and M. McKay. (2000). *The Relaxation and Stress Reduction Workbook,* Fifth edition. Oakland, CA: New Harbinger Publications.

Frankl, V., and G. Allport (Preface). (1998). *Man's Search for Meaning*. New York: Washington Square Press.

Holmes, M. M. (2000). *A Terrible Thing Happened: A Story for Children Who Have Witnessed Violence or Trauma*. Washington, DC: Magination Press.

Kushner, H. (1994). *When Bad Things Happen to Good People*. New York: Avon.

Matsakis, A. (1996). *I Can't Get Over It: A Handbook for Trauma Survivors.* Second edition. Oakland, CA: New Harbinger Publications.

Matsakis, A. (1998). *Trust After Trauma: A Guide to Relationships for Survivors and Those Who Love Them.* Oakland, CA: New Harbinger Publications.

Problem Solving/Planning/Judgment Deficits

Staff of the Tampa General Rehabilitation Center. (1996). *Brain Injury: A Home Based Cognitive Rehabilitation Program.* Tampa, FL: HDI Publications.

Recreational and Social Life Problems

Caplan, L. R., M. L. Dyken, and J. D. Easton. (1994). *American Heart Association Family Guide to Stroke Treatment, Recovery, and Prevention.* New York: Times Books.

Larkin, M. (1995). *When Someone You Love Has A Stroke.* New York: Dell Publishing.

National Stroke Association. (1986). *The Road Ahead: A Stroke Recovery Guide.* Denver, CO: The National Stroke Association.

Sexual Dysfunction

American Heart Association. (1995). *Sex After Stroke.* Dallas, TX: American Heart Association.

Butler, R., and Lewis, M. (1976). *Sex After Sixty.* New York: Harper & Row.

Comfort, A., ed. (1978). *Sexual Consequences of Disability.* Philadelphia: George F. Stickley.

Dell Orto, A. E., and P. W. Power (1994). *Head Injury and the Family: A Life and Living Perspective.* Winter Park, FL: PMD Publishers Group, Inc.

Speech Problems (Aphasia)

American Stroke Association. (unknown). *Caring for a Person with Aphasia.* Dallas, TX: American Stroke Association.

Ewing, S. and B. Pfalzgraf. (1990). *Pathways: Moving Beyond Stroke and Aphasia.* Detroit, MI: Wayne State University Press.

Lafond, D., Y. Joanette, J. Ponzio, R. Gegiovani, and M. Taylor-Sarno. (1992). *Living with Aphasia: Psychosocial Issues.* San Diego, CA: Singular Publishing Group, Inc.

National Stroke Association. (1986). *The Road Ahead: A Stroke Recovery Guide.* Denver, CO: The National Stroke Association.

Stimulus Neglect

Sacks, O. (1985). *The Man Who Mistook His Wife for a Hat*. New York: Harper & Row.

Substance Abuse

Fanning, P., and J. O'Neill. (1996). *The Addiction Workbook*. Oakland, CA: New Harbinger Publications.

Gorski, T. (1992). *The Staying Sober Workbook*. Independence, MO: Herald Publishing House.

Gorski, T. and M. Miller (1986). *Staying Sober: A Guide to Relapse Prevention*. Independence, MO: Herald Publishing House.

Karol, R., and F. Sparadeo. (1991). *Alcohol, Drugs and Brain Injury: A Survivor's Workbook*. Lynn, MA: New Medico Head Injury System.

Miller, W., and R. Muñoz. (1982). *How to Control Your Drinking*. Revised edition. Albuquerque: University of New Mexico Press.

Vocational/Educational Problems

Davis M., E. R. Eshelman, and M. McKay. (2000). *The Relaxation and Stress Reduction Workbook*. Fifth edition. Oakland, CA: New Harbinger Publications.

Smith, D. (1998). *Disability Workbook for Social Security Applicants*. Denver, CO: National Stroke Association.

Virginia Department of Education. (1993). *Guidelines for Educational Services for Students with Traumatic Brain Injury*. Richmond, VA: Rehabilitation Research and Training Center on Severe Traumatic Brain Injury.

Appendix B

INDEX OF DSM-IV™ CODES ASSOCIATED WITH PRESENTING PROBLEMS

Impulsivity
Recreational and Social Life Problems
Rehabilitation Noncompliance
Vocational/Educational Problems

Alcohol Abuse   305.00
Driving Deficiencies
Substance Abuse

Alcohol Dependence   303.90
Driving Deficiencies
Substance Abuse

**Alcohol-Induced Anxiety
Disorder**   291.89
Anxiety/Fear
Impulsivity

**Alcohol-Induced Mood
Disorder**   291.89
Depression/Grief

**Alcohol-Induced Sexual
Dysfunction**   291.89
Sexual Dysfunction

Alcohol Withdrawal Delirium   291.0
Impulsivity

**Amnestic Disorder Due to
(General Medical Condition)**   294.0
Confabulation
Memory Impairment

Amnestic Disorder NOS   294.8
Memory Impairment

**Antisocial Personality
Disorder**   301.7
Agitation, Aggression, and Violence

**Anxiety Disorder Due to
(General Medical Condition)** 293.84
Anxiety/Fear
Impulsivity

Anxiety Disorder NOS   300.00
Anxiety/Fear
Recreational and Social Life
   Problems

**Attention-Deficit/
Hyperactivity Disorder
(State Type)**   314.xx
Attention and Concentration
   Impairment
Impulsivity

**Attention-Deficit/
Hyperactivity Disorder NOS**   314.9
Attention and Concentration
   Impairment

Bereavement   V62.82
Depression/Grief

Bipolar Disorder   296.xx
Perseveration

**Bipolar I Disorder, Most
Recent Episode Depressed**   296.5x
Depression/Grief

Bipolar II Disorder   296.89
Depression/Grief

**Borderline Personality
Disorder**   301.83
Agitation, Aggression, and Violence
Chronic Pain
Rehabilitation Noncompliance
Substance Abuse

Cannabis Abuse   305.20
Substance Abuse

Cannabis Dependence   304.30
Substance Abuse

Cocaine Abuse   305.60
Substance Abuse

Cocaine Dependence   304.20
Substance Abuse

Cognitive Disorder NOS   294.9
Attention and Concentration
   Impairment
Confabulation
Denial and Impaired Awareness
Driving Deficiencies
Impulsivity

Initiation Difficulties
Memory Impairment
Perseveration
Problem Solving/Planning/Judgment
   Deficits
Sexual Acting Out
Speech Problems (Aphasia)
Stimulus Neglect
Substance Abuse
Vocational/Educational Problems

Communication Disorder NOS 307.9
Speech Problems (Aphasia)

Conversion Disorder   **300.11**
Initiation Difficulties

Delirium Due to
(General Medical Condition)   293.0
Agitation, Aggression, and Violence
Confabulation
Impulsivity

Dementia   **290.xx**
Confabulation
Driving Deficiencies
Impulsivity
Initiation Difficulties
Memory Impairment
Perseveration
Problem Solving/Planning/Judgment
   Deficits
Speech Problems (Aphasia)

Dementia Due to
(Axis III condition)   294.1
Agitation, Aggression, and Violence
Confabulation
Driving Deficiencies
Initiation Difficulties
Memory Impairment
Perseveration
Problem Solving/Planning/Judgment
   Deficits
Speech Problems (Aphasia)

Dementia NOS   **294.8**
Driving Deficiencies
Memory Impairment
Perseveration

Problem Solving/Planning/Judgment
   Deficits
Speech Problems (Aphasia)

Dependent Personality
Disorder   **301.6**
Dependency/Counterdependency

Depressive Disorder NOS   **311**
Depression/Grief

Diagnosis Deferred   **799.9**
Agitation, Aggression, and Violence
Anxiety/Fear
Chronic Pain
Confabulation
Denial and Impaired Awareness
Dependency/Counterdependency
Depression/Grief
Driving Deficiencies
Initiation Difficulties
Problem Solving/Planning/Judgment
   Deficits
Rehabilitation Noncompliance
Sexual Dysfunction
Substance Abuse
Vocational/Educational Problems

Dissociative Identity
Disorder   **300.14**
Confabulation

Dysthymic Disorder   **300.4**
Depression/Grief

Expressive Language
Disorder   **315.31**
Speech Problems (Aphasia)

Factitious Disorder   **300.xx**
Confabulation
Initiation Difficulties

Female Dyspareunia Due to
(General Medical Condition)   625.0
Sexual Dysfunction

Female Hypoactive Sexual
Desire Disorder Due to
(General Medical Condition)   625.8
Sexual Dysfunction

**Generalized Anxiety
Disorder**   300.02
  Anxiety/Fear
  Impulsivity

Hypochondriasis   300.7
  Chronic Pain

**Major Depressive Disorder,
Single Episode**   296.2x
  Depression/Grief

**Major Depressive Disorder,
Recurrent**   296.3x
  Depression/Grief

**Male Dyspareunia
Due to (General
Medical Condition)**   608.89
  Sexual Dysfunction

**Male Erectile Disorder
Due to (General
Medical Condition)**   607.84
  Sexual Dysfunction

**Male Hypoactive Sexual
Desire Disorder Due to
(General Medical Condition)**   608.89
  Sexual Dysfunction

Malingering   V65.2
  Confabulation
  Initiation Difficulties

**Mental Disorder NOS Due to
(General Medical Condition)**   293.9
  Agitation, Aggression, and Violence
  Emotional Lability

**Mixed Receptive-Expressive
Language Disorder**   315.32
  Speech Problems (Aphasia)

**Mood Disorder Due to
(General Medical Condition)**   293.83
  Depression/Grief
  Impulsivity

Mood Disorder NOS   296.90
  Depression/Grief

No Diagnosis or Condition   V71.09
  Agitation, Aggression, and Violence
  Anxiety/Fear
  Attention and Concentration
    Impairment
  Chronic Pain
  Confabulation
  Denial and Impaired Awareness
  Dependency/Counterdependency
  Depression/Grief
  Driving Deficiencies
  Initiation Difficulties
  Memory Impairment
  Perseveration
  Problem Solving/Planning/Judgment
    Deficits
  Recreational and Social Life Problems
  Rehabilitation Noncompliance
  Sexual Dysfunction
  Speech Problems (Aphasia)
  Stimulus Neglect
  Substance Abuse
  Vocational/Educational Problems

**Noncompliance With
Treatment**   V15.81
  Denial and Impaired Awareness
  Dependency/Counterdependency
  Depression/Grief
  Rehabilitation Noncompliance

**Obsessive-Compulsive
Personality Disorder**   300.3 or 301.4
  Anxiety/Fear

Occupational Problem   V62.2
  Vocational/Educational Problems

Opioid Abuse   305.50
  Chronic Pain
  Substance Abuse

Opioid Dependence   304.00
  Chronic Pain
  Substance Abuse

**Other Female Sexual
Dysfunction Due to
(General Medical Condition)**   625.8
  Sexual Acting Out
  Sexual Dysfunction

Somatization Disorder   300.81
   Chronic Pain
   Confabulation

Somatoform Disorder NOS   300.82
   Chronic Pain
   Confabulation

Specific Phobia   300.29
   Anxiety/Fear

**Substance-Induced
Anxiety Disorder**   292.89
   Anxiety/Fear
   Impulsivity

**Substance-Induced
Mood Disorder
(Specify Substance)**   292.84
   Depression/Grief
   Impulsivity

**Substance-Induced
Sexual Dysfunction
(Specify Substance)**   292.89
   Sexual Dysfunction

**Substance Intoxication
Delirium (Specify
Substance)**   292.81
   Impulsivity

BIBLIOGRAPHY WITH INTERNET SITES

Adams, R. L., O. A. Parsons, J. L. Culbertson, and S. J. Nixon. (Eds.) (1996). *Neuropsychology for Clinical Practice: Etiology, Assessment, and Treatment of Common Neurological Disorders.* Washington, DC: American Psychological Association.

Aloni, R., and S. Katz (1999). "A Review of the Effect of Traumatic Brain Injury on the Human Sexual Response." *Brain Injury,* 13, 269–280.

Aloni, R., O. Keren, M. Cohen, N. Rosenthal, M. Romm, and Z. Groswasser. (1999). "Incidence of Sexual Dysfunction in TBI Patients During the Early Post-Traumatic In-Patient Rehabilitation Phase." *Brain Injury,* 13, 89–97.

American Psychiatric Association. (2000). *Diagnostic and Statistical Manual of Mental Disorders, DSM-IV-TR (Text Revision),* fourth edition. Washington, DC: American Psychiatric Association.

American Psychological Association. (1992). *Ethical Principles of Psychologists and Code of Conduct.* Washington, DC: American Psychological Association.

Bergner, M., R. A. Bobbitt, W. B. Carter, and B. S. Gilson. (1981). "The Sickness Impact Profile: Development and Final Revision of a Health Status Measure." *Medical Care,* 19, 787–805. (Available from the Medical Outcomes Trust, 198 Tremont St., PMB #503, Boston, MA 02116-4705, phone: 617-426-4046. Internet: www.outcomes-trust.org.)

Bishop, D. S., and I. W. Miller. (1988). "Traumatic Brain Injury: Empirical Family Assessment Techniques." *Journal of Head Trauma and Rehabilitation,* 3 (4), 16–30.

Blanchard, E. B., and E. B. Hickling. (1997). *After the Crash: Assessment and Treatment of Motor Vehicle Accident Survivors.* Washington, DC: American Psychological Association.

Boyd, T. M., and S. W. Sautter. (1993). "Route-Finding: A Measure of Everyday Executive Functioning in the Head-Injured Adult." *Applied Cognitive Psychology,* 7(2), 171–181.

Brown, G. W., and M. Rutter. (1966). "The Measurement of Family Activities and Relationships: A Methodological Study." *Human Relations,* 19, 241–263.

Brush, J. A., and C. J. Camp. (1998). *A Therapy Technique for Improving Memory: Spaced Retrieval.* Beachwood, OH: Menorah Park Center for the Aging.

Culbertson, W. C., and E. A. Zillmer. (no date). *Tower of London^{DX}: Research Version* (TOL^{DX}:RV). North Tonawanda, NY: Multi-Health Systems Inc.

Cushman, L. A., and M. J. Scherer. (1995). *Psychological Assessment in Medical Rehabilitation.* Washington, DC: American Psychological Association.

DeGood, D. E., A. L. Crawford, and A. E. Jongsma. (1999). *The Behavioral Medicine Treatment Planner.* New York: John Wiley & Sons, Inc.

Derogatis, L. R. (1987). *Derogatis Interview for Sexual Function.* Baltimore, MD: Clinical Psychometric Research.

Dywan, J., and S. J. Segalowitz. (1996). "Self- and Family Ratings of Adaptive Behavior After Traumatic Brain Injury: Psychometric Scores and Frontally Generated ERPs." *Journal of Head Trauma Rehabilitation,* 11(2), 79–85.

Epstein, N. B., L. M. Baldwin, and D. S. Bishop. (1983). "The McMaster Family Assessment Device." *Journal of Marriage and Family Therapy,* 9, 171–180.

Evans/Abarbanel (Author/Editor). (1999). *Introduction to Quantitative EEG and Neurofeedback.* New York: Academic Press.

Frank, R. G., and T. R. Elliott. (Eds.) (2000). *Handbook of Rehabilitation Psychology.* Washington, DC: American Psychological Association.

Glosser, G., and H. Goodglass. (1990). "Disorders in Executive Control Functions Among Aphasic and Other Brain-Damaged Patients." *Journal of Clinical and Experimental Neuropsychology,* 12(4), 485–501. (The Tower of Hanoi is available from Western Psychological Services, 12021 Wilshire Boulevard, Los Angeles, CA 90025-1251. Phone: 800-648-8857. Internet: www.wpspublish.com.)

Hagan, C., D. Malkmus, and P. Durham. (1979). "Levels of Cognitive Functions." In *Rehabilitation of Head Injured Adult: Comprehensive Physical Management.* Professional Staff Association of Rancho Los Amigos Hospital, Downey, CA.

Haley, J. (1984). *Ordeal Therapy.* San Francisco, CA: Jossey-Bass.

Harrell, M., F. Parenté, E. G. Bellingrath, and K. A. Lisicia. (1992). *Cognitive Rehabilitation of Memory: A Practical Guide.* Gaithersburg, MD: Aspen Publishers, Inc.

Jongsma, A. E., and L. M. Peterson. (1999). *The Complete Adult Psychotherapy Treatment Planner,* second edition. New York: John Wiley & Sons, Inc.

Kames, L. D., B. D. Naliboff, R. L. Heinrich, and C. C. Schag. (1984). "The Chronic Illness Problem Inventory: Problem-Oriented Psychosocial Assessment of Patients with Chronic Illness." *International Journal of Psychiatry in Medicine,* 14, 65–75.

Kinston, W., and P. Loader. (1984). "Eliciting Whole-Family Interaction with a Standardized Clinical Interview." *Journal of Family Therapy,* 6, 347–363.

Kreuter, M., A. G. Dahllöf, G. Gudjonsson, M. Sullivan, and A. Siösteen. (1998). "Sexual Adjustment and its Predictors after Traumatic Brain Injury." *Brain Injury,* 12, 349–368.

Langer, K. G., L. Laatsch, and L. Lewis. (Eds.) (1999). *Psychotherapeutic Interventions for Adults with Brain Injury or Stroke: A Clinician's Treatment Resource.* Madison, CT: Psychosocial Press.

Lezak, M. (1982). "The Problem of Assessing Executive Functions." *International Journal of Psychology,* 17, 281–297.

McLellan, A., L. Luborski, C. O'Brien, and G. Woody. (1980). "An Improved Evaluation Instrument for Substance Abuse Patients: The Addiction Severity Index." *Journal of Nervous and Mental Disease,* 168, 26–33.

McLellan, A. T., H. Kushner, D. Metzger, R. Peters, I. Smith, G. Grissom, H. Pettinati, M. Argeriou. (1992). "The Fifth Edition of the Addiction Severity Index." *Journal of Substance Abuse Treatment,* 9(3), 199–213.

Meier, M. J., A. L. Benton, and L. Diller. (1987). *Neuropsychological Rehabilitation.* New York: The Guilford Press.

Melzack, R. (1975). "The McGill Pain Questionnaire: Major Properties and Scoring Methods." *Pain,* 1:191–197.

Melzack, R. (1987). "The Short-Form McGill Pain Questionnaire." *Pain,* 30, 191–197.

Millard, R. W. (1989). "The Functional Assessment Screening Questionnaire: Application for Evaluating Pain-related Disability." *Archives of Physical Medicine and Rehabilitation,* 70, 303–307.

Miller, G. (1985). *The Substance Abuse Subtle Screening Inventory (SASSI): Manual.* Bloomington, IN: Spencer Evening World. (Available from The Psychological Corporation, 555 Academic Court, San Antonio, TX 78204-2455. Phone: 800-211-8378. Internet: www.PsychCorp.com.)

Miller, L. (1993). *Psychotherapy of the Brain-Injured Patient.* New York: W. W. Norton and Company.

Miller, L. (1998). *Shocks to the System: Psychotherapy of Traumatic Disability Syndromes.* New York: W. W. Norton and Company.

Miller, L. (1994). "Sex and the Brain-Injured Patient: Regaining Love, Pleasure, and Intimacy." *Journal of Cognitive Rehabilitation,* 12, 12–20.

Moos, R. (1974). *The Family Environment Scale.* Palo Alto, CA: Consulting Psychologists Press.

Mueser, K. T., and S. M. Glynn. (1999). *Behavioral Family Therapy for Psychiatric Disorders,* second edition. Oakland, CA: New Harbinger Publications.

Office of Equal Opportunity. (1990). *The Americans with Disabilities Act: Your Responsibilities as an Employer.* Washington, DC: Government Printing Office.

O'Hara, C. C., and M. Harrell. (1991). *Rehabilitation with Brain Injury Survivors: An Empowerment Approach.* Gaithersburg, MD: Aspen.

Ohio Valley Center for Brain Injury Prevention and Rehabilitation. (1997). *Substance Use and Abuse after Brain Injury: A Programmer's Guide.* Columbus, OH: The Ohio Valley Center for Brain Injury Prevention and Rehabilitation.

Olson, D. H. (1986). "Circumplex Model VII: Validation Studies and FACES III." *Family Process,* 25, 337–351.

Olson, D. H., D. H. Sprenkle, and C. S. Russell. (1979). "Circumplex Model of Marital and Family Systems: I. Cohesion and Adaptability Dimensions, Family Types, and Clinical Applications." *Family Process,* 18, 3–28.

Practice Management Information Corporation. (1999). *International Classification of Diseases, 9th Revision, Clinical Modification (ICD-9-CM).* Los Angeles, CA: Practice Management Information Corporation.

Prigatano, G. P., J. P. Fordyce, H. K. Zeiner, J. R. Roueche, M. Pepping, and B. Casewood. (1986). *Neuropsychological Rehabilitation after Brain Injury.* Baltimore, MD: The Johns Hopkins University Press.

Prigatano, G. P. (1999). *Principles of Neuropsychological Rehabilitation.* New York: Oxford University Press.

Prigatano, G. P., and D. L. Schacter. (eds.) (1991). *Awareness of Deficit After Brain Injury: Clinical and Theoretical Issues.* New York: Oxford University Press.

Robinson, F. B. (1970). *Effective Study.* New York: Harper and Row.

Roueche, J. R., and D. J. Fordyce. (1983). "Perception of Deficits Following Brain Injury and Their Impact on Psychosocial Adjustments." *Cognitive Rehabilitation,* 6, 4–7.

Rutter, M., and G. W. Brown. (1966). "The Reliability and Validity of Measures of Family Life and Relationships in Families Containing a Psychiatric Patient." *Social Psychiatry,* 1 (1), 38–53.

Sandel, M. E., K. S. Williams, L. Dellapietra, and L. R. Derogatis. (1996). "Sexual Functioning Following Traumatic Brain Injury." *Brain Injury,* 10, 719–728.

Schover, L. R., and S. B. Jensen. (1988). *Sexuality and Chronic Illness.* New York: Guilford.

Selzer, M. (1971). "The Michigan Alcoholism Screening Test." *American Journal of Psychiatry,* 127:1653–1658.

Shallice, T., and P. W. Burgess. (1991). "Deficits in Strategy Application Following Frontal Lobe Damage in Man." *Brain,* 114, 727–741.

Sipski, M. L., and C. J. Alexander. (eds.) (1997). *Sexual Function in People with Disability and Chronic Illness.* Gaithersburg, MD: Aspen.

Snyder, P. J., and P. D. Nussbaum. (1998). *Clinical Neuropsychology: A Pocket Handbook for Assessment.* Washington, DC: American Psychological Association.

Sohlberg, M. M. (1992). *Manual for the Profile of Executive Control System.* Puyallup, WA: AFNRD.

Sohlberg, M. M., and C. A. Mateer. (1989). *Introduction to Cognitive Rehabilitation: Theory and Practice.* New York: Guilford.

Stringer, A. Y. (1996). *A Guide to Adult Neuropsychological Diagnosis.* Philadelphia, PA: F. A. Davis Company.

Vaughn, C. E., and Leff, L. P. (1976). "The Measurement of Expressed Emotion in the Families of Psychiatric Patients." *British Journal of Social and Clinical Psychology,* 15, 157–165.

Weinberg, J., and L. Diller. (1999). "Dealing with Rationalization and Unawareness in the Treatment of Visual Inattention." In K. G. Langer, L. Laatsch, and L. Lewis (eds.) *Psychotherapeutic Interventions for Adults with Brain Injury or Stroke: A Clinician's Treatment Resource.* Madison, CT: Psychosocial Press.

Williams, J. M., and Kay, T. (Eds.) (1991). *Head Injury: A Family Matter.* Baltimore, MD: Brookes.

Wilson, B. (1987). *Rehabilitation of Memory.* New York: The Guilford Press.

Wilson, B., J. Cockburn, and A. Baddeley. (1985). *The Rivermead Behavioral Memory Test.* Bury St. Edmunds, England: Thames Valley Test Company.

(Available from Psychological Assessment Resources, Inc., P.O. Box 998, Odessa, FL 33556. Phone 800-331-8378. Internet: www.parinc.com.)

Zasler, N. D. (1994). "Sexual Dysfunction" (pp. 443–469). In Silver, J. M., and S. C. Yudofsky, et al. (eds.). *Neuropsychology of Traumatic Brain Injury.* Washington, DC: American Psychiatric Press, Inc.

WEB SITES

Aneurysm

www.canisius.edu
   Brain Storm: resource directory for persons having brain aneurysms

www.westga.edu/~wmaples/aneurysm.html
   Support for persons having aneurysms and arteriovenous malformations.

Anxiety

www.adaa.org
   Anxiety Disorders Association of America

Brain Injury

www.biausa.org
   Brain Injury Association, Inc.

www.neuro.pmr.vcu.edu
   National Resource Center for Traumatic Brain Injury

www.cdc.gov
   Go to the National Center for Injury Prevention and Control; "Order NCIPC Publications"; request "Facts about concussion and brain injury"

Brain Tumor

www.tbts.org
   The Brain Tumor Society

Children's Books Regarding Dealing with Disabilities, Trauma, Death

www.maginationpress.com

www.biausa.org/medialib.htm

Dating and Friendship

www.dateable.org
Dateable: a dating service founded to combat the isolation and social discrimination often experienced by people with disabilities

Multiple Sclerosis

www.nmss.org
National Multiple Sclerosis Society

www.msworld.org
Support organization for persons having multiple sclerosis

Pain

www.painfoundation.org
American Pain Foundation

Social Security

www.ssa.gov

Stroke

www.americanheart.org
American Heart Association/American Stroke Association

www.stroke.org
National Stroke Association

Substance Abuse

www.na.org
   Narcotics Anonymous World Services

www.alcoholics-anonymous.org
   Alcoholics Anonymous

www.al-anon-alateen.org
   Al-Anon/Alateen

http://members.aol.com/picadainc/groups.htm
   Prevention & Intervention Center for Alcohol and other Drug Abuse

www.familiesanonymous.org
   Families Anonymous

Travel

www.aaa.com
   American Automobile Association

www.aarp.org
   American Association of Retired Persons

www.access-able.com
   Access-Able Travel Source

www.projectaction.org/paweb/
   Project ACTION Accessible Traveler's Database

www.gimponthego.com
   If you can forgive the title, you'll find good information here

Visual Impairments

www.hadley-school.org
   Offers free correspondence courses to persons with visual impairments, and family members

www.rfbd.org
   Taped text books and other reading materials for persons with reading disabilities

www.booksontape.com
   Catalog of tape-recorded books

www.nfb.org
   National Federation of the Blind
   Advocacy group.
   Medical equipment, kitchen items, and games designed for visually impaired persons

ABOUT THE DISK*

TheraScribe® 3.0 and 3.5 Library Module Installation

The enclosed disk contains files to upgrade your TheraScribe® 3.0 or 3.5 program to include the behavioral definitions, goals, objectives, and interventions from *The Rehabilitation Psychology Treatment Planner.*

Note: You must have TheraScribe® 3.0 or 3.5 for Windows installed on your computer in order to use *The Rehabilitation Psychology Treatment Planner* library module.

To install the library module, please follow these steps:

1. Place the library module disk in your floppy drive.
2. Log in to TheraScribe® 3.0 or 3.5 as the Administrator using the name "Admin" and your administrator password.
3. On the Main Menu, press the "GoTo" button, and choose the Options menu item.
4. Press the "Import Library" button.
5. On the Import Library Module screen, choose your floppy disk drive a:\ from the list and press "Go." Note: It may take a few minutes to import the data from the floppy disk to your computer's hard disk.
6. When the installation is complete, the library module data will be available in your TheraScribe® 3.0 or 3.5 program.

Note: If you have a network version of TheraScribe® 3.0 or 3.5 installed, you should import the library module one time only. After importing the data, the library module data will be available to all network users.

User Assistance

If you need assistance using this TheraScribe® 3.0 or 3.5 add-on module, contact Wiley Technical Support at:

Phone: 212-850-6753
Fax: 212-850-6800 (Attention: Wiley Technical Support)
E-mail: techhelp@wiley.com

---

*Note: This section applies only to the book with disk edition, ISBN 0-471-35179-2.

For information on how to install disk, refer to the **About the Disk** section on page 363.

WILEY
Publishers Since 1807